DISAFFECTION FROM SCHOOL

DISAFFECTION FROM SCHOOL

Ken Reid

METHUEN · *London & New York*

First published in 1986 by
Methuen & Co. Ltd
11 New Fetter Lane
London EC4P 4EE

Published in the USA by
Methuen & Co.
in association with Methuen, Inc.
29 West 35th Street
New York NY 10001

© 1986 Ken Reid

Typeset in Great Britain by
Hope Services, Abingdon
and printed by
Richard Clay, The Chaucer Press
Bungay, Suffolk

*British Library Cataloguing in
Publication Data*

Reid, Ken, 1946–
Disaffection from school.
1. High school students –
England – Attitudes
I. Title
373.18′1   LA635

ISBN 0-423-51540-3
ISBN 0-423-51550-0 Pbk

*Library of Congress Cataloging in
Publication Data*

Reid, Ken.
Disaffection from school.
Bibliography, p.
Includes index.
1. School attendance – Great Britain.
2. Problem children – Great Britain –
Discipline.
3. School vandalism – Great Britain.
4. Underachievers – Great Britain.
I. Title.
LC145.G7R45 1986   371.2′95′0941
86-677

ISBN 0-423-51540-3
ISBN 0-423-51550-0 (pbk.)

This book is dedicated to Auntie Elsie and Uncle Linton (Mr and Mrs A.L. Sims) who looked after me and brought me up in my difficult, adolescent days. Without your help, who knows what might have transpired.

CONTENTS

Acknowledgements ix
Foreword xi

1 Introduction 1
2 Absenteeism 16
3 Disruption in Schools 29
4 Aetiology of Disruptive Behaviour 46
5 The Broader Context of Disruptive Behaviour 70
6 The Search for School Factors 88
7 Schooling 104
8 Responding to Disaffection 125
9 School Initiatives 141
10 Formal Sanctions 177
11 Multidisciplinary Approaches 203
12 Conclusions 218

References Used in the Text 227
Further Reading Lists 247
Subject Index 259
Name Index 261

ACKNOWLEDGEMENTS

I wish to thank several people for their help during the preparation of this book. These include:

1) 'H', 'J', 'J2' and 'R' for allowing me to visit their institutions and interview selected staff and pupils;
2) All the pupils and professionals who agreed to be interviewed in connection with field work for the book especially 'Craig' and 'Jason';
3) Nan Davies, formerly tutor in education at University College, Cardiff, for generously giving up so much of her own time to advise and help me on educational topics of interest in my own dim, distant student days.
4) Dr David Fontana, Senior Lecturer at University College, Cardiff, for his inspirational teaching;
5) Professor David Pritchard for his advice when reading the final draft;
6) My former pupils at Bicester and Faringdon for giving me so many insights into the 'causes' of disaffection!

7) Mrs Denise Johns for typing the manuscript.

Finally, I would like to thank my wife Pat, children Rebecca, Nicholas and Joanna for their patience. Believe it or not, Daddy is coming out of solitary confinement soon!

The publishers and I would like to thank the Welsh Office and the ILEA Learning and Resources Branch for permission to reproduce extracts from their reports on *Disaffection From School* and *Improving Secondary Schools*. We would also like to thank the staff and pupils of George Green's School, London E14 for their time and help in preparing the cover photograph.

FOREWORD

This book endeavours to piece together the various facets of disaffected behaviour in schools. The text seeks to draw together a representative collection of the facts depicting the range of attitudes and practice which are to be found in work with disaffected pupils. The scope and subject matter contained in the book have been selected on the basis that many seemingly diverse aspects of policy and provision for disaffected pupils cannot be understood if divorced from one another. Up until recently, much published material tended solely to reflect the individual interests of researchers and ignore both the interdisciplinary and practical perspectives. Disruption, for example, is currently a vogue topic, although much of the literature on the subject ignores the part played by absentees and truants, and the contribution of such diverse profferings as educational psychology, teaching, social work and educational welfare.

This book sets out to achieve a number of distinct aims. First, it attempts to draw attention to the problems experienced by disaffected pupils at home and, particularly, at school in the hope that insights will lead to greater understanding and empathy on the part of many caring professionals, including teachers and social workers. Thus, it attempts to highlight similarities and differences which are known to exist between disaffected pupils, especially absentees and disrupters as, to date, much less is known about vandals and underachievers *per se*. The text also endeavours to show the limits which our knowledge in understanding disaffection has reached as well as some of the areas where further research is needed.

Second, the text suggests that many disaffected pupils are the unwitting victims of their home backgrounds and social circumstances, of school policies and of their own behaviour. Unless there is greater clarity about the guidance and remedial work which is undertaken by the numerous agencies who handle disaffected pupils and, at the same time, more understanding about their interface, especially between teachers and social workers, then the outlook for those caught up in the disaffection syndrome – the pupils themselves – is bleak and liable to get worse with the advent of the technological age.

Hence, one of the main thrusts of the book is directed towards understanding school-based problems such as absenteeism and disruption as well as the institutional and interagency responses to them. Although the text will be true to existing work, it will be argued that schools and caring agencies could do much more to assist in the prevention of disenchantment, alienation and the various manifestations of disaffection. This means that schools should and/or will have to devise their own policies to combat their disaffection problem (absenteeism, disruption, vandalism, underachievement and poor teacher–pupil relationships) based on agreed, united and workable schema. If schools do not tackle these problems in a systematic fashion soon, it may well be that disaffected behaviour will increase, with all the ensuing tension and disruption to schools and society this statement implies. If the remedial and treatment programmes which are currently implemented by schools are to be effective, then some teachers as well as disaffected pupils will have to change their attitudes. As a researcher, one is forced to the inescapable conclusion that the vast resentment which many absentees and disrupters feel toward their educational institutions, teachers, curriculum and general treatment within and outside schools has a legitimate basis, especially as so many schools reward their more able pupils at the expense of non-conformers and the less able. Failure at home, therefore, is exacerbated by a lack of success at school. This long overdue change in professional attitudes will not be easy to achieve, particularly as many teachers probably entered the profession to assist reasonably bright children to develop and progress, rather than to help difficult and less able pupils to conform and foster intellectual growth. If the truth were known, probably very few people train as teachers because they are genuinely concerned with the plight of such pupils as underachievers, absentees and disrupters. This is exemplified by the fact that up until very recently there were few, if any, major initial postgraduate courses in this field. Both research (Reid and Avalos, 1980) and my own teaching experience suggest that most secondary teachers like to work with as old and as able age groups as possible, given a free choice. There are not too many teachers around who willingly opt for work with 4X and 5X rather than 4A, 5A or the sixth form. In one sense this is what this book is really about: the failure of teachers, schools and pastoral care teams to come to terms with their disadvantaged, disaffected pupils. Rather, like priests, teachers should be prepared to help all pupils equally well; not some more than others.

The book has been written for students (student-teachers, social workers, educational psychologists), as a resource for practitioners (teachers, social workers and allied caring professionals), administrators, lecturers, advisers and researchers within education and related fields as well as for parents and other people who have an interest in and concern for young people in difficulty or trouble at school and the provision that is made for them. In order to make the book more enjoyable to read, examples of real case data are included at appropriate points throughout the text. These data were obtained from visits to selected schools and the Young Offenders Unit in one of Her Majesty's Prisons to interview teachers, pupils and young offenders. Some of these data were gathered during the field work for my study on persistent school absenteeism undertaken in South Wales between 1977 and 1980. But most of these data were collected especially for use in this book during 1984.

The text attempts to be jargon-free whenever possible. Although the book has theoretical underpinnings such as those described in *Truancy and School Absenteeism* (Reid, 1985a) and Chapter 1, it is meant to be practically rather than theoretically orientated. The plan of the book is to introduce the theme and follow this by a discussion of points related to the complex topics of absenteeism and disruption. Thereafter, from Chapter 6 onwards, absenteeism and disruption are linked as the text concentrates on the search for institutional factors and examines the critical influence of teacher–pupil relationships, educational responses to disaffection, school initiatives, formal sanctions and multidisciplinary approaches. Case data presented at various points in the book, especially in chapters 9 and 10, are used to highlight and reinforce points made throughout the book from the standpoint of disaffected and seriously disaffected pupils, young offenders and selected staff. The final chapter attempts to pull together and reiterate some of the major points covered in the earlier parts of the book. Another of the themes of the book is that disaffected behaviour and underachievement are closely related despite the absence of much research into this topic.

Owing to the imbalance in the amount of work which has been undertaken into disaffection, the references and further reading lists are necessarily more selective on some topics than on others. Explicitly, some of the areas on which a great deal of information is known include: the nature, extent and aetiology of absenteeism and disruption; the range of policies, provision and practice for coping with disaffected pupils; the role of schools and alternative education units; the operation of the law, and various exhortations to good multidisciplinary practice in casework. Much less is currently known about school differences and disaffection; the cognitive and non-cognitive aspects of schooling when related to disaffection; organizational matters and disaffection such as factors linked with the operation of pastoral care systems, home–school communication and curriculum development. Similarly, much more research is required into the links between disaffection and special educational needs; the professional concerns of agencies like the Educational Welfare Service, the School Psychological Service and Child Guidance Service; vandalism and disaffection; and the reasons given by disaffected pupils for their behaviour as well as their views on their social and educational treatment. Finally, further experimentation is required into good practice with disaffected children both in and out of schools. In particular, successful accounts of viable educational curricular and organizational innovations used with disaffected pupils are urgently required.

Ken Reid
Swansea, August 1985

1
INTRODUCTION

At the time of writing Jane is sitting at home wondering what her future holds. She has recently been sent home and suspended from school for the third time for throwing an object at Miss Burrows following a tantrum in class. The incident happened on her first day back at school after a lengthy period of truancy. She became agitated when some of the boys began calling her names behind the teacher's back. When Miss Burrows turned round, she spotted Jane out of her seat hitting a boy with a book. After Miss Burrows had told Jane to return to her seat, she responded by throwing the book at the teacher, hitting her on the forehead. In the ensuing struggle, Jane repeatedly swore at Miss Burrows as well as at some of her classmates who took their teacher's side. She then left the classroom and school premises without permission. The headteacher has since written to Jane's mother suggesting she keeps her daughter at home for the time being until a solution can be found. Jane is only fourteen.

Disaffected children like Jane who find themselves in trouble at school or who cause concern to the authorities because of their absence from school, disruptive behaviour or educational and social needs, are the focus of considerable attention at present. During the early to mid-1970s, genuine concern emerged amongst certain sections of the educational establishment about the number of children and young people who were reported to be regularly missing school, disrupting classes and underachieving. It seemed that academic and disciplinary standards in school were declining – something which the authors of the Black Papers on Education had been claiming for a number of years. Some of the agitation reflected the similar concern of the teachers' unions for the well-being of their members, who were reported to be dealing with intolerably difficult children in the classroom and, in extreme cases, facing physical threats. The media began to turn their wrath towards education, claiming that indiscipline in schools was mirroring and contributing to declining standards throughout society. Consequently, many parents, academics and members of the general public, as well as some educationalists, began to seize the opportunity to question the relevance of the educational experience on offer in schools for the needs of the children who behaved in such disaffected and alienated ways.

Feeling themselves under pressure, some local education authorities and funding agencies set about understanding the complex issues involved in disaffected behaviour. Thereafter, the literature on children in trouble reflects the peaks of frustration in public and academic concern. From the late sixties to mid-1970s the focus was on truancy and school refusal, indicative of the fact that the media and general public became aware that 10 per cent of secondary aged pupils missed school daily, with rates much higher in parts of Scotland, South Wales, North-West England, Inner London and some of the larger conurbations. Subsequently, it became disruption in schools which preoccupied commentators and researchers, giving rise to a spate of publications on the subject. These drew attention to the extent and genesis of the problem, the growth of on-site and off-site units for difficult and disruptive pupils and allied school problems. Interestingly, underachievement, a much more difficult topic to research when studied in its entirety, has never received as much acclaim or attention as truancy and disruption, although its consequences are at least as potent in the long run. Vandalism, too, has not been given as much attention as it deserves, possibly because of the complexities involved in finding suitable samples as well as the inherent difficulties in studying the interface of social, psychological and educational aspects of the subject.

Research in the 1960s and early 1970s largely concentrated on the social and psychological aspects of disaffected behaviour. This was in the belief that schooling was only a weak influence on pupil conduct when compared with the stronger influences of pupils' home and social backgrounds and individual traits. In the late 1970s and early 1980s research began to challenge the wisdom of these conventional views. Work began to show that there are differences between schools in, for example, their rates of attendance, delinquency, disruption and examination passes, which indicate that individual schools – their ethos, organization, teacher–pupil relationships and curriculum – do make a difference to pupil outcomes such as levels of attainment and disaffection. Since then, researchers have found that absenteeism is a multi-causal, multi-dimensional problem. Each absentee is unique with various combinations of social, psychological and institutional factors contributing to his or her non-attendance. Likewise, pupils are just as likely to misbehave in class because they dislike a teacher or subject as because of anxieties at home or psychological disturbance. Consequently, the search for school factors relating to disaffection has now begun in earnest.

Despite all this effort teachers continue to be fair game for politicians, the media and some of the general public. For example, on Thursday, 14 March 1985, and in the ensuing weeks, attacks on teachers and the teaching profession touched an all-time low. The Prime Minister, Margaret Thatcher, publicly blamed the alarming soccer violence which took place before, during and after the Luton Town–Milwall match the preceding evening on, amongst other things, the lack of discipline within schools and specifically made teachers the scapegoats for this rising trend. What nonsense! It was disgraceful and unworthy that a national leader and former Secretary of State for Education and Science should make such an unwarranted and unsubstantiated attack on the teaching profession, particularly as there was no evidence whatsoever to support her claim.

According to Her Majesty's Inspectorate, the vast majority of schools are well organized and controlled and free from large numbers of disruptive and difficult pupils. However, schools which contain a significant minority of disruptive pupils often have problems out of all proportion to the numbers involved. For instance, the Pack Committee (1977) which investigated truancy and indiscipline in Scotland, considered that the nature of disruptive behaviour in schools has changed over the years with certain pupils in some schools depicting far more brazen ill-conduct than ever before. Given the enormous changes which have taken place in education and society over the last two decades, it is to the great credit of teachers that they have managed to contain the situation at its present levels given their status in society, shortage of resources and lack of specific training in coping and dealing with difficult and disaffected pupils. In 1979–80, for example, there was no specific postgraduate main method course within universities in England and Wales which dealt with the training of teachers for work with difficult, less able pupils (Reid et al, 1981). Even now, many postgraduates, undergraduates and teachers continue to receive little, if any, worthwhile initial or in-service training in this complex field. Consequently, teachers have to rely far too much on their innate rather than acquired skills when they first begin, gradually, building up their own ways and means of coping with difficult pupils and demanding situations.

By blaming teachers for contributing to soccer violence, the Prime Minister was doing three things. First, she was irresponsibly diverting public attention away from the failure of the government to manage effectively by blaming a small and largely defenceless group within society – teachers.

Second, she was implying, if not acknowledging, that she was aware of existing deficiencies and the prevailing malaise within the profession. If she had come out publicly with a statement which recognized teachers' plights within schools and promised immediate action, she would have had the full support of teachers throughout Britain. After all, many teachers have been saying much the same thing openly because they are aware that events inside schools are becoming more difficult and, in some cases, getting worse. Most teachers feel a genuine concern for the well-being of present and future generations of pupils and dislike being put into a situation in which they cannot or are unable to give of their best. If, therefore, the Prime Minister was aware of the difficulties which existed within schools she should have started to examine the causes of these deficiencies rather than blaming schools and teachers for such things as football hooliganism, which they are powerless to prevent.

Of course, there is little doubt that a small minority of teachers are unsuitable for the profession. But this situation was partially caused by government policies in the 1960s and early 1970s when quantity not quality was the order of the day. This was an era in which, incidentally, Margaret Thatcher was Secretary of State for Education for part of the time. Rather than continually drawing public attention to the small number of teachers who are unfit or unsuitable for classroom leadership, the Prime Minister and her colleagues would have been better employed in manifesting their concern and goodwill for teachers and pupils alike by providing a massive injection of cash into education in order to give teachers and local education authorities the means to procure a better educational service, including a realistic recognition of teachers' in-service needs.

Third, the Prime Minister was publicly displaying her ignorance or deliberately ignoring the real causes of football hooliganism. It was quite ludicrous for any government to blame education for this present-day sickness because it is the government who are the leaders within society – not teachers. It is the government which determines public policy, thereby contributing, inadvertently or otherwise, to reaction or opposition from any section of the population, however deviant. Nevertheless, the Prime Minister's attacks on the subject, and the support she received in the media, are symptomatic of the low esteem in which the teaching profession is held in many quarters. Unfortunately, all this adverse publicity does is to lower the morale of the profession further, amuse disaffected pupils and make the job of maintaining control in the classroom harder rather than easier. Teacher-baiting is rapidly becoming a societal sickness. Furthermore, the policies adopted in the early to mid-1980s of 'cutbacks' in education, allied to falling rolls and low professional morale, are likely to create a climate in which disaffected behaviour will thrive – precisely the opposite outcome to the one which is required. The extent to which new policies on teacher assessments and the effects of youth unemployment will help counteract the educational malaise in which disaffection may rise must remain a matter for conjecture. Therefore, teachers do not *cause* football hooliganism.

If there was a direct causal link between teaching and football hooliganism, this would surely also apply to rugby, cricket, horse racing, athletics and fly fishing. The fact that such a relationship does not exist indicates that soccer hooliganism is a societal and political problem as much as a matter for the sport itself to rectify. It is a subject which is related to the infiltration amongst spectators of supporters of extreme right-wing ideologies; over-reactions by players and also by fans on the terraces; winning meaning everything, and unemployment more than classroom conduct.

An example of how teacher-baiting operates against the profession occurred in Manchester in October 1985 when five teachers were suspended for refusing to teach pupils who had daubed repugnant slogans on school walls, insulted staff and acted in a seriously disruptive manner. Rather than supporting the teachers' actions, the five found themselves suspended from duty by the local education committee for failing to teach the offenders. Surely this is the start of a very dangerous slippery slope. What chance has the profession when it fails to win the support of its employers? What sanctions are left for teachers to take if they can't even make a stand against blatantly offensive conduct? Teachers should not be blamed for contributing to declining standards in schools and in society when these circumstances occur. The Prime Minister and education employers would be better standing alongside teachers than lining up against them. After all, this is what normally happens in cases involving the police. Why make one rule for the police and another for teachers?

MULTIDISCIPLINARY PERSPECTIVES

As research initiatives into disaffection have been changing, so have the related professional attitudes and techniques. The discipline of psychology, for example, is currently debating the possibilities of changing the traditional role of psychologists and educational psychologists with all the self-anguish involved as old and new schools of thought clash. More specifically, in social psychology, the former emphasis on individual characteristics has largely given way over a period of time to more ecological approaches promoted by methodological developments. These developments have enabled psychologists to study people and their relationships within their social, cultural and historical context. As Frude (1984) writes 'the *in vitro* examination of people in contrived laboratory situations has been supplemented by *in vivo* observations in "real life situations" such as the home and the school'. Vigorous attempts, therefore, are being made to make psychology valid to people in everyday life rather than merely under experimental conditions. Increasingly psychologists are becoming more inclined to write about the implications of their findings as well as their conclusions, using actual case data and real-life situations. Although many educational psychologists remain 'psychometricians', a movement is growing from within educational psychology itself to allow members to engage in more problem-solving rather than diagnostic activities within schools and welfare agencies. Psychologists are coming out into the open to meet and talk to their clients more freely. Some now even resent being closeted behind closed doors guarding professional secrets.

Sociology, too, has changed. One significant change has seen sociologists become less dominated by 'macro-analysis' of large organizations in favour of smaller-scale 'micro-analysis' which examines in detail what goes on, for example, in individual schools and classrooms. Sociologists have been influenced by the work of labelling theorists, the interactionist school and ethno-methodology (Stubbs and Delamont, 1976).

Educationalists have been slow to respond to change, partly because, traditionally, education is not regarded as a discipline (Reid, 1984d). Hence, education has been too reliant on sociological and psychological rather than educational explanations for pupils' behaviour. This has led to an imbalance in work and much applied irrelevance. More recently, a new school-based, educationally-orientated movement has grown in momentum which is interested in the outcomes of educational systems and schooling upon pupils.

Therefore, a new era is dawning in studies into disaffection. For instance, from early work on clinical samples of truants (Tyerman, 1958; 1968), research has progressed from social and psychological explanations of the phenomenon (May, 1975; Galloway, 1976), to a stage where writers are beginning to show that the subject requires multidisciplinary approaches to be adopted which examine the interface of social, psychological and institutional factors (Reid, 1985a).

Such initiatives necessitate a meeting of professional minds leading to better interagency co-operation and more broadly-based initial and in-service training schemes which take account of the whole subject. Social workers following courses on absenteeism and disruption, for example, need to take cognizance of psychological aspects, the infuence of schools and related educational matters, as well as social and legislative issues. Guidance workers in schools need to be aware of the role and contribution of educational psychologists, social workers and child guidance as much as school factors and the operation of the *in loco parentis* concept. Without such training and understanding, professionals will at best only achieve partial and blinkered solutions.

Today, therefore, psychologists, sociologists and educationalists are beginning to step up their attempts to understand and seek explanations for disaffected behaviour. They are hampered by the individuality of each case, the different tolerance thresholds of pupils and teachers, differences between parental, teacher and social worker perspectives, differential local authority policies and practices, idiosyncratic court outcomes, regional variations in need, and by the fact that not all parents, schools, teachers and social workers are equally co-operative in helping collaborative or research ventures, given the delicate nature of the subject.

Likewise, the study of disaffection has been necessarily restricted by the normal practice of researchers concentrating upon aspects of the problem rather than on the whole topic. By and large, for instance, researchers have studied absenteeism and disruption as separate entities. This is not always the case. Some absentees are disruptive, some absentees are vandals, some vandals are disruptive, many absentees, vandals and disruptive pupils are underachievers.

Just as some researchers have tended to examine only the social (May, 1975) or psychological (Billington, 1978) aspects of absenteeism, so others have concentrated on limited approaches to comprehending disruptive behaviour. For example, recent studies into disruptive behaviour have tended to focus either on accounts of incident-analysis using teachers' reports (Comber and Whitfield, 1979), pupils' versions (Marsh et al, 1978), interviews with both teachers and their pupils (Galloway et al, 1982) or on individualistic explanations (Farrington, 1978) which seek to show that certain kinds of pupils are more prone to particular activities than others without explaining the links between the educational, social and psychological aspects of the problem.

Clearly, it is exceedingly difficult for researchers to attempt multidisciplinary approaches into absenteeism, disruption or disaffection when they are sponsored by specialist agencies on limited budgets with numerous time and resource constraints. But until social scientists stand up and insist that problems relating to disaffection – absenteeism, disruption, vandalism, violence and underachievement – are tackled from multidisciplinary perspectives, progress will continue to be slow and limited. The topic of disaffection not only requires multidisciplinary and interdisciplinary initiatives, it also requires global solutions.

SCHOOLS AND PASTORAL CARE SYSTEMS

Schools are beginning to lose their credibility with many youngsters today. Undoubtedly, amongst the numerous challenges which now face secondary schools is the requirement to meet the fluctuating needs of society and local communities during the dawn of a technological age. This is made more difficult in an era of change and decline in secondary education (Reid, 1983d). Nevertheless, schools are supposedly training youngsters for the twenty-first century; for increased leisure time and for the stark possibility that full employment is a myth. In such economic and educational climates, the onus upon schools to teach and train students using meaningful curricula is both fundamental and imperative to the survival of Britain as a trading nation. That schools are palpably failing to achieve these goals with a large proportion of their youngsters has been obvious for many years. Yet they are doing very little about it. Indeed, the educational response to changing economic and societal needs has been so poor that the Manpower Services Commission has begun to rival the Department of Education and Science as the main initiator of educational change and growth.

In some ways, previous research must take some of the blame for this trait. Too much research undertaken in the 1960s, 1970s and 1980s repeatedly let schools off the hook. Successive social and educational projects stressed that parents and individual pupils rather than schools and teachers were to blame for disaffected behaviour and underachievement. Simply put, this is not the case. All are equally culpable. Too many parents fail morally and educationally to support staff in schools. Conversely, too few teachers recognize the critical influence they have in detecting and overcoming disaffection and underachievement. Thus, teachers and parents need one another. They are both in the same boat – wanting their children to do as well as possible. It is in both their interests therefore to work more closely together. For example, underachievement, whether collective or individual, is linked with the degree to which those underachieving believe themselves valued by others or are trusted to take decisions for themselves. Whatever the resource level of an authority the real key to underachievement lies in the attitudes of people one to another within it (Brighouse, 1981).

Another reason for disaffection in secondary schools is the abject failure of pastoral care in many institutions. The separation of pastoral and curriculum work in the 1960s and 1970s was arguably one of the greatest disasters for schooling. There is very little evidence to show that the employment of vast numbers of pastoral workers in schools has reduced alienation, underachievement, disruptive conduct or absenteeism and improved educational standards. Arguably the move has been divisive, creating pastoral and academic empires, reducing the effectiveness of form tutors and resulting in more and more administration and bureaucracy. Indeed, some of the daily administrative tasks performed by middle management seem self-perpetuating rather than vital. Too few schools have devised successful strategies to link pastoral and academic work effectively. Again, it is not an 'either/or' situation. The promotion of pupils' intellectual and behavioural growth should be the mutual aim of both tiers within schools. Neither can achieve their promotional stage without the help of the other.

Poor pastoral work in schools is a failure of management. Sometimes schools lack clear job descriptions for postholders. There is no hierarchy of tasks. Pastoral appointees lack diagnostic skills. Most are insufficiently trained or totally untrained in such key subjects or issues as counselling, anxiety and maladjustment. Therefore, the talk of team work and systems training in schools is a fallacy. At best, many pastoral care teams are committed, with staff showing a high degree of caring and empathetic skills. But they lack training and understanding. Insight is no substitute for genuine knowledge.

The consequential stress upon pastoral workers in schools is much too high. Too many teachers are performing tasks as well as they can but, unfortunately, for which they are untrained or unsuitable. Thus, the demands of their job are unrealistic. By the end of term it is *they* and not their pupils who are exhausted. This is ridiculous. At the end of any school term, pupils and teachers should be equally tired; mildly so rather than exhausted.

In too many schools and classrooms, pupils look at their teachers with disgust or pity or are bored at the assignments given to them and by the kind of teaching they receive. This is particularly so in some classes for less able or middle-band pupils. There is a complete absence of structure in much of the secondary school curriculum in some schools. Far too many pupils learn little of value every day. In some form periods, for example, registration is stretched to take twenty minutes instead of two. Consequently, no worthwhile activities are taking place. All that is happening inside the room is of a negative nature – pupils learning to be late, whittle away time while beginning to despise and question the need for registration periods in the first place. This is a tragedy when well planned form periods can provide the very basis of a sound pastoral curriculum (Hamblin, 1986).

Teachers need to learn that good pastoral work is vital to positive outcomes in education and to real school effectiveness. Schools should devise suitable career and pastoral tuition at appropriate developmental stages for pupils. For example, the second year in comprehensive schools is the time when many pupils first begin opting out. Perhaps trouble begins to develop at home, younger siblings start to be seen as pests and maturation commences. None of these are major problems but are exacerbated by initial concerns over long-term job prospects, examinations, poor peer group relationships and learning difficulties. What happens? As some of the pupils start to gain in confidence, so they begin to rebel and are immediately punished for their conduct. In other words, the teachers or pastoral staff negatively reinforce the original deviant conduct at the expense of the real problem/s about which they know nothing – and probably never will. In the third year the problems ferment and grow. By the fourth, some of the pupils are persistent absentees, disrupters and underachievers, totally alienated from the system. It is then too late to rectify the situation. This is the story of any pupil in any school at any time, in any place. It is what I mean by the failure of pastoral care in schools: staff ignorant of their pupils' needs, problems and aspirations. Really good pastoral care and teaching is about knowing the total child – what makes a pupil tick as well as learn. This is why it is so silly to subdivide teaching into two distinct phases – learning and caring. In my view, good, successful teaching in classrooms is at least as important as competent administration and should be so rewarded. It is ludicrous that in order to climb the career ladder successful teachers have to leave the very job they are best at: educating children.

This is also why pastoral care should be seen as a skilled, trained, specialist job. Pastoral programmes in schools should be timetabled to stretch the judgement and decision-making skills of pupils. In the third year, for instance, these programmes should incorporate schemes to test pupils' motivation, achievement levels, ideas about success, gender stereotypes, and the community. Generally this is far from the norm. Equal opportunities for boys and girls in school, for example, continues to be a myth. Many fourth- and fifth-year girls have already formed very negative stereotypes of their careers and are diverted away from science. This is all wrong. It leads to disillusionment and female disadvantage. In this respect schools are in collusion with many of society's derogatory processes towards women. By the fifth year in schools, the pastoral curriculum should focus on examination anxiety, adjustment to work and learning to live as an adult in the community.

It is my firm belief that too many teachers experience the same routine in schools thirty or forty times throughout their careers. Apart from status, salary and resource deficiencies, this is one of the main reasons for the cancerous malaise in secondary education; a malaise which is recognized and felt by many pupils as well as teachers. It is about time that senior management in some schools started to combat staff disaffection – let alone pupil alienation. This will not be easy and poses a severe test for the managerial skills of headteachers, deputies, heads of year and heads of department. But there are some ways round the problems through imaginative job rotation and staff development schemes, school-based in-service and the promotion of tasks designed to foster a corporate spirit. Schools which do not have clear aims and objectives and united managerial strategies are likely to be those in which pupil and staff disaffection ferment and grow.

The Hargreaves Committee (1984, p. 89) make a profound statement on the manner in which schools and teachers currently perceive their disaffected pupils. This extract is so full of sound common sense that it is worth quoting in full because it expresses the sentiment behind this book.

> The most urgent need, we believe, is to change the way in which we perceive these (disaffected) pupils. At present in this country we tend to treat the pupils who do not fit into the secondary school as *problems*: they are pupils who are labelled as 'difficult', as 'deviants' or as 'misfits'. There is, it is said, nothing wrong with the school, but there is something wrong with the pupils who reject the school. Quite rightly, we try all we can to help such pupils to adjust to school like the majority of their peers but, when our attempts to integrate them fail, we tend to respond in one of two ways. The first response is often to be punitive by suspending the disruptive pupil. Schools may use

suspension also to demonstrate that continued disruptive or antisocial behaviour is unacceptable to the school community and to enable teachers and the other pupils in the class to get on with their work without disturbance while discussions take place with the parents. The second response is to reject them. The misfits are best catered for if they are placed outside the normal school, in a special class or a special unit, where people with the appropriate expertise, skill or interest can cope with these pupils, leaving ordinary teachers or ordinary pupils free to get on with the normal business of schooling.

We are not unsympathetic to these responses. Disaffected and disruptive pupils do indeed create real problems for teachers and other pupils. Not unnaturally, teachers often feel relieved when such pupils are absent. All this is true. But it is also true that the response of punishment and rejection tends to make the pupils worse, not better. They *know* [my italics] they are being rejected, and they resent it. They feel they have their own valid point of view, their own criticisms of the school and the teachers, and their own unmet needs none of which they believe are being taken seriously. The ensuing state of relationships between frustrated and rejecting teachers and resentful and rejected pupils is clearly unsatisfactory. Relationships can at this point only deteriorate. It is possible, we think, to break out of this vicious circle only by changing our general approach to these young people. The school's initial response to disaffection and disruptive behaviour should always be to seek the support and co-operation of the parents and to reintegrate the pupil into the normal life of the classroom. But when these attempts fail, as they do with a minority of pupils, there is no point in rejecting the pupils and blaming them for their refusal to conform or fit in. Instead, it seems more realistic and more productive to accept that the school has in some sense failed *them* rather than insisting that it is they who have failed *us*. Our school system can work for the majority, but we need not be afraid of recognising that for a minority the ordinary school, with its curriculum, teaching methods and organisation, is simply inappropriate. Instead of blaming and rejecting this minority, we can, if we recognise the limitations of the school to cater for the needs of every child, be ready to treat their rejection of school as legitimate and thus seek *positive alternatives* by which their needs can be met. The theme of our remarks on the severely disaffected and disruptive is this:

first, seek to integrate and, when that fails, find a positive alternative.

Finally, and it has to be said, the existing levels of quantifiable and unquantifiable pupil disaffection within many schools today is nothing short of a national disgrace. Some of the reasons why pupils manifest this behaviour is best summed up in the following incident which is an everyday occurrence inside some schools. One Tuesday morning in March 1985, I attended a third year careers convention in a large comprehensive school in South Wales. Sitting around the perimeters of a large, cold gym sat some twenty-five representatives of industry, business, tertiary, further and higher education, the police, armed forces and commerce. The session lasted two hours. During the whole of this time a large number of teachers stood in the centre of the gym talking amongst themselves. At no time did I see any member of staff liaise with any of the representatives or their pupils. Indeed, for half the time, some of the pupils ran around the gym completely unattended, manifesting their boredom. At the end of the session, the representatives left the hall without even a cup of tea.

The questions asked by the pupils indicated that some of them had received very little preparation or advice from staff on how to make meaningful long-term subject choices with their career aspirations in mind. Indeed, some of the pupils showed openly their concern and uncertainty by walking around the convention with their fourth- and fifth-year option programme sheets in their hands. It was apparent that many of the third-years were looking to the representatives to advise them on what subjects to take in their build up to future external examination programmes. However, even a cursory look at some of the pupils' option sheets showed that their choices bore little relationship to their future career needs. One girl, for example, hoped to become a vet. Yet she had been told by the school that she was not allowed to take more than two sciences in the fourth year as a matter of policy. Another hoped to become a maths teacher. He had been told to aim for a Grade 1 CSE rather than an 'O' level in maths because it was just as good. A third pupil asked my colleague and me if we could fill in her option sheet because she was so confused about what subjects she was supposed to or could take. In one sense this was hardly surprising. Three of the subjects she wished to take at 'O' level all appeared in the same column and she could select only one. In other columns, subjects appeared which she had no desire to take – precisely the scenario Hargreaves (1984) describes. Surely, therefore, the third-year tutors could have approached the career representatives with at least those pupils who were undecided or unsure about which subjects to follow during the next two vital years of their secondary education. After all, this would have shown the third-year pupils and the career representatives that their teachers cared – if nothing else. As it was, I am sure everybody drew their own conclusions. If teachers are not sufficiently interested in their pupils' careers and subject choices, in what are they interested? Therein lies the root of the problem: unprofessional, unscientific and unthinking work on the part of far too many teachers, often unwittingly so.

To summarize, schools must change. They must teach pupils what they *need* to know for their roles and jobs in society in the twenty-first century. They must improve their career guidance, pastoral provision, curriculum and home–school links. Schools must also work more closely and more harmoniously with external agencies concerned with helping disaffected and disadvantaged children. If schools do not change rapidly, then the present levels of disaffection and the various manifestations of this behaviour could continue to rise dramatically to a point where, in the long run, the consequences of having large numbers of unemployed, unskilled, disillusioned and alienated youngsters and adults alike will start to undermine society, as these people wittingly or unwittingly seek their revenge upon those who have let them down. In the final analysis, the prevention of such anarchy is what this book is really about. It endeavours to give professionals a basis in knowledge for the understanding and combatting of disaffected behaviour. Just as young seeds grow into large trees so disaffected youngsters can become dissatisfied, disgruntled adults. It is one of life's unsolved tragedies.

2
ABSENTEEISM

THE 'PROBLEM' OF ABSENTEEISM

There is currently a great deal of concern and disquiet about the large number of pupils who deliberately miss school daily. This anxiety is well founded because the consequences of consistently skipping school are very severe and suggest wider social, psychological and educational problems, disadvantage and disaffection.

One of the saddest and least publicized facts about persistent absentees is that many of them do not know what to do with their time when they are away from school. Some, for example, merely wander around their neighbourbood bored, engaging in such meaningless and monotonous activities as sitting in cafés, playing records at the homes of friends, visiting fairgrounds or getting themselves into further trouble with the authorities by stealing, trespassing or vandalizing public or private property. It is a tragic indictment of existing educational, pastoral and social provision that so many youngsters opt for this life-style in preference to learning in the classroom and socializing with their peers at school.

Absenteeism poses difficulties for the various educational and social personnel who attempt to cope with and cater for the needs of a large and deprived group of pupils for a variety of reasons. Legally, non-attendance at school is a problem because of the consequences for parents who break their statutory duties by failing to send their children to school. Psychologically, truancy and absenteeism are symptomatic of deeper disturbances within individuals which may foreshadow more serious manifestations in later child and adult life. Sociologically, truancy and absenteeism are known to be linked with multiple adverse home conditions, low social class and deprivation. Educationally, truancy and absenteeism are sources of concern because non-attenders tend to fall behind in their school work with all the consequences this statement implies. Finally, institutionally, truancy and absenteeism suggest disaffection with school.

At no time has the outlook for absentees looked so bleak than now as we move towards the so-called technological age. Of nowhere is this situation more true than in today's schools. Secondary education is in the midst of an era of change and decline exacerbated by acute shortages of resources. Similarly, the health and social services also lack certain professionally qualified staff as well as resources.

Consider the facts about education and absenteeism carefully. Teachers are extremely busy people. Few of them are experts on all the multi-dimensional facets of absenteeism. Their workloads and the organization of schools mean that not many of them have the time to know a great deal about some of their less able and deviant pupils like truants and absentees. In any event, few teachers are particularly sympathetic to pupils whom they classify as non-conformers. Consequently, a lot of teachers – being only human – are not too upset when they find only twenty instead of thirty pupils present in their classes. Such situations simply mean less work and more manageable units for them. Put another way, less time in dispute or cajoling some of the least able and occasionally difficult pupils who have openly demonstrated their rejection of schooling and other forms of social control by staying away.

ROOTS OF ABSENTEEISM

Previous research conducted before the mid-1970s tended to put all the blame for truancy and absenteeism on to a pupil's home background and related social factors (Tyerman, 1958; 1968). This is simply not the case, although the myth lingers on. While a very high proportion of truants and absentees come from deprived and unsupportive home backgrounds, fortunately not every pupil in these circumstances elects or is encouraged to miss school. Thus, home background is only one spoke in an extremely complex wheel.

Transferring all the blame for absenteeism on to the homes and social backgrounds of pupils and parents can best be described as a 'cop-out'. Too often, many professionals (especially teachers) conveniently ignore their own part and the role of their institutions in the process. Research has repeatedly shown that schools tend to be places which reward the able more than the less able (Hargreaves, 1967; 1982; Hargreaves et al, 1975). It must be very difficult being below average in such environments especially when long-term job prospects are so bleak; the school curriculum is palpably unsuited to the needs of many incumbents and individual attention in the classroom is often lacking because of such factors as size, staff uninterest, teachers' incompetence or inability to control or enthuse with middle and lower bands, as well as complications caused by teaching certain subjects in mixed-ability situations.

Recent research (Reid, 1985a) suggests, therefore, that teachers and schools can be blamed for absenteeism as much as parents and pupils' home backgrounds. It is probably not unfair to suggest that while many pupils 'mitch' illegally, their behaviour can be viewed as almost justifiable when the full extent of their individual social, psychological, and educational circumstances are known. Extortion and bullying at school and boredom in lessons as a result of perpetual inactivity or meaningless activity are three such educational examples. Another less overt one is the repeated failure of pastoral care teams, teachers and social workers to respond positively to the social and educational needs and pleas for help of some deprived pupils in empathetic rather than punishment-orientated terms.

Nowadays, only a small minority of protagonists continue to hypothesize 'causes' for absenteeism and truancy. One of the reasons for this trend lies in the fact that research has ascertained that while a high proportion of truants and absentees show certain social and psychological traits, they do not all share the same individual characteristics. Hence, every truant and absentee is unique.

Another fantasy is that all truants and absentees are difficult pupils. Again, this is simply not true of the majority. The real truth is that they tend to be very sensitive people. No one appreciates their limitations more than they. They are not ogres. Rather, they are frequently the victims of their own unfortunate social, psychological and educational circumstances. To be frank, many absentees can be classified as 'born losers'. Few of them are born or blessed with life's natural advantages and have little prospect of upward social mobility to look forward to in the future. Quite a number are shy, inward-looking people who are grateful for any help and interest they receive – provided no strings are attached. This 'difficult' fable partly grew because researchers tended to conduct their research into absenteeism on 'clinical' (the worse and most hardened cases – often truant delinquents) samples.

Another reason lies in the fact that until recently most research utilized conventional techniques of gathering data – demographic variables, standardized tests and the judgements of third parties such as teachers, parents (to a lesser extent) and education welfare officers in order to describe the characteristics of absentees. Consequently, many researchers did not know their absentee samples very well, if at all, and there was a marked lack of school-based research.

Between 1977 and 1980, Reid (1981; 1982; 1983; 1984; 1985a) undertook a two-stage school-based study which used a social anthropological (Stubbs and Delamont, 1976) and test-questionnaire approach. The first part of this study was based entirely on the perceptions of a large group of Persistent Absentees whose views were contrasted with two vastly different Control Groups (one from the same forms as the non-attenders; the other comprised of pupils from academic bands, both matched for age and sex) of good attenders. When added to the knowledge obtained from previous studies, these findings have helped to provide a comprehensive picture of many of the reasons why some pupils decide to miss school.

Certain aspects related to truancy and absenteeism continually recur in the literature. Taken together, recent research suggests that pupils skip school for three different but complementary and often linked groups of reasons – home background and social class origins; socio-environmental, social psychological and cultural explanations; and finally, school factors. Home and social class background aspects incorporate unstable home backgrounds (divorce, separation, death of a parent, parent in prison, one-parent families); large families; pupils with low birth order positions; unemployed or irregularly employed parent(s); fathers who are away from home for long or frequent periods (merchant seamen, long-distance lorry drivers); parental condoned absence for any reason (such as caring for a younger brother or sister while the mother is at work or undertaking the family shopping); short- or long-term paternal or maternal illness; defective home discipline; an 'unhealthy' atmospheric climate within the home; sibling friction; histories of paternal, maternal or sibling truancy within the family; homes with low incomes and low housekeeping standards; parents unable to cope with life or who demonstrate a variety of social pathologies (alcoholism, mental illness, violent conduct, family disorganization and associated stress factors); families in which the parents are uncooperative and/or hostile to authority in general, especially to school authorities; and families at the lower end of the social scale (especially when the father is employed either in unskilled or semi-skilled work).

Socio-environmental, social psychological and cultural explanations include poor housing; overcrowding; poverty; geographical location; urban and rural dimensions; racial and cultural traditions; community ethos and ethics; fear of attending school (realistic or irrational including school refusal cases); personality factors (such as a low self-concept, introversion or isolationism); free school meals; peer-group influences; the attraction of alternative employment; school community conflicts; and individual characteristics such as laziness (oversleeping, lateness and a dislike of walking or travelling to school).

School aspects include falling behind in classwork (often following an illness); form and school transfers for any reason; a dislike or fear of certain lessons (such as physical education), tests or examinations; boredom or inactivity at school; bullying; extortion; difficult peer-group relationships within individual forms or at school; teasing (due to personal characteristics – red hair, fatness, 'squeaky' voice or other reasons); the general lack of discipline and order in the school, form or the playground; noise levels; school rules and punishments; poor teacher–pupil relationships; organizational factors within schools (split-site, constantly changing classrooms after every lesson, assemblies); staff turnover (especially a change of form or subject teacher); staff attitudes; size of school; school ethos and atmosphere; lack of a school uniform, equipment or sports kit; and, finally, negative pastoral care systems.

The link between individual home background, social and school factors is perhaps best shown in families where the parents are uninterested in their children's progress at school, are the victims of dreadful environments, unsure of their constitutional rights and responsibilities and pass on their values to their children.

Reid's interviewing of persistent absentees revealed four further interesting trends. First, absentees tend to blame their schools rather than themselves or their families for creating the circumstances which first caused them to miss school. Second, many absentees make allowances for the treatment they receive from their parents at home but not for their teachers at school. Third, many absentees have more than one reason for missing or avoiding school. Fourth, there are significant differences between pupils' initial and later reasons for missing school. It seems that one event will often trigger off a pupil's desire to miss school. Thereafter, the number of reasons for skipping school tends to increase with time – presumably in order to justify the original action and because the longer pupils are away the harder it is for them to re-integrate successfully into school life. Recent findings clearly imply, therefore, that schools could do far more to detect initial rather than persistent non-attendance. When initial absenteeism and truancy lie undetected, schools stand little chance of preventing the behaviour from escalating and reaching the chronic stage in a large number of instances.

NIGEL

Many of the aforementioned points are highlighted in the following brief case history of Nigel who attends a large comprehensive school in South Wales.

Nigel lives with his father, mother, sister and three brothers in semi-squalid conditions in a three-bedroomed council house situated close to a busy industrial estate in a large conurbation. Since the age of two, Nigel has shared a bed with one of his elder brothers. The inside of his home shows signs of advanced decay – bare walls, damp and a considerable amount of disrepair. Much of the furniture is basic and old, the low quality carpets are well worn and the small garden is unkempt. Nigel's father is now unemployed. Formerly, he undertook unskilled work in a local factory and was employed as a long-distance lorry driver and merchant seaman.

Nigel first started to miss school at the age of nine ('When my father used to come home'). The volume of his absences increased shortly after he transferred to the local comprehensive school. ('I hate the place – everything about it. It's too big and the teachers don't care about you'). Nigel claimed that his troubles in school increased after he was put into a class in which he knew few of his peers. ('I didn't like the other children in my class. Sometimes I used to "mitch" with my old classmates – but now I hardly ever see them.')

School reports indicate that despite low ability, his lack of progress is entirely due to his absenteeism. In an average term, he misses about 85 per cent of possible attendances. Consequently, his parents have been prosecuted twice for his truancy and fined. ('My mother cares quite a lot. Sometimes she cries and gets depressed. I don't think my father is really bothered. He says that missing school never did him any harm.')

Psychological 'tests' showed that Nigel has a low academic self-concept and general level of self-esteem. When he attended, his behaviour in school was rated as quite good, although he manifested some neurotic rather than anti-social tendencies. Evidence obtained from a repertory grid technique (Kelly, 1955) revealed that he cared deeply for his parents despite their obvious neglect of him. This is a significant point because a social worker's report written about Nigel after he had been prosecuted for trespassing on a railway line and theft from a local store, suggested that he was a case of 'gross parental neglect'.

Nigel's circumstances reinforce the interface of social, psychological and institutional factors in school absenteeism and truancy. Although some of his personal characteristics are unusual, in some ways he fits Tyerman's (1968) description of the typical, isolated truant who comes from a deprived and unsupportive home background. But there is more to his case. Psychologically, he shows deficiencies in personality, intellect, motivation and socialization. Educationally, Nigel is a failure mainly because of his non-attendance. However, as neither he nor his parents attach much importance to his scholastic achievements at school, his failure is only to be expected. Using Reid's (1985a) categories (see Chapter 5), Nigel can be classified as a Generic as opposed to Typical, Psychological or Institutional absentee because his circumstances include elements of social, psychological and educational reasons for missing school.

TYPES OF ABSENTEEISM

Everybody thinks they know what constitutes absenteeism from school. Nevertheless, it is quite hard to define and there is a real danger of people using terms wrongly. Teachers, for example, frequently refer to 'truants' when they really mean 'non-attenders', 'parental-condoned absentees' or 'school refusers'.

Therefore, general labels such as 'absenteeism', 'persistent school absenteeism', and 'school non-attendance' have become increasingly used by recent researchers (Carroll, 1977). These terms have been preferred because they encompass truancy and the superficially less serious forms of poor attendance at school and recognize the fact that the same pupil can miss school for different reasons on different occasions. Moreover, terms like 'absenteeism' and 'non-attendance' do not carry with them some of the more emotive connotations commonly associated with labels such as 'truancy' and 'school phobia'. Hence, in modern day usage, 'absenteeism' and 'non-attendance' are global terms which denote all forms of absence except illness.

Nevertheless, certain distinct categories of absence have been studied and used by researchers for over 100 years. These include 'truancy' (originally 'wandering'), 'parental-condoned absence' and 'school refusal'/'school phobia'. Tyerman (1968, p. 9) defined a truant as a child who is absent on his own initiative without his parents' consent. School refusal or school phobia is a more complicated phenomenon which incorporates a variety of definitions in the literature depending upon researchers' standpoints. Typically, school refusal is manifested by cases of pupils who show outward signs of emotional upset when faced with the prospect of going to school for a variety of reasons. School refusal cases are often associated with pupils of higher than average intelligence, who inwardly fear failure and have over-demanding parents.

Parental-condoned absence is a category which is beginning to receive increasing attention as its importance is becoming more fully appreciated. For instance, research by Galloway (1976), Galloway et al (1982), and Caven and Harbison (1980) suggests that parental-condoned absenteeism can account for as much as half or three-quarters of all illegitimate non-attendance. An academic debate exists in the literature about whether parental-condoned absence is in fact truancy. The Pack Committee (SED, 1977), for example, which investigated truancy and disruptive behaviour in

Scotland, took the view that parental-condoned absence is in fact truancy. They went on to formulate their own definition of truancy which stated that: 'Truancy is unauthorized absence from school, for any period, as a result of premeditated or spontaneous action on the part of the pupil, parent or both.'

RATES OF ABSENTEEISM

Despite numerous difficulties in the collection and interpretation of reliable data on absenteeism (Williams, 1974), an historical and statistical analysis of the subject shows that pupil rates of non-attendance vary considerably – by country, region (even within comparatively homogeneous localities), sex, age, school and school type, race, season and week.

Historically, it is worth mentioning that the shift towards compulsory attendance was gradual. Radical changes were needed in the thinking and attitudes of Victorian and Edwardian society before the move towards compulsory schooling could take place. In the event, ruling classes in England changed their position from employing child labourers under harsh conditions to educating the same children, within a comparatively short period. The transition, however, was far from smooth. Between 1899 and 1939 schooling was in some aspects both stark and repressive and compulsory education was far from universally accepted by the entire population (Humphries, 1981), especially in regions like South Wales (Reynolds and Murgatroyd, 1977). Although attendance at school for all children between the ages of five and the recognized school leaving age has been partially compulsory since 1870 and entirely so since 1918, it took nearly forty years for average attendance to reach 80 per cent in London, Scotland and certain other urban and rural areas (Rubinstein, 1968; Roxburgh, 1971; Withrington, 1975).

During the early to mid-1970s, numerous attempts were made to measure the rates of attendance in schools during a day (DES, 1975; ILEA, 1976, 1980, 1981), a week (NACEWO, 1975), a term (Galloway, 1976), and a school year (Baum, 1978; White and Peddie, 1978). Researchers who have studied patterns of attendance generally agree that they show a marked reduction during the day, week, term, and school year (Baum, 1978), with the Spring Term being the worst, probably because of illness and inclement weather conditions (Sandon, 1961).

Absenteeism rates have been found to vary between 2 and 24 per cent depending upon who and what is asked. Usually, the figures have ranged in surveys between 2 and 12 per cent (DES, 1975; SED, 1977; Caven and Harbison, 1980) but individual reports by Her Majesty's Inspectorate show that certain schools in South Wales, North West England and Scotland have much higher rates of absenteeism: between 20 and 40 per cent is not uncommon in certain areas.

The one-day national survey of all secondary and middle schools in England and Wales (DES, 1975) reported that 9.9 per cent of all pupils were absent on the day. Of these, 2.2 per cent had no legitimate reason for absence. Subsequently, these latter figures are often quoted as probable national absenteeism and truancy rates (Carroll, 1977). By contrast, school refusal rates have been found to account for less than 1 per cent of all absences, probably even lower (Rutter et al, 1970; Berg, 1980).

A pressure group, the National Association of Chief Education Welfare Officers (NACEWO, 1975), carried out their own survey in October 1973, of all secondary schools in sixteen local education authorities. Their findings showed that 24 per cent of the secondary pupils were absent. Of these, it was estimated that between 3.5 and 7 per cent of the children were away from school without good cause. In another survey undertaken in Scotland (SED, 1977), which involved a six-week study of secondary pupils, 15 per cent were found to have been unaccountably absent on at least one occasion. Whichever findings are believed, the total number of children missing school daily is very high and these figures can be used as one measure of disaffection. Obviously, using such statistics for rates of disaffection is fraught with difficulty as they ignore disenchanted pupils who continue to attend school despite their feelings, including pupils in middle and academic bands.

The problems of school absenteeism are not solely confined to Britain. The United States has similar, if not greater, difficulties especially in parts of the Deep South, industrial North East and cities like New York where the attendance at some high schools is estimated in some academic papers to be below 50 per cent with black and immigrant pupils having lower rates of attendance than white (Abbott and Breckinridge, 1970). Even emerging African states are not immune, nor are developed and underdeveloped countries such as Spain and India. As far as is known, however, absenteeism is not a major concern in Eastern Europe. The lower incidence of absenteeism in countries like France and West

Germany is undoubtedly attributable in part to the earlier and more punitive measures taken against parents for their offsprings' non-attendance.

Evidence from the National Child Development longitudinal studies of children born in 1946 and 1958 has revealed substantial differences in rates of attendance in different regions throughout England and Wales. These differences have remained consistent over a considerable period of time (Douglas and Ross, 1965; Davie et al, 1972; Fogleman and Richardson, 1974). At the age of eleven, for example, almost twice as many pupils in Wales (14.6 per cent) than the south-west of England (7.5 per cent) failed to make 85 per cent of possible attendances. The truancy rate in Wales is also higher than in England: 4.1 per cent compared with 2.1 per cent. South Wales in particular has special problems (Carroll, 1977).

Most studies agree that more girls than boys are absent from school at both the secondary and junior school levels. In infant classes the reverse is true (Mitchell and Shepherd, 1980). By contrast, the Department of Education and Science and Welsh Office Survey of 1974 reported that there was only a slight difference between the attendance rates of secondary boys and girls. However, Tyerman's (1968) research, undertaken on a clinical sample, found that nine times more boys than girls are truants. At the junior school level, when teacher ratings have been used, a greater proportion of boys than girls have been considered or suspected of being truants (Mitchell and Shepherd, 1980). Some researchers, however, believe that far more girls than boys miss school with the consent of their parents. Truancy as a symptom of delinquent behaviour is more characteristic of boys than girls (Tennent, 1971; West and Farington, 1973, 1977; West, 1982). Irrespective of sex, once a pupil starts truanting, this behaviour is likely to persist (Davie, 1972; Fogleman and Richardson, 1974; White and Peddie, 1978).

Another quirk of published statistics is that rates of absenteeism and truancy vary between who and what is asked with major differences being recorded between estimates obtained from parents, teachers and the pupils themselves (Fogleman, 1976; Fogleman et al, 1980). In the National Child Development Study, for example, 52 per cent of pupils reported that they had truanted at one time or another in their final year of compulsory education although parents' reports claimed that 88 per cent of their children never truanted.

The peak age for absenteeism and truancy is now 14-plus with the final compulsory year of schooling the worst time (Galloway, 1980). Overall rates of absenteeism tend, therefore, to increase with age. Nevertheless, the importance of prevention in the primary school should never be forgotten. In Reid's (1982d) sample, for instance, nearly 20 per cent of the Persistent Absentees first began to miss school at the junior stage.

Truancy and absenteeism rates also vary considerably by school and school types. Gray et al (1980) found that absenteeism increases from about 10 per cent in primary and lower secondary age ranges to approximately 20 per cent in the last years of compulsory education. Their London statistics show primary school attendance rates to have remained fairly constant over a long period of time. In secondary schools in London, however, rates of non-attendance rose from between 9 and 10 per cent in 1966–77 to 14 per cent in 1978. Conversely, Moore and Jardine (1983) in their follow-up Northern Ireland study found a reduction in the number of absentees in 1982 compared with 1977. There was also a general reduction in the length of absences. It is difficult to be certain, therefore, whether absenteeism from secondary schools is rising as some protagonists believe (Boyson, 1974; Reynolds et al, 1976). Further research might reveal substantial regional differences on this matter.

Rutter et al (1979), in their notable study of twelve Inner London secondary schools, reported that the average attendance of fifth-year pupils during two weeks in September and January varied between 12.8 and 17.3 out of a maximum of twenty possible attendances. The proportion of poor attendances per school ranged from 5.7 per cent to 25.9 per cent. Similarly, Reynolds et al (1976) investigated comprehensive schools in a South Wales valley and found that rates of absenteeism between schools varied considerably. Therefore, the work of Rutter and Reynolds clearly implies that the school is one of several factors which affects attendance.

SUMMARY

The family and home circumstances of absentees and truants are usually characterized by multiple deprivation. Not only do many absentees come from unfortunate and unsupportive backgrounds but often from unhappy homes. They are also inclined to have low self-concepts and to have been schooled on a diet of unrewarding academic and educational experiences. In their personal lives, they are inclined to be loners and to have fewer friends in school than good attenders. Thus, absenteeism is nurtured on failure, confrontation and disadvantage at home and in school as well as anti-learning attitudes which permeate certain local communities. Recent research shows that absenteeism from school is the result of interaction between pupils' home and social backgrounds, psychological and institutional factors. Far more research is needed on the educational aspects related to absenteeism from schools, especially on such matters as the curriculum, discipline, teachers' attitudes and pastoral provision.

Viewed from these standpoints and irrespective of 'cause', absenteeism may be seen as a positive expression of disaffection from school, in the sense that pupils opt out, alone or in groups, in search of alternative ways of spending their time. The irony of their behaviour is that their actions inevitably compound their own long-term disadvantage.

3
DISRUPTION
IN SCHOOLS

It often seems that the mass media would like the general public to believe that educational standards are continually declining accompanied by alarming acts of disruptive behaviour in schools. This is hardly surprising. After all, such stories make good headlines and help to sell newspapers. In support of their claim, protagonists argue that increasing numbers of teachers are unable to cope in the classroom, teacher stress is high, teacher competence low, much of the curriculum is irrelevant and unstructured, school rules are constantly being changed and undermined, absenteeism rates are too high and in some schools pupils not only come and go as they please but act in undisciplined ways by being rude and abusive to staff and showing little interest in learning.

It is extremely difficult to assess objectively the merits of these claims because schooling has altered so much in character over the years. On one side of the coin, a higher proportion of pupils achieve passes in public examinations than ever before. Conversely, large numbers of parents and employers frequently suggest that standards of written English, mathematics and general levels of comprehension and understanding have declined. Either way, the simple truth is that such claims are almost impossible to verify and remain a matter of conjecture and belief.

The precise extent to which schools are prone to acts of disruptive behaviour by pupils is very hard to detect for a variety of reasons. First, there are differences between the general public's and teachers' views on the matter. Standards of behaviour in schools have changed as schools have become more liberal institutions. The cane, for example, is either banned or used very sparingly by headteachers these days whereas thirty years ago it was often used for minor offences. Second, as we shall see later in the chapter, the evidence from research points in certain directions but remains unclear and is not universally accepted. Third, there are disputes between educationalists about what constitutes disruptive behaviour and what is meant by the terms 'disruptive' and 'disrupters'. Finally, there are differences between schools, classrooms and individual teachers when analysed by intake, teacher expectations, levels of tolerance and actual everyday standards of conduct.

Obtaining objective data on disruptive behaviour is a difficult enterprise in itself. Whereas the media has a tendency to sensationalize some incidents in schools, such as acts of vandalism and assaults on teachers, this is balanced by the normal reluctance on the part of school personnel and educational administrators to admit too openly to their problems when questioned. Such reticence is understandable. Clearly, schools which are prone to high levels of disruptive activity would prefer to avoid unfavourable publicity if only for the sake of teacher and parent morale. In any event, a lot of abusive and disruptive behaviour in schools lies undetected or, more accurately, goes unreported. For instance, some teachers these days simply ignore what have become everyday outbursts by a few difficult pupils such as swearing or threats of retaliatory action following punishment for misdemeanours. It is the soccer pitch syndrome. If each footballer who swore, cheated or repeatedly fouled on the pitch was sent off every time, there would soon be no league soccer. So it is in schools. If every serious deviant or disruptive act resulted in suspension, many school rolls would soon fall dramatically. This would be especially true in some inner-city areas in large conurbations like Birmingham, Cardiff, Liverpool, London and Glasgow.

Therefore, aspects of school life have changed over the years. People educated in small, select schools between, say, 1900 and

1965 would probably find numerous organizational and behavioural differences today if they were enabled to return to the classroom. Experienced teachers, for example, often claim that confrontation in classrooms, along corridors and within the perimeters of schools used to occur less frequently. Whether this is merely a product of their imagination with the passing of time is hard to ascertain with certainty. Clearly, both society and educational practices have changed but not all change is necessarily for the worse. After all, schools are far more humane places today than ever before, whatever some pupils might care to think.

The fact remains that few teachers are adequately trained on initial or in-service courses to cope with acts of disruptive behaviour in class. After all, how can they be? Every instance is spontaneous and unique. Simulation exercises provide only a partial solution. Hence, it is the case that first-time events like being sworn at, being pushed out of the way or being given two-finger signs often form watersheds in the professional lives of many new male and female entrants to the teaching profession. How they cope and handle these potentially disruptive situations can be crucial to their future well-being, career development and health. Just explaining the action of offenders to superiors on such occasions for instance, is never easy, especially when one senses that those in authority are inclined to view the matter rather differently – taking teacher error or inexperience into account!

EXTENT OF DISRUPTIVE BEHAVIOUR

Given the sensitivity of teachers, schools and local education authorities, it is hardly surprising that the topic has received so little attention by way of research until fairly recently. Moreover, the dearth of acceptable evidence is in itself a considerable handicap in drawing too many firm conclusions.

A historical analysis of the literature shows that violent and disruptive conduct in schools has been displayed by a minority of certain pupils since the Middle Ages and has continued unabated into the nineteenth and twentieth centuries. This conduct has been as prevalent in the last 100 years in the United States as in Britain.

The advent of comprehensive schooling in Britain and the emergence of the Black Papers on Education gave rise to a number of research projects, reports and books which were published in the early and late 1970s (Lowenstein, 1972; 1975; DES, 1975b; NUT,

1976; SED, 1977) and have continued thereafter (Dierenfield, 1982; Galloway et al, 1982; Tattum, 1982; Frude and Gault, 1984). Evidence from these studies provides a fairly uneven and patchy picture. In 1976, for example, the Essex County Teachers' Working Party on disruptive behaviour in schools stated that there had been no wholesale breakdown of discipline in schools in the county. They added, however, that in recent years the disruptive influence of a minority of pupils had caused increasing difficulties. By contrast, giving evidence to the same working party (NUT, 1976), the Berkshire Association of Secondary Heads reported a rise in physical attacks on teachers and serious acts of disobedience.

The Pack Committee (SED, 1977), which investigated indiscipline and truancy in Scotland, gave some guarded support to the latter conclusion. They determined that indiscipline could be on the increase in some areas, but probably not others. They felt that there were no indications to show that acts of disruptive behaviour were out of control or of alarming proportions. Nevertheless, and here we come to the crux of the matter, the committee believed that the character of disruptive behaviour in schools had changed in recent years making it harder to control.

Consider the facts carefully. Only twenty or thirty years ago, most pupils in schools were meek and submissive and their teachers uniformly authoritarian in nature. As schools have changed and become increasingly humane places, so it seems that some pupils have become increasingly bold, leaving individual staff to determine their own standards of acceptable and unacceptable behaviour.

TEACHERS' VIEWS

This conclusion is borne out by statements made by teachers in comprehensive schools interviewed especially for this book.

Bill trained as a teacher immediately after the war on a short-entry scheme. He has taught in the same school all his professional life. For the first twenty-three years the school was the local grammar school. Thereafter, it became comprehensive. Since then, the size of the school has increased four-fold although the number now on roll is falling. When interviewed, Bill summed up his career in the following way.

I'm retiring next year. Looking back, I wish I'd gone earlier. Teaching is not what it used to be. Morale is appalling, standards are very low and discipline has become a dirty word. Today, I'm looked on as a kind of old-fashioned fuddy-duddy. Thirty years ago, my kind of outlook was the norm. Academic standards were everything and believe me very high. It was a pleasure and an honour to be a teacher. You were regarded with prestige by the community. Nowadays, teachers are looked down upon by all and sundry. In a way, I suppose we deserve it because there's a terrific gulf between the public and us now.

The first twenty years of my life as a teacher were fairly consistent and happy. Everybody knew where they stood. Since this school became comprehensive, everything has changed – catchment area, the curriculum, extra-curricular activities, discipline, the attitude of parents, moral standards and most of all the staff. I hate to say this but I think some of my younger colleagues are dreadful – no professional standards whatsoever. And as for the head. Well, that's another story . . . It's education down the drain if you ask me.

. . . mind you, they don't swear and cheek me. They'd soon find out who was boss if they did. But life is hell for some staff here I can tell you. How they can stand coming to school day after day defeats me. One of them pretends everything is fine in his classes when I've never heard such a din. I suppose he copes because he's on valium like the rest . . .

Another experienced male member of staff from the same school made much the same point. He had been trained in a college of education in the halcyon days of the mid-1960s.

The biggest change in my life took place about ten years ago when I suddenly realized that I couldn't rely upon anyone else ever again. I had to stand or fall by my own actions. Before then, the school had a wonderful spirit. All the staff acted as one. We were all on the same side. Today, the attitude is every man for himself and take what you can. I've never liked it. Nor do the pupils. They sense the values of staff and respond in kind. It's no wonder when the profession is riddled with so many misfits. Frankly, I wouldn't want my son to come here. It's an awful thing to say, but if I were some of the pupils here, I'd rebel as well. After all, some of them learn nothing of value from one day to the next.

A fairly recent female appointee made the following comment in response to a question:

Why should I control pupils in my class when my head of department only takes the brightest pupils because we all know she can't cope with the rest. She gets paid more than me so she should set an example to the rest of us. When she comes into my class, the pupils either snigger or jeer.

Finally, a mature female member of staff summed up her feelings in this way:

Most teachers these days have no idea what they're getting into. The whole profession has changed over the last fifteen years. Today, people seem to think that all you need to do is to teach your subject, mark books and go home. No one seems to think that there's more to teaching than this.

Here, unfortunately, it's the law of the jungle from the third form up. It never used to be. I understand that other schools are different. But here it's very difficult. Most of our pupils face bleak futures. I argue that we've got to adapt and change. But people won't. Maybe that's why the MSC (Manpower Services Commission) is taking over.

Look at it this way. From the pupils' perspectives, we've failed them. Last week, one of my fourth years told me that he wondered how I could take my subject so seriously when it had so little relevance for his future. Two days later he was sent to me by a colleague for disrupting his lesson. I wasn't sure which was the most important – answering his question or supporting my colleague. In the event, I suppose I did neither very well.

The evidence from these extracts suggests that some of the changes which have taken place in schools have confused pupils and teachers alike because of their pace and direction. Pupils find they can get away with certain things in some lessons but not in others. Maybe this reinforces the Pack Committee's view. There is no overall breakdown in discipline in education – just in certain areas, schools and classrooms.

WHAT IS DISRUPTIVE BEHAVIOUR?

Most children are not universally good or bad all the time. Sometimes their conduct is better than at other times. On one day, they can be the apple of their mother's eye; on another they can be the cause of her migraine! Similarly, children's behaviour at school does not fall into two neat groups of 'normal' and 'disruptive'. It consists of a continuum which ranges from extremely co-operative to totally unacceptable. The behaviour of children in school changes as their teachers, their age and their family circumstances alter and is influenced by teachers' tolerance levels, circumstances which pertain in classrooms and classroom mores (Galloway et al, 1982). Consequently, disruptive activity appears to take place more with some teachers than others.

Disruptive behaviour is a difficult concept to define. Topping (1983, p. 11) argues that 'like "intelligence", "disruptive" is a semantically loose, vernacular word and serves its function best by so remaining providing this is understood.' Galloway et al (1982) took a similar stance when they defined disruptive behaviour as 'any behaviour which appears problematic, inappropriate and disturbing to teachers.'

Lowenstein (1975) defined disruptive behaviour as 'any behaviour short of physical violence which interferes with the teaching process, and/or upsets the normal running of the school'. Therefore, Lowenstein distinguished between disruptive and violent behaviour.

Parry (1976) defines a disruptive child as one 'who knowingly or unknowingly effectively and frequently disrupts his own education and the education of others.' This straightforward definition has much to commend it – especially for educationalists.

Lawrence et al's (1981) definition encapsulates a common standpoint which interprets disruption in terms of its consequences for the institution. 'Behaviour which seriously interferes with the teaching process and/or seriously upsets the normal running of the school. It is more than ordinary misbehaviour . . . and includes physical attacks and malicious destruction of property.'

Tattum (1982) also stresses the context in which the behaviour takes place: 'Disruptive behaviour is rule-breaking behaviour in the form of conscious action or inaction, which brings about an interruption or curtailment of a classroom or school activity and damages interpersonal relationships.'

These definitions highlight the scope of a difficult and all-embracing concept which has to take account of serious and minor misdemeanours. Lawrence et al's (1981) study of teacher responses to disruptive behaviour, for example, provides a list of some of the types of pupil behaviour which they regarded as unacceptably disruptive. These were: 'blank defiance, rejection of reasoning, unacceptable noise levels, physical violence between pupils, threats to pupils or teachers, theft, extortion, graffiti and vandalism, verbal abuse, lack of concentration, boisterousness and lack of consideration to others.'

The Pack Committee (SED, 1977) attempted to describe behaviour which is typical of disruptive and deviant children. They borrowed their six categories from the Stirlingshire Secondary Headteachers' Association Working Party Report on *Discipline in Schools*. These were:

1) Pupil and authority – lateness, absenteeism, truancy, general non-compliance with school rules.
2) Pupil and work – repeated failure to undertake work given for home study, the non-production of requested written work, blatant opposition to projected work.
3) Pupil and teacher – use of abusive and foul language, persistent interruption of teacher, refusal to carry out instructions, disruptions of the teaching situation.
4) Pupil and pupil – bullying, intimidation, violent assault, extortion, theft.
5) Pupil and property – lack of care of books and equipment, defacing of furniture, deliberate vandalism of fabric.
6) Pupil and public – offences in private property, offences in public areas and public transport. (Not of general application, but in certain circumstances the school can properly take action and may be expected to do so.)

Certain specific acts therefore, are more closely associated with disruptive children in schools than others. These include: defiance of authority, sullen attitudes, low tolerance of frustration, a tendency to react explosively to being frustrated and frequent and extreme changes of mood by pupils and teachers alike (NAS/UWT, 1978).

INCIDENCE OF DISRUPTIVE BEHAVIOUR

Despite a number of large- and small-scale surveys, it is probably fair to say that there remain no reliable national statistics on the precise incidence of disruptive behaviour. There is, however, a certain amount of helpful and interesting, if much criticized, information available. For the purpose of this chapter, the findings from large-scale surveys will be considered first, followed by localized studies and evidence obtained from research conducted in the United States.

Lowenstein (1972; 1975) undertook two important but methodologically debatable surveys on behalf of the National Association of Schoolmasters in the seventies. In his first study, Lowenstein sent out questionnaires to NAS representatives in 13,500 schools. He received replies from 10 per cent of primary schools and 25 per cent of secondary schools. Of the 1065 secondary schools that replied, roughly 60 per cent (622 in number) reported violence of some kind. Of these, only twenty-four schools stated that violence was a common occurrence. Lowenstein concluded that violence was most frequent in urban secondary schools and amongst 13 to 14 year-olds.

Unfortunately, this study has been heavily criticized for its global approach, low response rate and, most crucially, because Lowenstein failed to define the meaning of his terms (such as violent conduct) on the questionnaire. Respondents were left to make up their own minds, therefore, on what constituted violent disruptive behaviour. It seems unlikely that all respondents viewed this notion uniformly.

In 1975, Lowenstein conducted a follow-up survey based on information obtained from a three-month period between October and December, 1974. Data came from 5 per cent of primary schools (825 out of 17,000), 15 per cent of middle schools (141 out of 909) and 18 per cent of secondary schools (846 out of 4675). Lowenstein reported an average of 0.53 violent incidents per 100 primary-school pupils, 0.41 violent incidents per 100 middle-school pupils and 0.64 violent incidents per 100 secondary-school pupils. Instances of disruptive behaviour averaged out at 1.62, 1.45 and 4.48 per 100 primary-, middle- and secondary-school pupils respectively. Lowenstein concluded that incidents of violent and disruptive behaviour are more frequent in secondary than middle or primary schools. He also found that boys were more likely to be involved in these forms of behaviour than girls and the final year of schooling was the peak period. Size of school was not a factor although he considered that the larger the school the more difficult it is to ensure that every member of staff co-operates in being observant and vigilant and willing to report incidents to senior colleagues.

Lowenstein (1975, p. 22) listed the types of violent and disruptive behaviour reported by the teachers in the survey in order of frequency – not intensity. These were:

1) physical attacks on other children;
2) disruptive or unruly behaviour;
3) truancy;
4) verbal abuse of teachers;
5) vandalism;
6) extortion;
7) breaking and entering of school property;
8) gang violence;
9) attacks on teachers by pupils;
10) attacks on other pupils;
11) other manifestations;
12) racial violence;
13) attacks on teachers by parents.

From his returns the most serious problems in primary schools would seem to be physical attacks on other children and disruptive and unruly behaviour. In middle schools, truancy appeared third on the list behind the other two. In secondary schools, disruptive and unruly behaviour and truancy easily come top, followed by physical attacks on other children, vandalism and verbal abuse of teachers.

Once again, this second study was criticized for its low response rate, lack of objectivity, disregard for the intensity of incidents (Tattum, 1982) and because Lowenstein assumed that such a survey could produce meaningful and reliable evidence. Laslett's (1977) concise review of disruptive behaviour suggests that Lowenstein took on 'an impossible task' in 'attempting to discover from teachers' opinions the national prevalence of violent and disruptive behaviour among children of different ages, in different areas and in different kinds of schools.'

A third but different kind of study for the NAS/UWT was conducted by Comber and Whitfield (1979) who sent out a questionnaire to a representative sample of 1600 union members and received a 40 per cent response rate. The researchers' aim was to gather 'first-hand accounts of recent incidents in schools, perceived as being stressful to the teacher which would serve as a basis for discussion on the nature and treatment of indiscipline.' The authors concluded: 'It is apparent that indiscipline in many schools is a serious problem impairing the efficiency of the school and imposing considerable stress on teachers.'

Tattum (1982) challenges this conclusion. He considered that in view of the low response rate and the fact that nearly half the respondents made nil returns and claimed that their school work never caused them considerable stress, the evidence led him to the opposite conclusion to Comber and Whitfield – namely that indiscipline was not a serious problem for the majority of teachers in the survey, and that these negative features of school life should not be over-emphasized.

The Department of Education and Science and Association of Education Committees (*Hansard*, 1975) undertook a survey of 100 local education authorities in January, 1973. A 60 per cent response rate was obtained from chief education officers. The main findings revealed that:

a) Just over 13 per cent of secondary schools admitted at least one incident of violence between pupils compared with only 2 per cent within primary schools.
b) Violence towards teachers was much less common.
c) The number of pupils involved in incidents within schools of all types was very low.
d) Three-fifths of the chief education officers thought there had been no significant increase in misdemeanours at this point in time.
e) Incidents of disruptive behaviour were found to be more common amongst boys, in more densely populated areas and in larger schools.
f) Much of the vandalism which affected schools took place out of school hours.
g) Home and social problems were largely blamed for the disruptive behaviour; in particular, marital break-up and domestic tension.

Finally, the remedies most often mentioned were better co-operation and communication within and between schools and local communities followed by improved pastoral care arrangements, firm and decisive school leadership and empathetic and appropriate concern on the part of the headteacher and senior staff for disaffected pupils. These were allied to good support from local social science departments.

The data obtained from this study have also been criticized, notably for the way they were obtained. For example, the survey found 768 incidents of pupil-to-pupil violence in secondary schools and 1.68 incidents of pupil-to-teacher violence per 10,000 pupils. Incidents of threats of violence towards other pupils and teachers were recorded at 3.36 and 0.11 respectively. Critics have suggested therefore, that the lower levels for threats as opposed to actual events are probably attributable to the way in which the survey was conducted. Chief education officers are so senior that there may be a natural tendency for them only to be informed about the most serious cases. In real life, it seems logical that more threats than specific acts of violence occur.

Towards the end of the 1970s, Her Majesty's Inspectorate (HMI, 1979) examined indiscipline and disruptive behaviour as part of their secondary school survey. This involved a 10 per cent sample of all maintained secondary schools in England (N = 384) with fourth- and fifth-year intakes. HMI asked headteachers to assess the extent of pupil behaviour problems in their own schools. Eight aspects were listed for comment.These were: indiscipline; violence between pupils; hostility towards teachers; truancy unknown to parents; absence with parents' knowledge; internal truancy and lesson-skipping; theft and vandalism in schools. Headteachers were asked to indicate the extent of their problems – whether they were nil, minor, considerable or serious.

The main findings revealed that:

a) Only 6 per cent of schools indicated they had a considerable problem of indiscipline. Less than 1 per cent thought it was serious.
b) Hostility towards staff was a minority problem. No school thought they had a serious problem over this matter.
c) Only seven schools expressed considerable concern over violence between pupils and only one regarded it as a serious problem.
d) Sixty per cent of schools considered that they had no disruptive pupils. Only 13 per cent thought they had more than ten disruptive pupils in their school. Thus, the overwhelming majority of headteachers claimed that their schools only suffered from minor problems of indiscipline.
e) Absenteeism was regarded as a much more serious problem, especially parental-condoned non-attendance. Over 20 per cent of all schools indicated they had a serious or considerable problem over this matter.

In common with other surveys of this kind, disruptive behaviour emerged as a much greater problem in inner-city schools, particularly those located in deprived areas with older housing and a large number of pupils with learning difficulties. Interestingly, however, many schools in similar environments reported few or no problems. HMI concluded that indiscipline and disruptive behaviour are small-scale in secondary schools in England, though when such behaviour takes place it is out of all proportion to the event. The report considers that discipline depends on good internal management of the curriculum, high teacher expectations of pupils, imaginative and varied teaching styles and an empathetic pastoral care system.

HMI have also been criticized for the way the information was collected, notably the fact that the data were based on headteachers' perceptions. It seems probable that few headteachers would be willing to criticize their schools in writing to Her Majesty's Inspectorate. As, however, a member of HMI visited each school to check the accuracy of the information provided, it is possible that this criticism has been overstated.

Briefly, a number of local and smaller-scale surveys have also been conducted into the incidence of disruptive behaviour, most notably by Cumbria's Education Committee (Sidaway, 1976; McNamara, 1975; Mills, 1976; and Rutter and his colleagues, 1979). The Cumbria Working Party on Disruptive Pupils found that 4 per cent of their total secondary-school population was described by their teachers as 'aggressive, bullies and disrupters.' The problem was seen to increase with the age of the pupils with 10 per cent of pupils in the fifth year included in the overall statistic. This might provide one pointer to where some resources need to be concentrated in secondary schools for less-able and difficult pupils, the exact opposite of much common practice.

McNamara's survey confirms one aspect of the findings reported earlier in the section. His investigation of forty-seven secondary schools ascertained that the average proportion of disruptive pupils varied from 15 per cent in selective grammar schools to 42 per cent in schools located in difficult and deprived catchment areas. It would be interesting to know today, with the advent of comprehensivization, whether these rates have remained static or risen.

Mills studied seriously disruptive pupils aged between thirteen and sixteen in sixty-one secondary schools in one local education authority. He found that there was a hard core of 3 per cent of disrupters in the schools, supplemented by another 10 per cent who sometimes became involved. The most common forms of deviant or disruptive behaviour were: the rejection of school standards in dress; persistent truancy; the cutting of individual lessons; refusal to work and co-operate in lessons; and misbehaviour intended to destroy lessons. Physical assaults on teachers were extremely uncommon. Bullying was assessed at a rate of eight per thousand pupils.

Finally, Rutter et al's research into twelve Inner London secondary schools over a twelve-week period records only one incident which brought a lesson to a premature conclusion and very little else which could be classified as 'severe' misbehaviour. They state that 'the "blackboard jungle" image of city schools was definitely not the predominant impression', although they did acknowledge that some teachers had more problems than others in handling classes.

The picture which emerges is that the number of disruptive (as opposed to occasionally naughty) pupils in schools is small as is the number of schools which continually experience difficult problems. Thus far, there is no large-scale evidence of a breakdown of discipline in secondary schools and virtually none in primary schools. But individual teachers and schools do have their weaknesses and problems. It may well be that the evidence to date is somewht rosier than the truth, given the inherent difficulties of collecting such potentially damaging and volatile data. What is clear from a full reading of the literature is that disruptive behaviour occurs more commonly in deprived inner-city areas, in urban rather than rural regions, amongst boys rather than girls, amongst secondary rather than primary pupils and amongst 15 rather than 11 year-olds. There is some conflicting evidence about the influence of school size, although, perhaps surprisingly, school size is not found to be a significant factor in a majority of studies. Above everything else, what really stands out is that further research is needed. In particular, much more evidence is required on the role and influence of individual schools and teachers in combatting and preventing indiscipline in schools.

EVIDENCE FROM THE UNITED STATES

If the picture in England and Wales is generally encouraging, the reverse is true in the United States.Successive studies conducted in the States reveal the stark and horrific facts that levels of disruption, anti-social behaviour, violence and crime in schools are not only high but increasing. A substantial proportion of teachers and pupils fear for their safety in schools and a large number of parents and of the general public are concerned about the safety of children when travelling to school and when attending classes.

The literature makes gruesome reading. In one nationwide survey (NEA, 1979), three-quarters of teachers polled claimed that disciplinary problems in schools impaired their effectiveness to teach and schools had not done enough to help them with their problems. Startlingly, the same survey revealed that 5 per cent of the respondent teachers had been physically assaulted in 1978–9 (approximately 110,000 assaults). Of these, 10 per cent required medical treatment for the physical injuries they received and 8 per cent required further treatment for emotional trauma. Another report accepted by Congress, estimated that 70,000 teachers are physically assaulted every year (Bayh, 1977).

Research undertaken in the States reveals that assaults on teachers and students are rising; so is teacher stress, vandalism, extortion, rape, robbery and weapon violence in schools. In one year alone, 100,000 teachers had their private property vandalized. In any given month, 2.4 million high school students have something stolen, 282,000 are attacked and 112,000 are forcefully robbed on school premises. The problem of violence, indiscipline and anti-social behaviour is especially concentrated at the junior high school (12–15 years) level (NIE, 1977). Over two-thirds of robberies and half the assaults on youths occur on pupils in this age group. These incidents occur more frequently in deprived urban areas in places like New York and Chicago.

GARETH

The case of Gareth demonstrates the kind of difficulties which teachers in some schools have to cope with and overcome on either a daily basis or over a period of time.

Gareth is 15, the last of three children – all boys. His parents were divorced when he was 6 years old. Since then, he claims he can count the number of times he has spoken to his father on one hand, although he often sees him around town. His mother has always had the greatest difficulty in coping with three boisterous children. Currently, she is employed as a part-time cleaner in a local factory for two hours in the early morning and a similar amount of time after office hours.

Gareth's two elder brothers both left school without obtaining any formal qualifications. John, the eldest brother, is currently in prison for theft and malicious wounding with intent to cause grievous bodily harm. The other brother, Martin, also has a criminal record but of a less serious nature. In their early teens, Gareth's two elder brothers were notorious local delinquent truants.

Gareth's academic performance at primary school was below average but his attendance and behavioural records were good. This standard soon deteriorated after his transfer to the local comprehensive school. He was first formally suspended from school at the age of twelve for 'persistently swearing at a teacher in class after refusing to carry out the tasks which had been set.' Since then, he has been suspended on four other occasions for: 'hitting another pupil without provocation causing severe distress and physical damage' (medical attention given to the victim on the school premises); 'stealing school property and attempting to sell it at a local shop' (police informed); 'knocking Miss Y over in her classroom after she had asked him to open a window – subsequently leaving the school premises without permission' (mother interviewed by headteacher and head of year before he was re-admitted to school); and, 'for repeated bad language and violence on the games field after refusing to play in goal during a game of football' (mother interviewed again). The latter three incidents took place during a six-month spell when Gareth was in his third year of secondary education.

In between the suspensions, Gareth's school record showed that he had been warned on numerous occasions for a variety of offences, while his mother had been seen by staff on several others. Both the educational psychologist and social services had been consulted and received written reports on Gareth's adverse school behaviour and home circumstances which, they agreed, were closely linked.

Gareth is unpopular with his peers (especially his classmates) and the teachers. School records indicate that the parents of some of the other children in his form regard him as being a disturbing influence on their offspring. Apart from his outbursts of disruptive behaviour, Gareth attends school infrequently, makes no effort with his schoolwork and appears to dislike his teachers. He holds those who endeavour to help him in contempt. His behaviour has undoubtedly worsened with age.

School records also show that the headteacher and senior staff have made repeated attempts to have Gareth removed from their roll and placed elsewhere. Despite repeated warnings to the mother and pleas for help to the social services, all these efforts have failed.

One reason for this may lie in a report writen by a social worker which argued that removing Gareth from the school would be a retrograde step. She considered it would be counter-productive to all personnel involved in his welfare in the long run owing to his home circumstances and fraternal background.

The aim of the social services appears to support Gareth within his family environment in the hope that he will eventually conform and not degenerate like his brothers. The critical stage in this process will probably be reached when Gareth leaves school and seeks employment. On the one hand, while such endeavour is to be applauded, it does seem doubtful whether it will succeed given, for instance, existing local employment opportunities for unskilled labour. In the meantime, the pupils and staff at school continue to shoulder most of the burden.

SUMMARY

The dearth of reliable statistical evidence is a considerable handicap in assessing the extent of disruptive behaviour in schools in Britain. Those surveys which exist suggest that with a few exceptions levels of disruptive and violent behaviour are low. Generally speaking, schools appear to be well controlled although the management of difficult pupils is not becoming any easier as future prospects for less able youths decrease.

The crucial stage in secondary schools appears to be the third year onwards which suggests that headteachers need to find and place competent, experienced staff in positions involving pupil care. The third year may not be the place to blood newcomers in posts of pastoral responsibility. The same point applies to the often neglected role of form tutor.

The evidence from the States suggests that when discipline does break down, the outlook and long-term consequences for teachers and pupils alike are very severe and should not be underestimated. Moreover, there is a corresponding overspill into the community in terms of crime and general anti-social conduct. The facts from the States do help put the prevailing situation in Britain into their proper perspective and counter those alarmist features which often appear in popular newspapers. Nevertheless, teachers in Britain should not become complacent. Collectively and individually, they must maintain control in their schools and classrooms if learning and purposeful activity is to ensue and they are to retain their dignity.

4

AETIOLOGY OF DISRUPTIVE BEHAVIOUR

This second chapter on disruption concentrates on one major aspect – the 'causes' and types of disruptive behaviour. The next chapter will focus on the academic debate about whether disruptive behaviour is in fact maladjusted behaviour; the place of disruptive behaviour within the general concepts of special educational needs and deviance; diagnosing disruptive conduct and the relationship between disruption and absenteeism.

A wide range of psychological theories exist to account for and explain differences in children's behaviour. These include psycho-dynamic, cognitive–developmental and social learning theories, the incompatibility of working- and middle-class values, sub-cultural and labelling theories (Docking, 1980).

In our present state of knowledge there are no clear-cut grounds for adopting one approach at the expense of others. Strategies recommended by professionals for dealing with disruptive behaviour will depend on the particular explanation favoured or on individual circumstances. Of necessity in schools, teachers usually adopt pragmatic rather than ideal approaches or solutions. Their main concern is generally to overcome the disruptive act as quickly as possible and to prevent the conduct from recurring. In any event, many teachers receive relatively little training in disaffection or disruption or about how to cope with deviant and disruptive pupils. Too often, such topics do not form part of their initial (Reid et al, 1980) or in-service training.

The so-called 'causes' of disruption can reasonably be sub-divided into seven. These are: underachievement, the family, links between schools and parents, peer-group relationships, the gulf between the general public and teachers, schooling *per se* and teaching. None of these facets should be considered in isolation. This chapter concentrates on the first five of these issues as schooling and teaching form an integral part of Chapter 7.

These seven items are not listed in any order of priority. No excuse however is proffered for placing underachievement first. It is not mere coincidence. What is surprising is that so many other texts or academic articles fail to consider the crucial importance of the relationship between underachievement to the study of disruptive behaviour and disaffection. In fact, this relationship is so obvious and vital that it is fundamental to an understanding of the subject. It is my firm belief that underachievement is the greatest single problem confronting secondary schools today, followed by standards of teaching and the lack of structure in the curriculum. Primary schools, too, are by no means exempt from this criticism.

WHAT IS UNDERACHIEVEMENT?

Underachievement is a massive educational problem. It should be a major concern for everyone involved in education.

Although underachievement is a commonly used term, its exact meaning is sometimes unclear, and often misused and misunderstood. In order to demonstrate underachievement, it is logically necessary to show first that the potential for achievement exists. Consequently, the debate about intelligence measurement (IQ) has partly been about the search for a reliable indicator of potential which is *independent* of achievement.

Chomsky (1968) makes the same point in his work on linguistic development when he uses the terms competence and performance. For both IQ and language the problem which faces researchers is that the only way to estimate potential (competence) is by means of the assessment of achievement (performance). Independence of the two measures has not, to date, proved to be possible.

Despite this lack of precision, it is essential that the concern felt by many secondary teachers about their pupils' lack of achievement is not ignored. Many teachers who use the term underachievement asssume, because of their general knowledge of the pupil, that the necessary potential is there. This is a reasonable assumption to make. Most young children have the potential to learn to read although, for some, progress is slow. Similarly, most adults who wish to eventually learn to manipulate the complex controls of a car. There are, of course, some tasks that are beyond the capabilities of most of us: rapidly understanding complex scientific theories; gaining complete fluency in a new language in a short period; and becoming a first-rate musician if we are born tone deaf. Thankfully, however, for most tasks undertaken in secondary schools careful tuition, hard work and a high level of motivation can lead to the growth of skills and understanding.

Achievement is not, however, uniform. Because there are clear differences in all three of these components (tuition, application and motivation), pupils vary markedly in their performance. At the level of individual pupils this is understandable. After all, talents and motivation occur to quite different degrees. Naturally, the quality of teaching also varies. The situation is less straightforward, however, for whole groups of pupils where ability and motivation are likely to be reasonably distributed. If some groups of pupils are underachieving, teachers will, therefore, be especially concerned (Mortimore, 1982).

DISAFFECTION AND UNDERACHIEVEMENT

One of the biggest drawbacks to establishing the precise link between disaffected behaviour and underachievement lies in the fact that underachievement is a difficult and imprecise concept to measure. Underachievement is not a stable or single commodity. For this reason, researchers tend to measure aspects of under-achievement by using such instruments as standardized achieve-ment tests in, for example, reading or mathematics which provide only partial answers. These endeavours rarely take account of behavioural underachievement or mass underachievement in schools or throughout a region. Moreover, most projects on underachievement are unable to glean accurate information on the quality of teaching or unsuitable curricula and so on.

As an education tutor, I have sat at the back of lessons on teaching practice observing student-teachers teaching and inwardly recoiled in horror at the content of their subject matter rather than their teaching ability. In one school, the head of department asked a maths student to teach fractions and decimals to middle-band fourth-year pupils. It struck me that these 14- and 15-year-old pupils should have learnt these mathematical concepts years earlier. When I investigated the matter further, some of the pupils told me they were learning fractions and decimals for the second or third time while others had never done so. This incident exemplifies the lack of structure in the curriculum. In some schools the content of a subject's curriculum changes with every new teacher which must confuse many parents and pupils alike. In this respect, the absence of agreed national guidelines for the secondary school curriculum is a handicap and can spur both disruption and disaffection – particularly when pupils become bored or uninterested in the content of their lessons. Sometimes, who can blame them? Sitting at the back of the class watching my student teach, I found myself wondering what the pupils had been learning in their primary schools and during the first three years of their secondary education.

On another occasion, I looked through the English exercises of groups of pupils from one secondary school because of comments made by a student-teacher. I found that there was not a single grammatical correction or comment made by the subject teacher throughout the exercise books – only an overall grade at the end of each piece of work. Therefore, it came as no surprise when a year later my wife was asked by the parents of one boy from this school to coach him privately in English language in an endeavour to get him through his 'O' level resit examination. Apparently, the parents had been given the impression by the school that their son was very able and so they could not understand why he had fluffed his 'O' levels. A glance on their part at his English exercise book would at least have provided a partial answer. Although his conceptual development was good, he had no idea how to write a paragraph, punctuate or spell. In my opinion, at least one teacher at his school is being paid for failing to do her job adequately. The progress made by this boy in the first few weeks of his private coaching showed that he had the ability to grasp some of the fundamentals of the English language if he had ever been taught the subject properly. Following intensive tuition using a twenty-year-old text on English grammar, the pupil passed his 'O' level resit in English language three months later.

There again, consider this true story. At the age of 21, Caroline Jones, who has been unemployed for the last three years, and whose school refused to give her good job references because she did not do well enough in her final examinations, discovered she had an IQ which put her in the top 1 per cent in the country. Her measured IQ of 155 placed her well above the national average of 100 and made her eligible to join the élite ranks of MENSA, the organization you need an IQ of 148 to join.

Caroline discovered she was among the most intelligent people in the country after entering a national magazine competition for young women who thought life offered them little hope. She was tested by MENSA along with a hundred other young women and judged to be in the top five. Since then, she has received a day's career counselling in London and discovered she is capable of far more than her teachers or prospective employers could ever have realized.

Caroline started work after leaving school with four 'O' levels on a government training scheme at a hospital in Wales as a clerical assistant. When that finished, she did secretarial work for a small business until it folded. Since then she has been unemployed.

When interviewed, Caroline made the following revealing statements:

a) 'I used to feel angry when I was forced to do something menial and I know a lot of people who are fed up because they are doing jobs beneath their intelligence.'

b) 'Unemployment is degrading. You think people are looking down on you. Even if they are not, you think they are. You get fed up on the dole. Things just don't seem to be going anywhere.'

c) 'When I found out the results of the MENSA test I felt puzzled and a little bit angry. But I know there are a lot of people who have to do menial jobs and are not happy with their lives because they know they are capable of more.'

The extent to which Caroline's frustration is typical is hard to gauge. There are undoubtedly countless numbers of pupils who underachieve because of bad teaching, the lack of structure, purpose and coherence in the curriculum, frequent changes of schools or teaching staff, poor school organization and unfavourable learning climates within classrooms. Despite pronouncements on accountability, schools and individual classrooms remain essentially very private places. According to some, teaching is the second most private activity.

Not all pupils are or need be as unfortunate as Caroline. Take the case of Michael, a 10-year-old pupil in a J4 class in Swansea.

Michael comes from a single-parent family with an insecure domestic situation. However, his mother originates from an affluent family background. As a child she attended a girls' public school but fell on hard times after becoming an unmarried mother. Since then, she has been shunned by her parents, and been at odds with the mores of working-class neighbourhoods in whose vicinity she has resided in a variety of caravans, flats and council homes, cohabiting with a succession of men. For instance, Michael and his mother recently moved to a new council flat in another district after neighbours deliberately set fire to their previous property. The neighbours took revenge upon Michael's mother by throwing a lighted cloth through the letter box after she had reported them for displaying repeated cruelty towards their dog.

Upon entry to his new school, Michael exuded his confused state by continually drawing attention to himself by disrupting lessons at every opportunity. His activities included: vandalizing school property; verbal violence towards staff; and persistent fighting with other pupils.

Fortunately, Michael's enlightened headmistress, Miss Willis, realized that part of his problem lay in underachievement.She soon ascertained that Michael was potentially the most able pupil in the class. So she specially arranged for him to have individual tuition for an hour a day at school on a one-to-one basis. This work was carried out by a peripatetic teacher supplied by the local education authority. In addition, she ensured he had the means to join a local boys rugby club by providing his kit. Since then, rugby has become his all-embracing passion. One Thursday, for instance, he was in a state of high excitement after playing his first match for his new team after only a few weeks' training and previously sitting on the bench as a replacement.

Within the last six months Michael's academic and behavioural improvement has been remarkable. Whether this gain will continue into the secondary stage remains to be seen. Hopefully, the secondary school will continue Miss Willis's enlightened approach.

On the other hand, Michael could very easily regress as the school is not only much larger but has a reputation for having a considerable number of disaffected pupils on its roll.

There have been no completely satisfactory explanations put forward to explain fully the causes of underachievement. There are, however, a number of important correlates of group underachievement (Mortimore, 1982). These include social disadvantage, peer influence, school influence, the secondary system, sexism and racism.

Although it is wrong to blame home background for underachievement at school, it is clear that, in general, pupils who experience social disadvantages such as low income, poor housing, marital disharmony, inconsistent discipline, paternal unemployment or come from one-parent families are less likely to do well at school than their more advantaged peers (Mortimore and Blackstone, 1982). The evidence overwhelmingly suggests that the combination of poor housing, low income, worse health care and familial stress has a powerful effect on the school performance of some pupils. Nevertheless, it needs to be borne in mind that some pupils from deprived working-class backgrounds achieve well at school and in later life.

From a variety of data sources it is clear that from the age of seven onwards there is a considerable difference in achievement between pupils from homes where the parent has a non-manual occupation, and those where the parents are considered 'working class'. In reading, mathematics and referral rates for special education, these class differences persist over time (Davie et al, 1972; Fogelman et al, 1978).

Halsey et al (1980) reported that, despite the increase in the provision of higher education, the chances of a pupil from a working-class home going to university are no better now than before the First World War. Therefore, even after accepting the fact that many of these pupils may not have chosen to go on to higher education, the occupational limitations remain considerable. Upward social mobility remains the exception rather than the norm for children from working-class origins (Murphy, 1981). Paradoxically, in this era of high unemployment, the consequences of underachievement may be particularly serious.

Rutter (1979) suggests that the influence of peers is especially influential on pupils as they make their educational choices (subject choices etc.) during their secondary education. Even in schools where teachers highlight the advantages to pupils of taking a wide curriculum, some pupils will insist on following rigidly stereotyped choices. Thus, although research on the influence of peer groups is not as fully developed as studies of family background, it seems probable that friendship influences have a strong effect on certain children – especially teenage pupils. In some cases this peer pressure is only part of a much wider influence encompassing family and society.

Recent studies of school effectiveness have shown that individual schools can have a powerful effect on pupil achievement (Edmonds et al, 1978; Rutter et al, 1979). The impact of the school *may* not, however, be sufficient to overcome the combined effects of social disadvantage. The available evidence seems to suggest that good schools appear to raise the performance of *all* pupils. The reverse is also probably true. Poor schools have negative effects on the achievement of their pupils. Critical factors which impinge on pupil performance appear to be effective teaching strategies, positive teacher expectations, well-structured courses, favourable school ethos, adequate resources, well-managed departments and schools, homework and detailed feedback given to pupils and parents (Brophy and Good, 1974; Rosenshine, 1978; Mortimore and Mortimore, 1981). Of course, it is easier to be a good teacher in some schools than others. Researchers have frequently drawn attention to the negative effects of bad behaviour, high absence rates, low morale and the generally unfavourable school climates within some institutions.

Whilst the organization and curriculum of secondary schools remain dominated by public examinations it is difficult to see how, even with 'good' schools, the underachievement of some groups of pupils can be avoided (Mortimore, 1982). Conventional examinations are highly competitive. Pupils from disadvantaged home and social backgrounds compete with those who, throughout their lives, have experienced every possible support. For most pupils in secondary schools the chances of achieving sufficiently high grades to pass external examinations like 'O' level are low. Small wonder then that so many pupils give up towards the end of their secondary schooling or once they perceive their limitations. Consequently, truancy and disruption present alternatives which, for some pupils, are probably very hard to resist.

Sexism is commonly associated with certain kinds of under-achievement particularly for girls in science subjects and for girls raised within, for example, Asian homes where women are treated as inferior to men. Sexism can influence the expectations and career aspirations for girls, held by teachers, parents, male peers, employers and, indeed, the girls themselves. But the evidence about sex differences in achievement is not straightforward. Overall, girls appear to perform as well or slightly better than boys at all stages up to 'A' level examinations. In some subjects, however, there appear to be major differences by sex. For example, the Assessment of Performance Unit (APU) surveys show that girls underachieve in most mathematical tests (HMSO, 1980; 1981b). Boys appear to underachieve in French and some other modern languages. In the physical sciences, girls are under-represented. But they do not underachieve. In fact, although the proportions of girls entering physics and chemistry examinations are relatively small, those who do enter perform rather better, on average, than boys. Needless to say, the proportions, for instance, of girls entering technical subjects and of boys entering home economics are minimal.

Even though a larger proportion of girls than boys go on to higher education, a much smaller number go on to high status courses. In 1981, for the first time, a slightly higher proportion of female than male applicants for university places were successful. Overall, however, there were still far more male applicants – and thus entrants – to university (UCCA, 1982). For girls, therefore, the term 'underachievement' is somewhat misleading. In reality, it is a combination of underachievement and under-representation that creates barriers to equal opportunity.

Women graduates on teacher-training courses within universities in England and Wales predominate in modern languages and arts subjects. Males continue to be in a majority in maths and physics and to a lesser extent in chemistry. Biology and primary education are female dominated. Teaching is increasingly becoming a female-dominated profession (Reid et al, 1981a and b).

Racism and differences between races are other important contributory factors in some underachievement. Racism, however, is an extremely complex subject as the variation in school performance between pupils of different Asian family backgrounds demonstrates. Racism, in the form of direct aggressive actions, such as bullying in school, clearly causes concern to many pupils from minority groups and this worry undoubtedly affects pupils' learning. However, in describing ethnic groups, there is always a danger of over-generalization, particularly when pupils from so many different cultures are involved. Similarly, most black pupils now in school are of British nationality, and have been born and fully educated in this country.

Generally speaking, evidence on the achievement of black pupils is difficult to find, as ethnic background has seldom been systematically researched – partly because of the delicate nature of the topic. To date, research suggests that:

a) The proportions of black school leavers going on to some form of further education are high.
b) The parents of some black pupils are especially keen for their children to do well at school.
c) Underachievement amongst black pupils with family backgrounds from the Caribbean is common (HMSO, 1981; Taylor, 1981).

The HMI survey (Welsh Office, 1984) of selected secondary schools in Wales makes interesting reading and provides considerable insight into the relationship between underachievement, disaffection and curriculum organization and planning which is worth reporting in detail.

Most schools adopt a mixed ability organisation in the first year, coupled with some kind of special provision for slow learners, usually in the form of at least one separate class, but in a few cases through various arrangements for withdrawal from main stream classes. A significant number divide the first year into two or three according to ability – again excluding special classes; some still stream pupils on entry. Examples of all three types were included in the Autumn 1983 sample. Setting by ability in year I, where it is practised at all, is nearly always confined to English, Welsh, French or mathematics and in most cases the sets come into operation after Christmas. A number of schools with mixed ability groups in year I introduce banding in year II, though the coincidence of setting in all schools tends to increase sharply at this stage. By year III most academic subjects are taught in ability groups based either on sets or ability bands; only a minority of schools retain a substantial measure of mixed ability teaching at this level.

Some curricular differentiation is usual in years I, II and III in those schools with banded organisations. In most cases there is a smaller allocation of time for modern languages in the second band, while some abler pupils are offered a second foreign language. There may also be some differentiation in science, lower ability groups being offered general science and abler pupils the three single science subjects, sometimes on a reduced time allocation. Most schools, however, provide a common 3-subject science programme for all in year III. It is often the case that little thought is given in years I to III to the adaptation of schemes of work for pupils of lower ability. Especially in subjects such as science, history and geography, they find increasing difficulty with the more theoretical aspects of the work and with the sheer volume of material which for them becomes progressively less manageable. Although they may have been subject to no differentiation of curricular pattern in years I to III, less able children may approach the time of subject choice in Year III in a state of discouragement which reduces the value of any efforts the school has made to develop new, appropriate and interesting courses in years IV and V. Some schools on the other hand (and particularly some individual departments) have succeeded in providing a common syllabus framework for all pupils in year I to III, in which approaches, materials and the amount of content covered can be varied according to the needs of pupils of varying ability.

Early decisions to vary the provision for different ability groups often provide the first negative signals to pupils of lower ability. It is not unreasonable that schools should seek some degree of differentiation of provision in accordance with their perception of the varying needs of pupils – though in the first 3 years there is a case for keeping to a minimum overt differentiation of curriculum patterns which, for some pupils, unnecessarily limits opportunities and forecloses certain options. What is unacceptable is that provision for the less able pupils should be less well planned and resourced. For example, a disengagement from foreign language study may provide an early experience of failure, especially in the many cases where schools have not yet succeeded in devising an appropriately differentiated foreign language course for less able pupils in the early years. The alternative of French studies or European studies often turns out to be an eclectic information-laden study which pupils variously join or leave at the end of the third year, or even, in some cases, the second year, in a way which frustrates plans to ensure progression in learning. Attempts to provide some flavour of the culture and lifestyle of the foreign country may founder on a lack of the necessary resources – pictures, tapes, up-to-date books, projected aids and classroom displays. Many pupils who fail to profit from a straightforward foreign language course have weaknesses in basic skills which the 'studies' courses rarely help to remedy – though if appropriately planned, they could do much to meet these needs. Where pupils do abandon foreign languages either partially or altogether, a possibility which more schools might explore is to use the time thus made available to provide support for them in their other academic subjects. For example, they could be helped with reading, organise their work more effectively so that it is completed and well-ordered, especially in subjects such as the humanities and science where deficiencies in basic skills can easily hinder progress and cause early discouragement.

All schools operate (for abler pupils, at least) a system of a common core plus optional courses in years IV and V; a substantial minority now structure one or more of their option lines to provide compulsory science, practical subjects or humanities courses, while others provide miscellaneous groupings but counsel pupils, with varying success, on the virtues of pursuing a balanced curriculum. The core invariably includes English and mathematics, taught in ability sets; careers, religious and physical education are also included, though in variable measures, and it is increasingly common for schools to provide some kind of social education, usually in the form of a module in a rotational programme. Welsh is a core subject to 16+ in the Gwynedd schools, in designated bilingual schools and in some schools in Welsh speaking areas of Dyfed and Powys. Few schools include any other subjects in the core curriculum. Schools usually offer either 7 or 8 time blocks for academic subjects. One school visited in Autumn 1983 offered 8 for the abler band and 7 for the less able; this was a commendable attempt to vary provision to meet the needs of pupils who would find the pace of work too fast in many subjects which could be allocated only 4 lessons in a 40-period week.

Some schools retain separate provision for a small non-examination group in years IV and V; in these cases the remedial or special education department often has responsibility for basic subjects while the remaining programme is taught by a variety of specialists. In some instances, where departments have given thought to the needs of these pupils, the provision is commendable. For example, certain schools have recently planned a range of fresh syllabuses co-ordinated by a senior member of staff. Some kind of work experience or community service often forms part of the programme for these pupils (though this is usually not well-related to the rest of the curriculum) and some may enter CSE classes in one or two subjects. In some cases, the curriculum of these pupils is fragmentary; it varies from year to year according to which teachers are available and, where they exist at all, the written schemes of work are often rudimentary, reflecting a lack of proper planning at departmental level. In a few schools, co-ordinated cross-curricular packages have been introduced for a proportion of pupils (up to 30%) in years IV and V.

Apart from this kind of provision for a small minority, most schools arrange optional subjects in groups which are timetabled simultaneously across the whole fourth or fifth year groups. However, the choice available to less able pupils in such arrangements is usually significantly more restricted. Many will have already abandoned the study of foreign languages, while other subjects may also, to varying degrees be regarded as mainly the preserve of the abler pupils; these often include the separate sciences (especially physics and chemistry), computer studies and craft, design and technology, and in some cases history and geography also. Pupils of modest and lower ability thus tend to choose from general science, human biology and rural science and, in the humanities, to take some kind of interdisciplinary programme, such as social or community studies, taught in many cases by teachers or small teams of teachers functioning largely independently of the major subject departments. A few such courses are of high quality; many risk being regarded by pupils as having lower status than traditional subjects and few would not benefit from being taken into the mainstream of departmental provision.

Of the schools with open option systems, only a minority have successfully created the general expectation that all subject departments or faculties will plan rigorously for the full range of ability, though many have made substantial progress towards this goal, often following recent new appointments at senior staff level. In many cases, the 'chosen' curriculum of pupils of modest and lower ability includes several subjects in which preparation for external examinations proceeds with few concessions to limited basic skills or the need for a motivating variety of experience. Where schools have devoted substantial resources to the planning of one or two specific courses (eg science and community studies) most lower ability children may be expected to take them; this reinforces the expectation that the single-subject courses in these areas are mainly the preserve of abler pupils, effectively reducing the choice available to less able pupils. In a few schools, the self-esteem of less able pupils also suffers when a popular course, from which they could profit or which is capable of being adapted to meet their needs, becomes over-subscribed, and as a consequence a selection occurs on the basis of ability in the subject concerned. Some pupils then become reluctant students of a different subject. This is a most unfortunate practice; if selection is unavoidable, consideration should be given to the overall needs and interests of each pupil involved before decisions are made. For various reasons therefore, even in schools which offer a wide range of 'open' options, the choice of course available to less able pupils may be much more restricted than is immediately apparent. It is not intended to suggest that schools should seek to maximise choice for its own sake; the question of how much and what kind of choice should be offered in the last two years of compulsory schooling is a very large and separate issue outside the scope of the present document. What is at issue is the question of the relative degree of priority ascribed by the school to the curricular programmes of various categories of pupils, as it may be perceived by pupils of modest and lower ability.

A significant minority of schools provide a separate optional curriculum for a lower ability band ranging in size from about 12% to around 40% of the fourth and fifth year group. In most cases, the choice of course afforded these pupils is overtly more restricted than that offered the abler band, though, for the reasons given above, no more so in practice than in many 'open' structures. The target often remains the CSE examination in most subjects. The same observation that curricular initiatives are sporadic and uneven, can sometimes be made of this lower band provision. However, one potential advantage of such an arrange-ment lies in the relatively greater consistency of teaching group which occurs from subject to subject and several schools have sought to exploit this in order to provide a measure of cross-curricular coherence in the pupils' programmes. 'Packages' have been developed in which individual CSE courses are modified and combined to conform to the requirements of City and Guilds Foundation level courses; other initiatives are based upon the co-ordination of courses for pupils of lower ability (including some non-examination work) under the leadership of a senior member of staff.

The detailed planning of syllabuses and learning approaches is in the hands of subject departments or, in a minority of cases, faculties. Although, as indicated, only a few schools have achieved a successful review of provision for pupils of lower ability across a wide range of subjects, encouraging examples of effective development are to be found in most areas of the curriculum.

The extent to which practice and performance in secondary schools in Wales is applicable to establishments elsewhere is, of course, a matter of debate. However, the underlying realities are probably not too dissimilar.

Until ways are found of adequately measuring and overcoming individual and mass underachievement, disaffection from schools is unlikely to be overcome. Apart from anything else, the present organization of schools, falling rolls and subsequent pressure on teachers as well as aspects of government policies on education all militate against successful outcomes. Simply put, teachers have too little opportunity to help underachievers in large classroom situations unless they do so in their own time without financial reward. And there should be no doubting the strong correlation between underachievement and frustration, with all this statement implies.

THE FAMILY

Although unhappy childhood experiences are no longer considered to be irreversibly damaging, Rutter (1975) believes there is little doubt that 'parents help shape the child's behaviour by means of their selective encouragement and discouragement of particular behaviours, by their discipline and by the amount of freedom which they allow.' Inconsistent and lax discipline as well as parents adopting different criteria and operating on different planes within the home, appears to have negative effects on children. So does the timing and quality of parental responses.

Maintaining effective and consistent standards of discipline in the home is never easy as any parent would testify. Parents have to cope with a number of pressures and distractions on a daily basis. Nevertheless, Rutter claims that the parents of troubled children differ quite early on from other parents in being less good at intervention, in giving encouragement and praise for good behaviour, by responding erratically to bad behaviour and in giving children too much attention for their misdemeanours.

In a particularly revealing study, Rutter et al (1975) compared families in two contrasting geographical locations – the Isle of Wight and an Inner London Borough. They found that parents in the inner-city region suffered from more social disadvantages including worse housing conditions, greater family discord, more mental disorder and an increased incidence of criminality. In addition, their offspring were twice as likely to have emotional, behavioural and reading problems. Broken homes were associated with delinquency and psychiatric disorders in children. Varlaam's (1974) ILEA literacy survey accords well with Rutter et al's work and shows similar associations between home and social background, behaviour and reading attainments. Such findings led the Court Committee (1976) to conclude that there is now extensive evidence to show that adverse family and social environments retard physical, emotional and intellectual growth, educational achievement and personal behaviour. Interestingly, however, outcomes for single-parent homes are no different from two-parent homes once allowance has been made for economic factors (Davie et al, 1972; Mortimore et al, 1983).

Other home factors, too, can affect the natural development of children and have consequences for school behaviour. These include:

1) Children who through their domestic and personal circumstances are forced to acquire adult status too early either by their domestic circumstances or for other reasons. Thereafter, school life can seem boring, irrelevant, petty and restrictive. Such attitudes often lead to withdrawal and conflict (Jones, 1976; Bird et al, 1980; Grunsell, 1980).
2) Well-integrated families who are notably anti-school, anti-authoritarian and anti-establishment. Sometimes these negative familial attitudes are supported by a prevailing neighbourhood culture which devalues schooling and over-values alternative ideals like work and fostering anti-social tendencies sometimes

through group indentities (teddy-boys, skinheads, punks) (Mays, 1972; Phillips, 1978; Grunsell, 1978).

3) Families which suffer from too much intra-familial friction such as unstable parental relationships (constant arguing), violence in the home, difficult sibling relationships and very poor parent–child relationships which can be hurtful, derisive, neglectful, punitive, harsh, over-demanding and suffer from minimal contact or affection (Seabrook, 1974; Bird et al, 1980; Grunsell, 1980). Families which suffer disproportionate economic or drink problems can sometimes exacerbate these problems. The stress of unemployment, poverty, living in poor or sub-standard housing conditions and familial illness should never be forgotten or underestimated. One of the least publicized facts about some teachers and social workers is that they themselves have often never had to endure social or familial deprivation like so many of their pupils. Such teachers and social workers can sometimes find it harder to relate to children and clients from less fortunate social or home backgrounds because of the culture gap which exists between them. Although many studies have found that a high proportion of non-graduates or college-trained teachers come from working class backgrounds (Lacey, 1977), there is now good evidence to show that a clear majority of university postgraduate-trained teachers emanate from favourable social class origins (Reid et al, 1980; Patrick, Bernbaum and Reid, 1982).

THE HOME AND THE SCHOOL

Few studies exist on differences between good and badly behaved pupils related to home background. One of the most impressive studies of those conducted into the relationship between a student's home and social background and school indiscipline remains the work of Feldhusen et al (1973) which was undertaken in the United States. Feldhusen et al investigated 1550 children in grades 3, 6 and 9 who exhibited persistent pro-social or aggressive–disruptive behaviour. They found that aggressive–disruptive youths were disadvantaged in terms of their home, family and parental backgrounds when compared with pro-social peers. Their list of 'psycho-social' correlates of classroom misbehaviours and home circumstances include:

1) lax or inconsistent paternal discipline;

2) maternal inadequacy in the supervision of her offspring;
3) poor parental–child relationships including indifference and hostility;
4) a disunified family in terms of their corporate spirit and social and household activities;
5) disagreements between parents about child rearing;
6) poor husband–wife relationships;
7) parents who found many traits of which they disapproved in their children;
8) mothers who felt unhappy in the community in which they lived;
9) parents who were unable to control their tempers and who had a tendency to resort to angry, physical punishment when their children misbehaved;
10) parents who belittled their own influence upon their children and who thought that other children exerted bad influences upon them as well;
11) parents whose leisure time was devoid of purposeful activity or included few cultural or intellectual engagements;
12) parents who were not members of a church or only attended spasmodically;
13) parents who were less well educated than the average population and, if employed, were in lower-level occupations of a semi-skilled or unskilled type.

Analysis of the school factors showed that the disruptive children had an average nine points deficit in their intelligence quotient (IQ) levels, significantly lower reading and mathematics test scores and were more inclined to drop out of school. In a follow-up study, Feldhusen et al (1977) found that some of the best long-range predictors of disruptive behaviour were the original behaviour status as identified by teachers, IQ, reading scores and father's educational level.

British studies confirm many of Feldhusen's findings. Rutter (1975) reports that conduct-disordered children tend to be impulsive, unpredictable and unmalleable; aggressive and assertive in their relationships, to be less responsive than their peers to praise and encouragement; and to show little concern or feelings for others. Rutter also found that conduct-disordered children tend to be educationally backward. The Cambridge longitudinal study of delinquency (West and Farrington, 1973) ascertained that the best predictors of delinquency were teachers' and peers' ratings of troublesomeness in earlier years.

In Reid's (1984b) study into persistent school absenteeism, the form teachers completed Scale B of the Rutter (1967) Children's Behaviour Questionnaire. The results showed that the persistent absentees (*note*: not disrupters) tended to behave worse in class than good attenders from the same forms and from academic bands. They also depicted higher levels of anti-social and neurotic tendencies in a minority of cases. When the criterion variables (such as 'truants from school') were excluded from the analysis, the differences between the groups were much reduced. Like most earlier work on truancy and absenteeism (see Chapter 2), the non-attenders in Reid's sample came from significantly more deprived home backgrounds than the good attenders with lower social class origins.

Tattum (1982) has suggested that many disruptive children are socially inept and lack the skills necessary to handle difficult situations. Such pupils can, for example, be verbally abusive when disciplined as part of a 'normal' reaction. Whereas other children tend to be quiet when problems arise in class; some disrupters appear to feel the need to defend themselves irrespective of cause, thereby attempting to save face even when there is no need. This is part of the 'it's not my fault' syndrome.

Taken collectively, most studies tend to suggest that much more thought and attention needs to be given to combatting early signs of behavioural problems. Unless action is taken at its inception, disaffection and disruption are likely to develop as pupils grow in confidence with age. Amongst other aspects to which people should pay particular attention are: early signs of behavioural problems in primary schools; problems which manifest themselves during the crucial period of transfer between primary and secondary schools (often badly handled) and between years, especially for 'at risk' pupils; overtly unfavourable parental attitudes towards school; *and* repeated parental non-attendance at parents' evenings or meetings arranged in schools.

Generally speaking, liaison and communication between schools and parents and vice versa is not always as efficient or effective as ideally required. Whether increasing parental involvement in schools will improve this matter must remain an open question. Given the present nature of governing bodies, it seems unlikely that too many of them will concern themselves with such matters as disaffection, disruption and absenteeism. If they did, things might start to improve. Who knows, some radical attitudinal changes and innovations might even take place.

Despite the aforementioned evidence, it is quite wrong to assume that all disruptive pupils come from lower streams and unfavourable home circumstances. Most probably do. When, however, an able child from a favourable home background manifests disaffected or disruptive conduct, the hue and cry is often out of all proportion to the circumstances.

Simon, for example, is one of the most volatile and disruptive pupils in 4AB at a large comprehensive school in South Wales. His father is a university lecturer and his mother a teacher. An only child, Simon boasts every modern convenience and natural advantage. Amongst his possessions are a home computer, personal television and stereo system in his bedroom. Yet one member of staff at his school recently walked out of a lesson after being verbally abused repeatedly by Simon. In a note written to the deputy head, the teacher stated: 'Teaching 4AB at the moment is no joke. Simon James is worse than any other thirty pupils put together. His rude and bolshy behaviour is disgraceful. A solution to his anti-social and abusive conduct must be found. I refuse to take this class again until something is done about him.'

Therefore, although most disaffected and disruptive pupils come from unfavourable home backgrounds and low social class origins, this is not always the case. Care should be taken by teachers not to generalize in specific cases as the circumstances in every incident normally differ; at least in certain aspects.

PEER-GROUP RELATIONSHIPS

The influence of peers and friendship groups on behaviour in schools, inside classrooms and within the local environment should never be underestimated, especially amongst teenagers who are at a vulnerable age. Sociologists have found that deviance is often associated with the prevailing neighbourhood culture. The 'Tiger Bay' and 'Toxteth' way of life often transcends generations (Mays, 1972). Miller (1958), for instance, argues that lower working-class culture is characterized by trouble, toughness, smartness, excitement, fate and autonomy – the kind of behaviour depicted by James Dean and Marlon Brando in films of the 1950s and 1960s and which is manifest by Clint Eastwood et al today. These so-called 'focal concerns' are in theory supposed to motivate working-class youngsters in their search for status in their surrounding neighbourhood.

Likewise, strong feelings can bind peer groups in schools and can and do lead to 'counter cultures' within schools. These friendship or common culture groups can develop into strong anti-school feelings within classrooms and schools and have profound consequences upon teacher–pupil relationships (Hargreaves, 1967; Lacey, 1970; Hargreaves et al, 1975; Willis, 1977).

Teachers today need to recognize that pupils belong to a variety of peer groups within schools, notably in their registration and teaching forms. Many pupils will have been together for a number of years since they started in nursery or primary schools. Consequently, the influence of such sub-cultures are all-important in learning situations. Each form, for example, tends to have its own 'heroes', 'wags', 'loners', and potential disrupters. Competition between groups, pupil harassment, polarization of attitudes and in-cliques can all affect and/or influence classroom outcomes. How teachers react to and handle each sub-group is often vital to learning and conduct within the classroom.

Some pupils, though they lose all formal interest in school, continue to use its facilities for their own compensatory social reasons. Reid (1985a), for example, found that good attenders sometimes have lower opinions of their teachers and schools than bad attenders even though they are in the same form groups. He suggests that some less-able working-class pupils may attend school regularly partly because of their higher number of social friendships within their form groups and throughout the school – the lesser of two evils syndrome. 'Stay home and be bored or go to school and see yer mates.' This finding accords well with the work of Mitchell and Shepherd (1967, 1980) who found that many absentees have friends attending other schools.

Reynolds (1975) argues that some non-conformist pupils deliberately subvert order in the classrooms for their own ends. He contends that such premeditated conduct sometimes leads to the establishment of truces between individual teachers and pupils to guarantee good behaviour. The 'you behave and I'll let you have your own way' syndrome. Reynolds suggests that such truces occur more frequently in the final compulsory year of schooling than before. Generally speaking, one feels that Reynolds is right. There are schools, however, where 'truce' situations begin much earlier and are common by the third year of secondary education. In these schools, the fourth year is often as difficult as the fifth.

Jim Davis is a teacher who exemplifies this trait. He detests having to teach 3X, 4X and 5X. In the days when Manover had been a grammar school, he had few disciplinary problems. Since the school became comprehensive and saw the arrival of new heads, deputies and heads of department, his sheltered existence has changed. One Wednesday, despite a previous agreement, he walked into 4X seemingly unaware that a researcher was present. 'All right get on with it. Get your books out. If you're good and there's no noise you can forget homework this week. Come on John, there's a good lad. Sit down . . . Billy . . . Sîan. Sit down . . .'.

Jim looked up and spotted the researcher. He then bellowed at the class for a full five minutes trying to restore order. Then he told the form to open their textbooks at page twenty. Silence reigned for a minute quickly followed by a mass of insults as the pupils realized that Jim had left the textbooks in the staff room. The lesson degenerated from that point. After fifteen minutes, the researcher left the room pretending he needed to be elsewhere, but, in reality, trying to hide his embarrassment as verbal disorder turned into uncontrollable chaos.

THE ATTITUDE OF THE GENERAL PUBLIC

No single social trait emerges from the literature to explain disciplinary problems in schools satisfactorily, but there is ample evidence to show that teachers need the support of parents in their fight against disruption and disaffected conduct. However, many members of the general public today have little idea of modern schooling and the gulf between parental expectations and educational standards and practices may be widening. The Certificate of Secondary Education, for example, is a much misunderstood and maligned examination in populist literature where conventional attitudes towards academic standards reign. As mentioned in Chapter 3, the Pack Committee (SED, 1977) considered that the gap between society's expectations and schooling has increased in recent years and may be more unevenly distributed throughout different sections of the community. Certainly, there are 'double standards' at work. Some members of the community expect their children to develop into intelligent, decent, moral, law-abiding citizens with the minimum of personal effort. Although they expect teachers to work towards these desirable ends, they themselves merely pay lip-service to such outcomes. In fact, many parents behave very differently themselves from the standards they set their children. In one survey, for instance, Hartshorn (1983) found that a surprisingly high percentage of schoolchildren now view 'video nasties' including many who are in their early teens and younger. Little, however, is known about the real effects of uncensored sex and violence on young, immature minds.

Reid and Reid (1983) suggest that the influence of so-called video nasties may be much greater than has hitherto been appreciated. For example, in one case in Swansea in 1983, Daniel was rushed to hospital after displaying alarming symptoms – shaking profusely and continually accompanied by intermittent screaming 'fits'. The medical staff were baffled by the behaviour until the following day when a bashful group of his friends reported the fact that his hysteria began immediately after the conclusion of watching a particularly sinister video. It transpired that the group had been watching the video at Daniel's home while truanting from school without the consent of their parents. It later emerged that these 'video parties' had become a unifying feature of these truants' behaviour. Unusually, some of this group were highly intelligent and emanated from favourable middle-class home backgrounds. Worryingly, the group also included pupils of primary as well as adolescent age. Clearly, this is an example where teachers could not be blamed for the children's conduct. Why then, had Daniel's parents not taken steps to ensure that the adult video could not be seen by their son? Did they not consider the temptation they had placed in his path? Fortunately, Daniel's hysteria appears to have been cured. Both he and his parents, however, have learnt a painful lesson.

In fact, the adverse influence of the mass media – especially large doses of violence on television, freely available pornographic literature, 'video nasties' and sensationalized reporting of un-savoury crimes or factual material – have all been blamed for the perceived decline in the moral standards of young people. So have teenage sex, under-age drinking, 'gangland' activities, drugs, the decline in the role of the church, the family and extended families since the end of the Second World War.

The real effects of the pressures such materials and activities impose upon young, immature minds can only be guessed. Evidence from the States is mounting that violence breeds violence. Tattum

(1982, p.32), for example, cites the case of 15-year-old Ronald Zamara who was tried for murder in the States in 1977. In Zamara's defence, his lawyer claimed that the teenager had become so 'brainwashed' by over-exposure to violent television that he was unable any longer to distinguish between right and wrong. Too many people forget that teenagers have adult bodies with children's minds; a situation fraught with danger without wise handling on the part of parents and teachers alike. In 1985, at the notorious trial of the so-called 'Fox' who raped several women in southern England, it was alleged that the character of this married man and father of three children completely changed after he became addicted to watching pornographic videos.

The Pack Committee (SED, 1977) drew a parallel between society's negligent attitudes towards child rearing and the rise in crime when they stated that: 'The same problem of double standards arises in relation to violence and crime, which is increasing and to which children are more and more exposed through what they see and experience. Like disruptive behaviour this, too, poses a dilemma for children – to imitate or not.'

SUMMARY

The aetiology of disruptive behaviour in classrooms and within schools is the product of a number of complex, wide-ranging and interrelated features. Apart from school and teacher-initiated aspects (considered in Chapter 7 onwards) and differences between the personality, temperament, ability and motivation of individual pupils, these include features linked with underachievement, familial factors, links between schools and homes, peer-group relationships, the neighbourhood culture and the mores of society. All these aspects can cause certain pupils to erupt more frequently than others, including on the spur-of-the-moment over-reactions in class after, for example, having a row with one's parents before leaving for school, falling out with a friend or being 'zonked' after a late night out. Despite this information, being able to spot potentially difficult or volatile situations before they occur is an immensely skilled task which most teachers acquire with experience and which some never achieve.

5

THE BROADER
CONTEXT OF
DISRUPTIVE
BEHAVIOUR

A common omission in much of the literature on disruptive behaviour is the failure to acknowledge the links which exist between serious acts of misbehaviour and maladjustment, children with special educational needs, deviance, psychiatric disorders, diagnostic work and absenteeism. This chapter is a succinct attempt to remedy some of these deficiencies.

MALADJUSTMENT AND DISRUPTIVE BEHAVIOUR

There is an interesting academic debate in parts of the literature about whether disruptive behaviour is in fact maladjusted behaviour. Such arguments are less important than an understanding of the relevant facts.

Maladjustment itself is such a broad concept that countless definitions exist to clarify the term. Many of these definitions are influenced by the numerous schools of thought on the subject. For instance, theories on the causation of maladjusted behaviour include explanations in terms of: emotional problems (Laufer,

1974); personality disorders (Younghusband et al, 1970); inter-family relationships (Mitchell and Shepherd, 1966); maternal deprivation (Bowlby, 1953); social and economic deprivation (Douglas, 1964); developmental difficulties (Erikson, 1963); the socio-economic structure of society (Stott, 1960); the education system (Tizard, 1973; Laslett, 1977; Millham, 1977; Lawrence, 1977); contemporary patterns of child rearing (Tutt, 1977); and social learning (Bandura and Walters, 1963). Present-day levels of unemployment, familial life, standards of housing, societal change and the little positive advice on action to remedy or alleviate maladjusted behaviour only serves to highlight the complexity of the subject.

After the 1944 Education Act, the Handicapped Pupils and Schools Health Service Regulations (Ministry of Education, 1945) described maladjusted pupils as those 'who show evidence of emotional instability or psychological disturbance, and who require special educational treatment in order to effect their personal, social and educational readjustment.' This is a meaningless and vague definition and serves only to reveal that 'maladjustment' is a 'rag-bag' (global) term. Discrimination between the 'maladjusted' and 'non-maladjusted' is always highly arbitrary (Galloway and Goodwin, 1979).

Maladjustment is not a category in the most widely used classification system in child psychiatry (Rutter, 1965; Rutter et al, 1969). The chief function of the term, therefore, was to provide a label under which special education could be provided under the terms of the 1944 Act.

According to research, levels of maladjustment amongst the school population are much higher than those obtained for disruptive behaviour previously discussed in Chapter 3. One possible explanation for this may be that local education authorities and headteachers are more prepared to admit to the fact that their schools contain maladjusted as opposed to disruptive pupils; after all, this appears to remove the 'blame' from them on to the parents.

Studies into levels of maladjustment in the normal school-age population are very much in accord. Rutter (1970) reported that 13 per cent of the school population were 'possibly' maladjusted. Chazan (1970) similarly ascertained that 13 per cent were 'somewhat disturbed'. Pringle et al (1966) found that 11.6 per cent of 1,130 11- to 15-year-olds were maladjusted. In all these studies, the boys outnumbered the girls by a ratio of 2 : 1. The boys also scored significantly higher than the girls on the behaviour scales used for gathering the data. This suggests that when they display symptoms, on average, boys are inclined to be more maladjusted than girls.

Davis (1977), in a study of children in their final year of primary education, identified 14.6 per cent as being maladjusted and worthy of further investigation. Of the total children tested, 7.4 per cent and 6.7 per cent of the boys and girls respectively displayed an appreciable to severe over-reaction on Stott's (1971) Bristol Adjustment Guide. Davies concludes that even at the pre-adolescent stage, there are a number of children who depict hostile attitudes to school. This reinforces the need for preventative work to begin in primary schools.

None of these surveys differentiate between emotional disorders and conduct disorders, between the disturbed and the disruptive. Therefore, the statistics hide the fact that the same pupils can display symptoms of emotional and conduct disorders on different occasions. The picture is further complicated by the fact that both the disruptive and the emotionally disturbed can show similar behaviour traits such as using bad language, being disobedient or committing acts of vandalism on different occasions to different degrees. Over-riding everything is the ineffectiveness of normal disciplinary measures to combat severe outbreaks of misconduct, the problems created for staff when these incidents occur and the resultant consequences upon classmates especially when teachers fail to regain control.

Thus, labelling pupils as either emotionally or behaviourally disturbed is a risky business. Too often labelling pupils as either disruptive or maladjusted is sometimes premature, made on insufficient information and counter-productive. Diagnostic difficulties will only ever be resolved after in-depth, multidisciplinary investigations have taken place and these usually cannot be undertaken in the normal school situation. Consequently, it makes no sense to suppose that children can be neatly divided into the disruptive and non-disruptive, with appropriate educational placements or remedies being automatically found from the application of these 'very sticky labels' (Topping, 1976; 1983).

For the time being, both the causative factors and the various manifestations of disruptive and maladjusted behaviour will continue to be common to each group. This philosophical and practical dilemma is likely to carry on confusing teachers in the foreseeable future. All that can be written with safety is that there always have been, and will continue to be, a significant number of disturbed and disruptive pupils whose social and educational needs have to be recognized, met and supported by schools either on their own or in combination with the other 'caring' agencies which have proliferated since the late 1960s and early 1970s.

It is obvious from this discussion on the link between maladjustment and disruption that all severely disruptive pupils could be classified as being maladjusted, if any useful purpose would be served by doing so. In practice, disruptive pupils are generally only considered to be maladjusted when special schooling is being seriously considered (Galloway et al, 1982). But even this simplistic distinction has been thrown into confusion by the 1980 Education Act.

SPECIAL EDUCATIONAL NEEDS AND DISRUPTIVE BEHAVIOUR

Prior to the Warnock Committee's Report and the ensuing 1980 Education Act, pupils could be categorized as possessing various handicaps from an official list. Most of these categories related to physical disabilities. Two particular categories were related to educational needs, behavioural and emotional handicaps. These were 'educationally subnormal' (ESN) and 'maladjusted'. For some years another academic debate ensued about the unsatisfactory nature of these categories (Younghusband et al, 1970) and alternative schemes (Regan, 1977). Many argued that the term 'maladjusted' was meaningless except for special education purposes and only invoked by educational psychologists as a means of obtaining special education places for children.

After the 1970 (Handicapped Children) Act, the ESN category was sub-divided into two. These were moderately mentally handicapped (ESN(M)) and severely mentally handicapped (ESN(S)). Although there was some agreement on the level of IQ which defined ESN(M)) children, assessing related behavioural problems continued to be exceedingly difficult (Galloway and Goodwin, 1979). In theory the 1980 Education Act has abolished all the old categories and replaced them with an over-riding concept of children with special educational needs. Therefore, all needy children are given individual assessments and receive treatment suitable to their particular circumstances and requirements.

Thus, Warnock (DES, 1978) has done a great deal to redefine and broaden the concept of special educational needs. Warnock concludes that up to one in four pupils will need some form of special educational provision at some stage in their school careers for a variety of reasons. Hence, by definition, all the pupils considered and discussed in this book now fall within the remit of pupils who require some form of special educational provision to overcome their learning and/or behavioural difficulties. Missing school or creating trouble in school or in class can in one sense be seen as a plea for help requiring specialist treatment.

Since the late 1960s a considerable lobby has grown in Britain which argues that children with handicaps should be integrated into ordinary schools and live as full lives as possible within the community after making every allowance possible for their disabilities (Thomas, 1978; 1982). The Warnock Committee supports this trend stating:

> There will be a need for the increasing development in ordinary schools of special facilities, and of teaching in a variety of ways, to enable as many children as possible who require special educational provision to receive it in ordinary classes.

They recommend that 'some form of resource centre or other supporting base should be established in large schools to promote the effectiveness of special educational provision.'

As the Warnock Committee did not commission their own research, they were unable to state with conviction the number of pupils with special educational needs who would present substantial behavioural problems in schools. Presumably they were mindful of the statistics on disruptive behaviour and deviance and psychiatric disorders which are discussed in the next section and in chapters 3 and 4.

At the time of writing it is difficult to judge the real effects *Warnock* is having upon schools. Teachers are probably becoming more mindful of children with special educational needs. However, in-service provision to acclimatize teachers to the new concept are at best patchy. Given the shortage of resources and staff in most schools, it does seem that progress in meeting the requirements of the 1980 Act, which followed publication of *Warnock*, is slow. Moreover, a large number of new teachers continue to be inadequately prepared for dealing with children with special educational needs (Reid et al, 1980; Patrick, Bernbaum and Reid, 1982) and course planners face difficulties in deciding just what to include and exclude from such courses (Thomas, 1985). What is certain is that throughout England and Wales, important educational and research initiatives are afoot, implementing and monitoring the progress of the 1980 Education Act.

In the United States, a similar integrationist lobby has been in existence for a number of years. Thus far, it seems that attempts to integrate handicapped pupils into ordinary schools have met with considerable progress, particularly since the passing of the Education For All Handicapped Children Act.

DEVIANCE

Evidence from research suggests that disruptive behaviour causes more concern to teachers than any other form of deviant behaviour (Blackham, 1967; Dunham, 1977). This is because it destroys the learning process, produces threats to the teachers' established order and cannot be ignored. The intention behind much disruptive conduct is to inflict physical or psychological discomfort or pain on the recipients.

Studies into the behaviour of children in school can be sub-divided into three types: local; national and epidemiological; and longitudinal. Perhaps the best known local study is the work of Shepherd et al (1971) who studied over 6000 Buckinghamshire schoolchildren in 1961 which, incidentally, was prior to the raising of the school-leaving age. Teachers were asked by the researchers to assess children's behaviour from a list of twenty-one statements such as 'not interested in school work'. The findings obtained from these data showed that:

a) A slight majority of the children depicted no manifestations of behaviour problems.

b) Boys were more likely than girls to depict adverse behavioural traits.

c) Girls were more often rated as being quiet or withdrawn. By contrast, boys were more frequently reported as aggressive, lacking interest, uncooperative, lying and stealing.

d) Across the entire age-range of pupils, only 4 per cent and nearly 2 per cent of boys and girls respectively were considered to be uncooperative in class. Like surveys on disruptive behaviour reported earlier in Chapter 3, there was a marked increase in prevalence amongst pupils in their final two years of compulsory schooling.

e) There was striking evidence that poor behaviour and poor attainment are inextricably linked.

The National Child Development (NCD) Study is probably the most widely regarded and acclaimed national investigation into the health, educational attainments and behaviour of children in England and Wales. Successive teams of researchers studied cohorts of all children born in one week in March 1958 in England and Wales. These children have been followed up at different periods from early childhood to adulthood from a variety of standpoints.

When these children were aged seven, their form teachers were asked to complete an original version of the Bristol Social Adjustment Guides (BSAG) devised by Stott (1963). From the findings, Davie et al (1972) reported that teachers regarded 64 per cent of the children as stable, 22 per cent unsettled and 14 per cent maladjusted.

At the age of sixteen, Rutter's (1967) twenty-six item behaviour questionnaire was preferred and used instead of the BSAG. From these data, Fogelman (1976) found that 18 per cent of the children were regarded by teachers as being disobedient. Irritation and over-hasty reactions applied to some extent to 20 per cent of the pupils.

Both the Buckinghamshire and National Child Development Studies have strengths and weaknesses. Their strength lies in the originality, size and location of their cohorts which provide country-wide and national pictures. Their weaknesses lie in the fact that the Buckinghamshire children may not be representative of pupils in places such as Liverpool, Glasgow, Belfast, Cardiff, London or Birmingham, while the NCD teams had to rely on screening techniques completed by a wide variety of professional personnel throughout the country.

The most detailed and widely accepted epidemiological studies of behaviour problems in English children were conducted by Rutter and his team in the Isle of Wight and in an inner London Borough (Rutter et al, 1970; 1974; 1975a,b,c) previously referred to in Chapter 4. These studies analysed the pupils' health, educational attainment and family backgrounds as well as their behaviour. As would be predicted from the chosen locations, almost twice as many children in London (19 per cent) as the Isle of Wight (11 per cent) were found to be deviant on the basis of their scores on the Teachers' Behaviour Questionnaire (Scale B) devised by Rutter in 1967. Two important findings stand out from these data. First, considered overall, parents expressed concern about roughly the same number of children as the teachers when interviewed by a social scientist or psychiatrist, using an interview schedule of known reliability (Graham and Rutter, 1968). Second, however, children who were regarded as disruptive at school were not always so regarded at home, nor vice versa. Therefore, although the parents and teachers were agreed on the percentage of children with behavioural problems, they did not always agree on their assessment of individual children. It seems that teachers are prone to associate disruption more with persistent extroverts rather than occasional or introverted offenders. Parents, who probably know their offspring better, appear to be more ready to identify withdrawn children as disruptive. This suggests that teachers often fail to recognize signs of disturbance which do not involve noisy or aggressive outbursts in class or in school. Finally, information obtained from the schools and the families in Rutter et al's comparative study conclusively showed that the greater prevalence of deviant behaviour in London children than those in the Isle of Wight was associated with higher rates of disadvantage within the pupils' home backgrounds and inside the schools rather than with other factors.

PSYCHIATRIC DISORDERS

Like the difficulties outlined earlier in defining differences between maladjustment and disruption, similar problems arise when considering whether disruptive pupils should be regarded as psychiatrically disturbed. In this instance, much depends upon how psychiatric disorders are defined.

Rutter and Graham (1968) define psychiatric disorders as: 'Abnormalities of emotions, behaviour or relationships which are developmentally inappropriate and of sufficient duration and severity to cause persistent suffering or handicap to the child and/or distress or disturbance to the family or community'.

They add one caveat. 'Our use of the term does not involve any concept of disease, nor does it necessarily assume that psychiatrists are the right people to treat such disorders.'

Galloway et al (1982) are amongst others who believe that this definition encompasses the majority of severely disruptive pupils. They contend however, that 'it is doubtful whether any useful practical purpose would be served by regarding disruptive pupils as just one group of psychiatrically disordered children.'

Rutter et al (1975c) in their comparative study of London and Isle of Wight children found that roughly twice as many of the former (25 per cent) as the latter (12 per cent) showed signs of psychiatric disorders. Like their findings for deviant conduct, Rutter and Quinton (1977) concluded that the differences between the two regions in psychiatric disorders amongst children were entirely due to differences in family and school conditions. It seems therefore, that irrespective of whether pupils manifest deviant or psychiatric symptoms, family and school circumstances are prime suspects when looking for causes.

Finally, it should be noted that Rutter et al (1976) found a slight increase in the rate of psychiatric disorders with age: when the pupils were fourteen rather than ten. Conversley, there were no statistically significant increases in the number of children with 'conduct disorders' or those manifesting disruptive tendencies.

DIAGNOSING DISRUPTIVE BEHAVIOUR

There are no simple formulae which can be used for providing early warnings of disruptive behaviour in class apart from common sense and intuition. Much depends upon the 'mood of the moment', the subject and preceding events.

Disruptive acts vary by degree and kind and in whether they are original or repetitive. Calling out in class, for example, might provoke confrontation one day but not on another. A great deal depends upon teachers' individual tolerance thresholds, charisma and their feelings on the day.

Researchers have made a number of attempts to quantify behavioural traits by devising rating scales or questionnaires. Two of the best known of these are Rutter's Children's Behaviour Questionnaire and Stott's Bristol Social Adjustment Guides (BSAG) previously referred to in this chapter. Like many others (Cohen, 1976), the Rutter Scale consists of checklists of misbehaviours which respondents rate as representing actions of particular pupils. Usually, respondents either mark or underline statements or tick appropriate categories on the instruments. The findings are then examined for the details provided on individual children or aggregated to give total scores so that overall trends can be ascertained. Reid (1984b), for example, used the Rutter Scale to ascertain overall differences in behaviour between good and bad attenders.

Behaviour scales are helpful guides but their true value should not be blown up out of all proportion. They do have their limitations and disadvantages. First, they tend to treat misbehaviour as if it is the sole responsibility of the pupils. Clearly this is not the case. Poor teachers, for example, may well attribute a larger number of problems to certain pupils than good disciplinarians or competent classroom managers. Hence, the assessment of two different teachers with the same pupils is liable to show some variations.

Second, findings obtained from scales only reveal overall trends. They are not sensitive enough to measure classroom interaction accurately. The fact that one class receives a lot of ticks on the inventories does not mean it is the worst behaved class in school. Teachers are only human. Teachers with poor relationships with pupils like truants, deviants or disrupters are often inclined to tick a greater number of categories for these pupils than others. In any event, such outcomes are often demanded by the scale as, for example, statements relating to non-attendance can be included in the check-list.

Third, there is sometimes a danger that researchers will go overboard and attribute collective results obtained from certain groups of children to all similar kinds of pupils whose life-styles, origins and educational circumstances may be entirely different. Researchers should always consider the possibility that their findings are due to quirks in their sampling procedures such as a lot of weak teachers, inadequate teaching, a poorly structured curriculum, a badly run school or particularly difficult, unusual or ebullient pupils. Equating findings obtained for pupils in Toxteth with those in Exeter is always a risky business. To give another example, Reid (1982a) found that, taken overall, persistent absentees tend to have lower self-concepts than good attenders. But some absentees had very high self-concepts, higher than some of the good attenders. Therefore, overall findings should not be confused with individual cases.

The danger of teachers blaming deviant pupils excessively for misbehaviour in class is a very real one (Hargreaves et al, 1975). In one experiment Wigley (1980 cited by Mortimore et al, 1983) found that bad behaviour occurred no more frequently amongst teacher-rated deviants than so-called good behavers. Teachers need to remember that it is quite natural for all pupils to misbehave occasionally as most parents will testify. The question is whether the misbehaviour is excessive or disruptive rather than merely experimental.

Classroom observation studies in primary (Galton et al, 1980) and secondary (Rutter et al, 1979) schools are beginning to gain in popularity and prestige. They, too, have their problems. They are time consuming, expensive and have reliability and validity difficulties to overcome. Another major concern lies in the fact that the very presence of researchers in classrooms (or observing lessons through screens) can drastically alter the normal day-to-day behaviour of teachers and pupils alike. In some ways it is not dissimilar to tutors and heads of departments observing student-teachers on teaching practice. The extent to which findings obtained from classroom observation studies are accepted by the teaching profession as 'gospel' will remain a matter of conjecture and opinion until such time as everybody is convinced of their total reliability.

DISRUPTIVE BEHAVIOUR AND ABSENTEEISM

Research by Tyerman (1958, 1968) into truancy suggested that many truants are shy, introverted loners. By implication, therefore, they are unlikely to be disrupters. More recent research by Reid (1984c) now indicates that the characteristics of absentees are far more complicated. Using the Anti-Social Sub-Scale on the Rutter Children's Behaviour Questionnaire as a guide, Reid ascertained that approximately one in three of his group of persistent absentees were assessed by their form teachers as manifesting disruptive characteristics. Of these, a greater proportion tended to be boys. Interestingly enough, however, the case data suggested that in some ways the female disrupters were more difficult to cope with than the boys, in the experience of the personnel involved. Indeed, a higher proportion of the female than male absentees – whether disrupters or not – were found to be involved with the local social services departments, often for their own rather than their parents' problems. A catalogue of these problems indicated the scope and serious nature of the absentees' own and familial difficulties (such as child abuse, neglect, prostitution and vandalism) which, in some instances, may have contributed to their non-attendance and deviant or disruptive conduct in school.

On the basis of his data obtained from 128 persistent absentees, Reid tentatively sub-divided his non-attenders into four categories – Traditional (or Typical) Absentees, Institutional Absentees, Psychological Absentees and Generic Absentees. He considered that two of these categories – Institutional and Generic – are more liable to contain disrupters in them than the others.

Before discussing these categories in greater detail, it is sensible to note that Reid cautions that much more research is needed before these classifications are tightened. In devising these categories, Reid is anxious to highlight that teachers and researchers alike should avoid generalizing traits common to all absentees. Non-attendance at school is a multi-causal, multi-dimensional problem. Each absentee is unique. To assume that all absentees miss school for the same reasons is at best unhelpful and can be misleading (see Chapter 2).

Reid considers that *some* of the characteristics shown by absentees in each category include the following aspects.

The Traditional (typical) Absentee

It is likely that the Traditional Absentee will be shy, introverted, have a low self-concept, few friends, come from an unfortunate home background and be the victim of deprived social circumstances. By nature, the Traditional Absentee will be pleasant, if reserved, when spoken to and liable to acquiesce rather than search for confrontation. The Traditional Absentee is probably well aware of his or her own social and educational limitations and less likely than Institutional Absentees to blame schools and teachers for his or her plight.

The Institutional Absentee

Institutional Absentees miss school for purely educational reasons. Unlike the Traditional Absentee, the Institutional Absentee can be an extrovert and look for and engage in confrontation when in school. They may even remain on the school premises although out of lessons. Institutional Absentees are more likely than other categories to indulge in 'on the spur of the moment' absence from lessons and be selective about days and classes to miss.

Institutional Absentees can have higher self-concepts than Traditional Absentees and larger numbers of friends. Sometimes they may even be the leader of a group of absentees and have a complete disregard for authority as well as being unconcerned about the outcome of any punitive measures taken against them. Like Traditional Absentees, they probably come from deprived and unfortunate home backgrounds. Reid considers that some Institutional Absentees will have been 'nurtured' on a diet of 'squabbles' at home, in their immediate neighbourhood and in their schools and classrooms.

The Psychological Absentee

Psychological Absentees can be the classic school refusal cases or miss school mainly for psychological or psychological-related aspects such as illness, psychosomatic complaints, laziness, a fear of attending school for any reason (such as a teacher, a lesson, an impending confrontation, bullying or extortion) and because of other notable physical or temperamental features or disadvantages like handicaps, tantrums, red hair, fatness, excessive tallness and a squeaky voice. Educationalists should note that Psychological Absentees will probably need specialist counselling or psychological or psychiatric help to assist them to overcome their irrational or justified fears or prejudices.

The Generic Absentee

The Generic Absentee is a pupil who misses school for two or three different reasons either at the same time or over a longer period. For example, a Generic Absentee may miss school on one occasion because her mother needs help, while on the next she misses school because she dislikes a particular teacher or lesson. Unlike their peers, Generic Absentees' temperament and behaviour do not fix them firmly into any of the three preceding categories.

Another interesting feature of Reid's (1983b,c) work is that many absentees (disrupters or otherwise) tend to blame their schools and their teachers rather than their parents, social backgrounds or psychological aspects for their conduct. Whereas absentees will make excuses for their parents' conduct, they do not make any allowances for their teachers or schools. Presumably this is part of the natural loyalty of family ties.

Despite Reid's work, the phenomenon of disruptive behaviour in school being related to truancy and absenteeism is not new. Over the last decade interest in this topic has increased and there have been a number of reports and research projects on disruptive behaviour which have been linked to school absenteeism (UCAC, 1975; SED, 1977; Davie, 1980; Davie et al, 1985; NAS/UWT, 1981) as people increasingly begin to appreciate that what happens within schools influences pupils' decisions about whether to attend or not. For example, as a teacher at Bicester School in the early 1970s I can remember that there was a better attendance in my social studies lessons on days when feature films were shown or there was a school trip than on occasions when hard work was planned!!

SHIRLEY

Shirley is fifteen. She began missing school at the age of twelve. She first decided to remain away from school when her brother was ill. She claims that she remained at home to help her mother. In reality, the reason probably had more to do with the fact that she did not fancy the long walk to school on her own.

Unlike those of many absentees, Shirley's parents are both employed in fairly secure and stable occupations. Her father is a motor mechanic while her mother works as an office clerk. They own their own semi-detached three-bedroomed house on a modern estate in an older part of town.

Shirley is considered by the school to be 'reasonably bright' and placed accordingly in a 'good middle band' after transferring from her primary school. At first, her reports in her new school were quite encouraging and her attendance was stable. Her primary school grades and transfer report were also very good. In theory, therefore, there was no reason for Shirley to clash with the authorities at school. But clash she did and this behaviour has continued ever since.

The following verbatim extract gives Shirley's version of events for the sudden deterioration in her school behaviour.

RESEARCHER: How then did you start acquiring your so-called bad reputation?
SHIRLEY: It happened after I had been away ill. Miss T. asked me for my maths homework. I told her I hadn't done it. She said she

would report me to Mr J. I asked her why, when she knew I had been off school with a cold. She just laughed at this which made me mad. Then she said that my attendance had better improve because I had a lot of other work to catch up on. I told her I'd like to but she had left me behind. She never helped me at all with anything I had missed. I didn't understand the new work. Then she said something about my attitude which got up my skin. So I told her to — off and learn to do her job properly. I was mad – really angry. This led to a dreadful row in front of everyone until she sent me out of the room and down to Mr J.'s office. Honestly, I'd never done anything like that before. Well, after that things got worse. Every maths lesson was the same. Either she'd pick on me or I'd cheek her. Then I started to argue with other teachers because of her. It was always the same. Everyone believed Miss T. No one thought I had a point. It made me sick.

RESEARCHER: So what you are claiming is that you used to cheek and argue with staff because of your poor relationship with only one teacher?

SHIRLEY: Yes, in a way. Well, it was like that at first. You see, it's her fault. She started everything. She's to blame. If she had helped me more at first rather than picking on me all my problems would never have happened. When you get a bad reputation here, there's no going back. So now I just give as good as I get. You have to, don't you – to defend yourself?

RESEARCHER: How do your parents feel about this?

SHIRLEY: Not very good. Sometimes my father gets really mad with me. So does my mother. They can't understand it. My brother has never caused any trouble at school. Once they threw me out of the house after I got a final warning from the deputy head and I spent the night with an aunt. But it's like I said before — there's no going back, is there?

RESEARCHER: Why then did you get sent home from the school the other week?

SHIRLEY: In a way that was also Miss T.'s fault. I'd just had her for maths and that always makes me furious. She knows I don't understand her lessons but she never cares or offers to help me. She just gloats when I get a low mark and makes sarcastic comments to the rest of the form. It really upsets me because maths is so important, isn't it? My brother is quite good at the subject. Well after maths we have games. I was late getting on to the pitch because I had to stay behind to see Miss T. Because of this Mrs R. (the PE mistress) put me in goal (at hockey). I hate playing goalkeeper. It was freezing. I wanted to play as a forward. So I refused to go in goal. Well, you know the rest don't you.

RESEARCHER: But surely there was no need to swear?

SHIRLEY: Probably not. At the time you don't think do you? Like I said, I was already angry.

RESEARCHER: Where are things going to end Shirley?

SHIRLEY: I don't know. I really don't. Sometimes I get really scared thinking about things. It's unbelievable. It really is. Basically I'm a nice person. I shouldn't always be in trouble.

RESEARCHER: How do you see things improving?

SHIRLEY: When I get a new maths teacher. I've had this cow now for three years and learnt nothing. The other kids feel the same. Why should we always have Miss T. when the other lot get someone like Mr A. It's not fair is it?

Shirley's interview data highlights the fact that attempting to re-integrate absentees back into the norms of school life is a hazardous exercise demanding much care, attention and thought. Both teachers and pupils have to readjust; a situation which calls for give and take.

Falling behind in classwork after illness or non-attendance is a perennial problem in schools. When pupils fail to catch up, then further bouts of illegitimate absence are likely, partly because frequent absentees feel uncomfortable in class when they are unable to comprehend the lesson. Sometimes frustration at falling behind in school work can lead to confrontation – as in Shirley's case – if the situation is not wisely handled.

Unfortunately, given time constraints, class sizes and teachers' workloads, it would be surprising if all transitions following illness or bouts of absenteeism went smoothly. In Shirley's school life, things went from bad to worse. In the space of three years, she changed from a good attender with reasonable grades to a persistently bad attender with chronic outbreaks of disruptive conduct. The latter trait is manifest by the fact that she was suspended from school twice in Year Four for 'gross verbal insolence to members of staff', sent home on others and reported on numerous other occasions to the head of year and deputy heads.

From Shirley's point of view, it seems that she has abandoned conventional behavioural patterns in school. Instead of attempting to achieve high educational standards she has settled for much less with all the confrontation involved. Surely this should never have been allowed to happen in the first place?

Perhaps Shirley's circumstances say something about the implementation of modern-day pastoral provision in schools – or the lack of it – but more on this subject in later chapters. Shirley's circumstances are not unusual, nor very special, indeed, rather common in underachievement cases. It is sad, therefore, that her deterioration took place against a background of stability and parental support – something which is far from the norm in absentee cases.

FUTURE OUTLOOK

It is depressing to report that the number of pupils whose home lives are unsettled, at least temporarily, is likely to increase in future years. Despite improvements in child health which have been made in this century, the psychological pressures on pupils have undoubtedly grown, due partially to the increase in divorce – often preceded by a great deal of acrimony – the effects of recession, unemployment, strikes, declining moral standards, changes within society, violence on television and in films as well as a host of other factors.

Given the well-known link between adverse home and social conditions and absenteeism, disruption, underachievement, maladjustment and vandalism, the prognosis for schooling must be bleak. It may well be that the number of disruptive pupils and incidents in schools will also rise in association with discord at home. If so, this challenge is unlikely to be met and rebuffed very easily by teachers in an era of low professional morale, cutbacks and falling rolls. All we can hope is that schools in Britain do not follow some of their counterparts in the States too quickly. This may sound pessimistic but it is also being realistic.

Paradoxically, if control in some schools is lost, attendant public outrage and media publicity could force a re-think on educational policy. Although not all will agree, some aspects of schooling today are achieved on the cheap, notably facilities for less able and difficult pupils. In these circumstances many pupils are bound to suffer. This is wholly wrong. Educationalists have a responsibility to future generations to ensure that every child is educated to the best of his or her ability. In the long run, this is the wisest safeguard against rising disaffection in schools.

SUMMARY

This chapter has provided insights into the broader context and meaning of disruptive behaviour when considered alongside maladjustment, children with special educational needs, deviance, psychiatric disorders, diagnostic work and absenteeism. Only the future will show how effective post-Warnock provision will be in providing suitable educational treatment in schools for all children with special educational needs including absentees and disrupters. A significant proportion of absentees in some schools can be classified as disruptive, especially those whose genesis has an institutional basis. There is a danger that if societal pressures continue to increase the number of pupils whose home lives are unsettled, then a related rise in absenteeism and disruption, may ensue. If so, teachers are going to need all their managerial skills to survive in the years which lie ahead.

6

THE SEARCH
FOR SCHOOL
FACTORS

The importance of the school as a contributory factor in pupils' disaffection is beginning to receive increased attention from a variety of sources. These include educationalists (teachers, administrators, lecturers and researchers), politicians, professionals in the health and social services as well as the media.

In earlier times, apart from a limited number of secondary moderns, few schools were thought to experience major problems of violence, vandalism, disruption, absenteeism and pupil disaffection. After all, at the end of the 1970s, HMI (DES, 1979) commented that the great majority of schools were orderly, hard working and free from any serious problems. Moreover, estimates of prevalence by McNamara (1975) of 1.5 per cent disruptive pupils at grammar schools and only 4.2 per cent in socially deprived areas led to similar conclusions being drawn (see Chapter 3).

Today, this view is increasingly being challenged (Reynolds, 1984) as more and more evidence begins to show that:

a) absenteeism is a major problem in parts of Britain;
b) 2000 out of 30,000 schools were the victims of suspected arson in 1979 (Geddes, 1982);
c) underachievement is considered the disease of the age especially amongst lower and middle ability band pupils who receive too little of everything in secondary schools – resources, the best teachers, adequate curriculum, praise and parental support. Hence, the number of disaffected, if not disruptive, pupils is thought by some to be rising.

The educational significance of research into disaffection is, correspondingly, also starting to rise for several reasons. First, recent legislation and DES policies are increasingly making schools more accountable for their actions and outcomes. Influential in this trend have been the publication of findings of: HMI inspections following school visits; schools' annual examination remits; and the findings obtained from the school differences group (Reynolds, 1985), notably after the impact made by *15,000 Hours* (Rutter et al, 1979). The opportunity for parents to have a greater say and choice in their children's schools is also playing its part.

Evidence on the impact of the school in contributing to and combatting disaffected behaviour is beginning to mount, although a great deal of further research is required before too many firm conclusions are drawn. Before considering this evidence, it is important to understand why the search for school factors suffered from a very slow and uncertain beginning. There were several reasons for this state of affairs.

Much educational and social research conducted before the mid-1970s emphasized the strong association between a variety of social variables like pupils' home backgrounds, social class origins, housing and location with absenteeism, truancy, disruption and underachievement. The view was often expressed that teachers and schools were the victims of their pupils' home and social backgrounds and intellectual capabilities rather than schooling (Tyerman, 1968). After all, these opinions did appear to have a factual base. For example, important work carried out in the United States suggested that individual schools had only weak and few independent effects upon their pupils when compared with the greater effects of social class (Jencks et al, 1972; Bowles and Gintis, 1976). Similarly, in Britain. For instance, Galloway's (1976a,b) work reported that the strongest link between persistent absentees and their schools lies in the number of pupils who have free school meals.

It is now known that these pioneer studies were heavily laden with familial and social rather than educational variables. Hence, a relationship between identifiable school attributes and pupil outcomes could not have been achieved (Reynolds et al, 1980; Reynolds and Reid, 1985).

This led to a secondary problem. Researchers who attempted to undertake school-based studies into institutional factors involved in absenteeism, disruption, underachievement and other manifestations of disaffection were hindered by the lack of clear leads from earlier studies. Looking back, it is now possible to see that a tradition of research into school factors could have existed much earlier if hints which were available from a large number of theoretical and empirical studies which linked or commented upon the relationship between school policies and social outcomes had been acted upon (Hargreaves, 1967; Lacey, 1970). The William Tyndale Enquiry (Auld, 1976) is but one practical example which showed that a clear relationship existed between perceived bad practice in schools and educational outcomes.

Educational researchers can partially be excused for failing to take these leads earlier for a variety of reasons. These aspects include the shortages of funds which were available for research and methodological difficulties which even now have only been partially overcome (Reynolds and Reid, 1985). Probably the greatest drawback, however, lay in the fact that some early studies in Britain into the relationship between schools and their effects upon pupils met with considerable opposition from teachers, teachers' unions and local education authorities. Such work was perceived as posing ideological, practical and political threats to schools. Thus, potentially important work by Power and his colleagues (1967, 1972), for example, into the link between schools and delinquency was stopped by the Inner London Education Authority and the National Union of Teachers before meaningful results were achieved – partly, if not wholly, because of the delicate and threatening nature of the subject. It is to be hoped that the emergence and publication of HMI reports will forestall and help avoid these kinds of difficulties (subversive pressures) in the future.

Of course, it has always been the case that some educationalists have welcomed research into such topics as reading and designing aids for physically handicapped children, far more than potentially threatening investigations into differences between schools and the link between school variables (such as classroom teaching, the curriculum and pastoral care) and truancy, maladjustment, under-achievement, vandalism and delinquency.

Confidentiality and territorial imperatives are two further difficulties which can hinder research. A number of teachers, parents and local education authorities for example, dislike researchers having access to pupils' records, often those even of a non-confidential nature. It is not unknown for parents to throw their weight around to prevent their children from completing 'tests' for researchers; nor for teachers to fail to complete questionnaires; nor for teachers to be as unco-operative as possible with researchers. Quite clearly therefore, social scientists who seek delicate information into the link between disaffection and schooling often walk a tightrope. Such people need to be diplomats as well as good researchers. Moreover, it is vital that the way they handle and present their findings is given as much thought as possible. There is nothing more likely to bring educational research into disrepute than educational researchers breaking the trust placed in them by their fellow professionals.

Set against this background, therefore, a great deal has been achieved in the search for school factors in a comparatively short period of time. Explicitly, evidence obtained from studies into differences between schools relating to disaffection show that substantial variations exist in rates of delinquency (Power et al, 1967, 1972), child guidance referrals (Gath et al, 1972), behavioural problems (Rutter, 1972), use of off-site units for disruptive pupils (Bird et al, 1980); action taken to cope with disruptive behaviour (Tattum, 1982), rates of suspension (Grunsell, 1980; Galloway et al, 1982) and absenteeism (Reynolds et al, 1976; Rutter et al, 1979) which are not solely attributable to differences between catchment areas.

MEASUREMENT

Research into differences between schools is beset by methodological and measurement difficulties (Acton, 1980; Goldstein, 1980; Hargreaves, 1980; Reynolds and Sullivan, 1981). This statement is true irrespective of whether the proposed research utilizes qualitative or quantitative approaches or both. For instance, school-based case study work is subjective and idiosyncratic and can suffer from technical difficulties of authenticity and/or 'con-tamination'. Narrow perspectives provide at best only partial insights or answers to a problem.

Let us take an example. Researchers wish to examine links between schooling and absenteeism. Owing to constraints imposed upon them by resource limitations they determine to investigate the relationship between pastoral care and absenteeism. Immediately they ignore most of the other possible school factors, such as teachers and teaching, the curriculum and a number of possible organizational variables. Moreover, as each pastoral care system in schools is different, if only in terms of staff personalities, they have to find a common way of presenting their findings. So they devise questionnaires. And so the difficulties are partially surmounted but . . . .

Worthwhile research into school absenteeism requires all facets of the subject to be examined because the social, psychological and institutional aspects are inextricably linked (Reid, 1985a). Therefore, to tackle any one part of the topic in isolation, although valuable, is potentially misleading. Ideally, researchers into absen-teeism require access to pupils, teachers and school records, education welfare officers, counsellors, social workers, social service records, educational psychologists, parents and others besides. Only then will an authentic multidisciplinary picture be painted. To date, research findings have been remarkably short of such generic approaches which probably accounts for the limited progress which has been made into research into absenteeism over the last 100 years.

Of course, limited approaches do have their value. In the search for links between school factors and disaffection much more school-based, teacher-initiated research is needed providing teachers understand how to undertake research in their own schools and classrooms (Hopkins, 1985). Given the dearth of research funds which are available, it is unlikely that there will ever be a lot of large-scale multidisciplinary projects into disaffection. Hence, despite its limitations, each small step is potentially very important. Every little bit of information will add to the picture until such time as the jigsaw is pieced together.

One note of caution is advisable here. As each pioneer study is unique, whether conducted on pupils or schools, and affected by a host of 'local' factors (geographical location, socio-economic aspects, teacher–pupil ratios etc.), researchers or teacher researchers are well advised to be cautious about generalizing traits from individual or small-scale data. This statement is written very much tongue in cheek because, judging from the literature, not everyone agrees.

Quantitative studies have special problems; at least as many as qualitative work. Given the present state of our knowledge, researchers are unable to measure accurately every aspect of school life because of constraints made worse by imperfect instruments, statistical limitations, time and, often, inherent conceptual difficulties. For example, without wishing to be too technical, most researchers are able to measure only some of the cognitive outcomes of schooling, whichever they select. These might include the number of external examination passes, pupils' academic self-concepts and reading attainment levels. Ways of measuring non-cognitive aspects of schooling such as a school's aesthetic tradition, the effects of geographical location upon say, learning and the influence of the built environment upon behaviour remain to be devised.

Future studies may be able to show that school timetables, the extent and quality of home–school liaison, the development of teacher support systems within schools and the speed of change inside schools (Gross et al, 1971; Schein, 1980) may all shed new light on the equation when they are included in research ventures. Irrespective of scope, therefore, most quantitative studies like *15,000 Hours* (Rutter et al, 1979) tend to provide only partial, if very important, pictures into effective schooling.

Despite earlier cynicism, British researchers have tended to be rather cautious about what they measure, how and why. In the United States however, no such caution exists in some circles. Some researchers in the States have found ingenious ways of measuring most things about school life. These include such esoteric aspects as school climate, school ethos and school environment. The extent to which such work is universally accepted remains a vexed question.

SCHOOL ORGANIZATION AND DISAFFECTION

Research into differences between schools highlights some of the organizational features associated with differing rates of pupil absenteeism and disaffection. Reynolds et al (1976; 1980) investigated eight secondary schools in a homogeneous South Wales valley. They found that these schools varied considerably in the amount of non-attendance they experienced. They reported that high attendance schools were characterized by small size, lower institutional control, less vigorous enforcement of certain key rules on pupil behaviour, higher co-option of pupils as prefects and closer parent–school relationships. The high truancy schools appeared to be narrowly custodial in orientation, with high levels of control, harsh and strict rule enforcement and an isolation of the formal staff organization of the school from potential sources of support amongst both pupils and parents.

Rutter et al's (1979) research undertaken on twelve inner London comprehensives found that in the most successful schools there was a prompt start to lessons, strong emphasis on academic progress and attainment, generally low frequency of punishment and a high rate of recognition for positive achievements, well-cared-for buildings and a feeling by pupils that they could approach teachers for help when they had a need.

Rutter et al (1979) reported that the more emphasis there is on pastoral care, the worse the academic attainment. MacMillan and Morrison (1979) agree with this conclusion. They point out that when a reduction in disruptive behaviour is a school's prime objective, it is likely to be achieved at the expense of attainment.

The HMI Report (DES, 1977) on ten good schools reinforces many of Rutter's findings. Their work suggests that favourable regimes are characterized by good preparation, variety of approach, regular and constructive correction of pupils' work and consistent praise and encouragement being given to pupils for their endeavour.

The work of Ayllon and Roberts (1974) provides some evidence to the contrary. Their study shows that disruptive behaviour can be reduced and academic achievement maintained, if not actually improved, when proper guidelines are followed by staff in schools. Like most other things about education, it seems that everything probably depends upon the calibre of staff in schools – particularly levels of motivation, competence and professional interest. Generally speaking, research to date suggests that academic criteria in schools have to take precedence over social criteria when choices have to be made if attainment is the prime goal. This is acknowledged by schools in their hierarchical patterns: deputy heads (academic) for example, generally take precedence over deputy heads (pastoral) in terms of seniority.

The effect that school policies and staff attitudes can have upon pupil outcomes had been commented upon repeatedly in the literature even before the school differences studies were conducted. For instance, Clegg and Megson (1973) were particularly concerned with the way in which school practices sub-divided the slow children from the bright, reinforcing the disadvantages of the weaker children. Hargreaves (1967) was among the first to draw attention to the alienation felt by low achievers in many schools. A lot of schools inadvertently operate double standards, rewarding the able over the less able, leading the latter to draw their own conclusions by manifesting disaffected behaviour. Despite the introduction of comprehensive schooling, one of the greatest remaining challenges facing educationalists today is providing equal opportunities and equal facilities for all pupils (Hargreaves, 1982). Too many schools are comprehensive in name only. In some parts of South Wales, for example, they are really neighbourhood rather than comprehensive schools in the true meaning of the word.

SCHOOL MANAGEMENT

The exact relationship between school systems and disruptive and disaffected behaviour is a complex subject because schools vary so much. There is some evidence which shows that disruptive behaviour is more likely to happen in long lessons, at the end of a school day when teachers and pupils are tired and comparatively minor incidents can erupt, in mid-week, mid-term and mid-year, especially November, February and March (York et al, 1972; Lawrence et al, 1981; Galloway et al, 1982).

The Pack Committee (SED, 1977) took the view that difficulties in schools could be related to the raising of the school leaving age; the maturation of pupils earlier than in previous generations; pupil confusion and unsettlement arising from a period of rapid educational change in schools; disenchantment and apathy with the curriculum and the kind of secondary education provided, especially amongst non-academic groups; teacher shortages and/or high rates of staff turnover; and poor and weak teaching in some cases. Undoubtedly today, unfavourable or uncertain employment prospects can be added to this list.

There appears to be a measure of agreement between writers on the need for schools to introduce coherent staff policies on organizational matters if they are to combat disaffection and disruption. There is however, some disagreement on the best way of introducing these schemes and the kind of detail which is required.

Hastings (1981) suggests that many schools need to change radically their timetabling structure so as to reduce the 'slack' time when vandalism and conflicts between children, and children and teachers tend to occur. Effective measures include the use of staggered lunch-breaks and reducing the number of pupils out of class at any one time, so making for easier control and less pressure on open space.

Gillham (1984) suggests that institutions need to develop their own guidelines for policy and practice based on general agreement amongst staff which aim at reducing opportunities for deviant behaviour to take place. To this end, he began some experimental work in a Nottingham comprehensive school which minimized opportunities for teacher–pupil confrontations to occur. As a result of his deliberations with staff the following practical scheme emerged. Staff agreed to a new managerial system based on four governing principles. These were: enforcing a minimum number of indispensable school rules; careful planning and manipulation of the timetable; providing an adequate system of remedial education and ensuring good lesson plans and classroom management. The logic behind Gillham's scheme should be fully understood as it has considerable potential for adoption by other schools.

a) Reduce school rules so that those which are left are both necessary and enforceable. Maintaining a large number of un-necessary and/or unworkable school rules is one of the functions that puts teachers most at risk of confrontation. When a rule is unreasonable, unnecessary or incapable of enforcement, then the vulnerability it creates for the teacher is unwarranted. In order to ensure that pupils understand the reasons for implementing rules, it makes good practical common sense to give them every opportunity to get to know school rules well. When pupils are unaware of school rules they will either fall foul of them unwittingly or 'test out' limits to find what behaviour is acceptable to staff. Gillham suggests that providing 'home-base' tuition on institutional practice in the first year is essential. This should include a substantial amount of form-tutor time to ensure that pupils entering the secondary school have a gradual induction into the rule system and prepare themselves accordingly. It also provides a means of form tutors and pupils 'breaking the ice'.

b) Like Hastings, Gillham suggests that timetabling is important in two respects. It can be used as a means of avoiding too much free time when there are not clearly defined activities. It can also be used to ensure an even distribution of lessons throughout the week and between and across years so that some pupils are not coping with the most demanding subjects on top of one another when their peers are engaged in day-long non-academic work; to ensure that pupils are not involved in key work at times of the day or week when their motivation is low, such as double English last thing on a Friday afternoon.

c) An adequate system of remedial provision is very important to ensure that pupils are not faced with work demands they cannot meet. Dissemination of appropriate information to subject staff is vital in this process, especially for those engaged in mixed-ability work. Detailed support from specialist teachers through the provision of alternative work materials being devised for use with retarded or underachieving pupils is also very important.

d) Good well-planned lessons and classroom organization are fundamental, especially with less able groups or in academically demanding situations. Staff who participated in Gillham's experiment felt these goals could be achieved by the implementation of the following policies:

1) Ensure the work is suitable to all levels of ability in the group.
2) Have clear rules and routines in class that pupils get to know quickly and understand. Pay particular attention to organization at the beginning and end of lessons to avoid confusion. Specify seating arrangements to keep mutually provocative children apart and so prevent unseemly scrambles for seats.
3) Ensure that less able children experience success in terms of short-term and well-defined objectives.
4) Avoid shouting or 'gunning' for pupils. This is likely to be provocative. The occasional confrontation between teacher and pupil can be worthwhile when followed by a constructive action. Sometimes misdemeanours can be more successfully dealt with privately after the lesson rather than immediately – after the situation has calmed down and rational processes are at work.

Gillham points out that staff saw the management of confrontation situations largely as a function of individual teacher's skills. He suggests that there are two main procedures for dealing with confrontation: de-escalating the process and/or getting the child out of the classroom and away from potential peer support. This avoids potential 'loss of face' situations on both sides. Not all educationalists will agree with this latter suggestion since in one sense removing a pupil from a classroom is by itself an admission of failure.

Based on the findings from *15,000 Hours*, Mortimore (1980) suggests that schools have it within their own means to improve their levels of academic achievement and reduce their levels of misbehaviour by following five particular guidelines. These are:

a) Instigate a common staff plan on pupil behaviour to foster consistent policies and overcome erratic, unfair and idiosyncratic sanctions. Such unity of purpose limits the number of chances for spontaneous disruption to occur in response to teachers' actions.

b) Place an emphasis on academic achievement for *all* pupils in the school irrespective of ability. This means that all pupils should receive homework, have their work marked in detail and be expected to achieve to their maximum potential. Careful lesson preparation is also associated with better pupil behaviour.

c) Ensure conscientious behaviour on the part of teachers in starting and finishing lessons on time. It is often forgotten that teachers have a legal duty to start classes at the designated time. Moreover, such promptness avoids the slack time between lessons when pupil confrontations occur and spirits rise. It also reduces the amount of time needed to re-control classes. Finally, it suggests to pupils that their teachers take their work seriously, care for their academic progress and mean to complete their syllabuses.

d) Make use of effective rewards. Regular praise for the recognition of good behaviour, work and achievement are strongly associated with high-achievement schools.

e) Promote pleasant working conditions in schools, with pupils encouraged to take an active part in the daily life of the institution. Mortimore suggests that this includes ensuring the physical conditions within the schools are as pleasant as possible, giving pupils opportunities to assume responsibility through monitor and prefect schemes and for looking after resources and equipment, as well as encouraging their participation in meetings and assemblies.

Lawrence, Steed and Young (1984) argue that teachers too often feel ashamed at their failure to cope with disruptive children in class. They believe that teachers should be more honest and open about their difficulties and not regard them as a sign of professional incompetence. Case studies taken from their work show that even the most experienced teachers make mistakes in their handling of classroom crises. Based on staff notes kept at two London comprehensives, they found that there were seventy-seven 'incidents' at the first school (1250 pupils) in a week, ranging from fighting in class and insolence, to talking, whistling and eating sandwiches during lessons; a ratio of one incident per 15.6 pupils. About half the incidents were reported by the teachers to more senior staff.

The authors' advice to teachers is:

1) Nip the incident in the bud. If a problem is brewing up, try warning the child off or take practical action such as ordering him to switch seats.

2) Take account of group dynamics in class. Look for leaders or troublemakers. Find ways of changing the group layout. Stand in a different place at different times throughout lessons.

3) Do not accuse groups of troublemaking when only one or two pupils are involved.

4) Talk to invididual troublemakers outside lesson time, especially when a pupil is becoming a persistent nuisance over several lessons.

5) Give children the benefit of the doubt if they make excuses which cannot be checked – such as a stomach-ache.

6) Defuse potentially dangerous situations by cracking a joke.

7) Think carefully before getting too angry about pupils eating in class.

8) Avoid becoming personally involved. Be alert to your feelings and state of mind. A teacher who is in a bad mood may over-react.

9) If you do decide to have a confrontation, do it on your own ground and on your own terms. Never be rushed into events. Know exactly what you are going to say.

Lawrence et al indicate that schools themselves can help to cut down on disruptive behaviour by changing their timetables, curricula or internal organization. They suggest spacing out periods with the same class, cutting down the length of time a group of pupils is together, finding efficient means of making changeovers between lessons as smooth as possible and avoiding over-rigid sanctions for minor misbehaviour.

IN-HOUSE TRAINING

Evidence is beginning to mount that schools have it within their own means to combat disaffection through good in-house training schemes. Apart from anything else, good innovative programmes can raise staff morale as well as combat disaffection. In these difficult times in education, good staff development programmes including school-based in-service work and job rotation are essential to combat the malaise which is endemic amongst the teaching profession.

Systems intervention programmes along the lines suggested by Reid (1982c) for absenteeism and Gillham (1984) and Mortimore (1980) for disruption require considerable attention to mundane detail and dedicated hard work on the part of staff. A united and coherent staff policy may at first glance not look very exciting on paper, when compared with many existing professionalized treatment procedures and their attendant rituals (specialist titles, offices, salaries and facilities) but it is by far the most effective way of combatting disaffection. Controlling and caring for pupils is the responsibility of all staff, not a select few. Pupils need to observe, feel and believe for themselves that their teachers care about them and know something about them as individuals. When good, empathetic pupil–teacher relationships exist, opportunities for disruption are much reduced – especially in well organized and managed schools where there is an overriding sense of purpose. More than anything else, staff policies, attitudes and the quality of teacher–pupil relationships probably explain real differences between schools. Indeed, it is in the search for these factors that researchers should be spending their time; not in fruitless examinations on the state of school buildings, capitation allowances and resources – important though the latter may be.

In any event, the permanent features of schools like the buildings have little effect on pupil outcomes according to research. Rutter et al (1979) report that sex composition, school size, age of buildings, physical space and perhaps most surprisingly, class size, are unrelated to school outcomes. However, both Reynolds et al (1976) and Rutter found that split-site schools are faced with a number of disadvantages especially in fostering a corporate spirit. Thus, it is the 'internal' features of schools rather than their fixtures which are related to measurable outcomes – academic attainment, and pupil conduct. It is people who matter most – the staff and pupils of individual schools rather than 'fixtures'. In one sense this is encouraging because it is a justification for teachers and teaching and is an argument which can be used against the profession's 'knockers'. It is not, however, a justification for bad teaching; nothing is. The amount of harm which bad teaching does for pupils is a subject of untold complexity and emotion. All that can be written with safety is that it seems more likely that some schools have more weak teachers than others and some pupils are taught by poorer teachers than their peers. The correlation between weak teaching and disaffection and disruption seems so obvious that it is often taken for granted. It is not a topic, however, about which very much is known or has been written. Presumably research into weak and effective teaching is too sensitive to be contemplated by many.

To summarize, successful schools appear to prevent too many difficulties from arising rather than being exceptionally skilled in coping with them once they have occurred (Ouston, 1981). But schools can prepare teachers in how to manage confrontation situations in two ways. First, by providing staff with a means of discussing management strategies at the school level through staff meetings. This ensures that teachers take common stands in similar situations. To outsiders, confrontations often appear spontaneous. Pik (1981) shows that this is rarely the case. Quite regularly situations can drift to the point where confrontation is almost inevitable as in the case of Shirley cited in Chapter 5. The lessons to be learned from outbreaks of severe disruption can be lost unless schools have the means to discuss and disseminate as well as providing guidance and support for staff.

The other essential feature according to Gillham (1984) is to ensure that schools have an established and reliable procedure for enabling teachers to get assistance in removing severely disruptive pupils from classrooms. He considers that schools which do not have this safeguard are failing staff and laying themselves open to more serious difficulties which could be avoided.

THE STATE OF PLAY

Research into school differences has begun to reveal that there are substantial variations in the effectiveness of different schools.

Reynolds (1982) and Rutter (1983) suggest that the effects of schools upon pupils may seem small by comparison with those of the home. Nevertheless, the difference of seven or eight points in pupils' verbal reasoning scores which appears to be gained by attending effective rather than ineffective schools is clearly not inconsiderable. To date, Madaus (1980), in a sample of Irish schools, is the only researcher who has reported that school effects are greater than home effects. This may be due to the present state of research into school differences, as much less is known about school than home background and social effects.

In any event, all these data must be viewed with some caution for the moment because Reynolds' work was conducted in secondary schools in a homogeneous South Wales valley. His schools are atypical of the national comprehensive pattern in most parts of England and Wales. Likewise, Rutter's London comprehensives were unusual in some ways such as their resource allocations. Moreover, school patterns in Ireland are different to England and Wales. Even the Scottish data (Gray et al, 1983) must be viewed with the greatest caution since Tibbenham et al (1978) reported major differences between comprehensives in Scotland when compared with the rest of Britain. What seems to be lacking from all these studies is representativeness. Future studies should aim to include the full range of school types and school variables since only then will the complete extent of differences which institutions have upon their pupils be ascertained (Reynolds and Reid, 1985). In this respect, the homogeneity of the Rutter and Reynolds schools is a drawback as was their relatively small sample sizes.

There is also a need for studies of primary schools to be conducted (Mortimore et al, 1985). The important suggestion of Jencks et al (1972) that ineffective primary schools serve ineffective secondary schools, generating an added disadvantage for some pupils, needs to be tested. Finally, some comparative studies between schools in the United States and Britain might be very revealing as would some cross-cultural work.

Taken overall, a reading of the relevant literature on British studies into school differences seems to indicate that pupil–teacher ratios, class sizes, the amount of capitation spent per child and the quality of school buildings, do not have major effects upon pupils' outcomes. Similarly, the formal organizational structure of the school appears to be less important in determining effectiveness than the informal, unstructured atmosphere or 'ethos' which the school embraces. By contrast, high levels of pupil involvement within schools, a balance between over-strong and weak disciplinary measures, a combination of firm leadership by headteachers which allows for some teacher participation and a system of schooling which praises and rewards good behaviour rather than merely punishing bad conduct, seems to be associated with being effective institutions (Reynolds and Reid, 1985). Clearly, the part played by individual teachers, pastoral care teams and the curriculum in schools is crucial in these processes – as are the examples set by the headteacher, senior management staff and the aims and objectives of schools. The passing of the 1981 Education Act's regulations on the publication of examination results could also have important local effects in the future. However, the number of parents who opt to send their children to one school or another on the basis of public examination results will probably be small, since most parents will continue to opt for their neighbourhood school for reasons of convenience and economy. Yet, there are already hints that choice based on examination results could become a growing practice, especially if and when the media begin to highlight these local differences. Whether local education authorities will manage to contrive ways of overcoming parental choice is another imponderable as parental choice is acceptable only when alternative places are readily available.

SUMMARY

Despite methodological complexities and initially slow progress, the search for school factors relating to disaffection is gaining momentum. This escalation of interest has been encouraged by work into school differences. Encouragingly, this research suggests that schools have it within their own means to determine the changes which they need to make in order to improve the educational experiences of their pupils, thereby diminishing opportunities for misdemeanours to occur. Writers are in accord that institutions need to develop their own policies for preventing and overcoming disaffected and disruptive behaviour in schools. Although there is some disagreement on the best ways of achieving these ends, all writers agree that the free, systematic use of praise and recognition of achievement is one of the most effective ways of preventing undesirable behaviour in class.

7
SCHOOLING

The link between schooling and disaffection is an extremely complex one partly because of the substantial variations which exist between geographical regions, pupils' socio-economic backgrounds, the curriculum, teachers' attitudes and school ethos and organization. This chapter concentrates on those aspects of schooling which are known to be related to disaffection. These include pupils' perceptions, parental perspectives, the curriculum, school rules, teacher expectations, teacher–pupil relationships, classroom management and bullying.

PUPILS' PERCEPTIONS

Comparatively few studies have investigated pupils' perceptions of their own schools, probably because of the delicate nature of the topic. Such work, however, does have considerable potential for providing useful insights into educational processes. Some of the findings obtained from these studies will be discussed at appropriate points later in the chapter. This section, therefore, is limited to a consideration of two recent projects.

The first is the work of Phillips and Callely (1981) who arranged for a group of forty postgraduate student-teachers from Cardiff to spend twelve days in twenty-six schools. The student-teachers interviewed 433 fourth-year pupils in an attempt to ascertain their views on aspects relating to their life in schools. In particular, the pupils were asked to say what they particularly liked or disliked about their school day.

In order, elements of the pupils' school day which they 'liked' were: breaks and lunchtimes; games/physical education/sports; teachers' attitudes; school buildings; English; mathematics; peers' attitudes and behaviour; out-of-class organized activities; art; history; journeys to and from school; timetables; school dinners; biology; cookery; woodwork; registration; commercial subjects; geography; needlework; chemistry; metalwork; school uniform; physics; technical drawing; rules and sanctions; lesson organiz-ation; assembly; option choices; social studies; French; length of school day; religious education; music; examinations; homework and careers lessons.

Aspects which the pupils disliked were in rank order: assembly; teachers' attitudes; breaks and lunchtimes; journeys to and from school; timetables; length of school day; school buildings; mathematics; rules and sanctions; school uniform; games/physical education/sports; lesson organization; out-of-class organized ac-tivities; religious education; school dinners; peers' attitudes and behaviour; English; homework; registration; physics; examinations; commercial subjects; history; careers lessons; option choices; geography; chemistry; music; technical drawing; art; French; social studies; metalwork; biology; cookery; woodwork and needlework.

For what they are worth in an *ad hoc* survey, the findings show that some parts of the school day are strongly liked and disliked by different pupils, which explains the high rankings in each of the two dimensions. Teachers' attitudes and mathematics are two such categories which highlight the polarization between the sampled pupils' views based on their own school experiences. However, the results do suggest that some elements of the school day are more strongly liked than disliked by pupils in schools. In this survey, these elements included art and English. Conversely, a number of aspects are more strongly disliked than liked by pupils. This applied to assemblies, journeys to and from school, timetables, rules and sanctions and school uniforms.

The work of Phillips and Callely is indicative of some of the diverse and idiosyncratic views which fourth-year pupils hold about those aspects of schooling which impinge upon their daily lives. Hence, the implications of the work are more important than particular findings. Explicitly, the results suggest that educationalists have little to fear when findings are published from detailed surveys undertaken on pupils' perceptions because their usefulness is limited without the contextual data. At best, rank order positions of individual categories are only useful in showing overall trends. Placings and percentages will inevitably vary from survey to survey dependent upon such factors as the age of the respondents, pupils' in-school experiences and geographical location.

In some ways Phillips and Callely's findings are quite encouraging. They indicate that as far as these fourth-year pupils are concerned, not everything about their schooling is distasteful. In fact, the authors conclude that many fourth-year pupils look forward to their time in school because they like the work involved, they enjoy learning and being with their friends. Phillips and Callely do comment however, that the highly articulate remarks which proliferated about and against school assemblies, the way rules and sanctions are applied in schools, the wearing of school uniforms and religious education, could be an indication to teachers to investigate the importance of these items amongst their own pupils.

In another study based on the perceptions of good and bad attenders, Reid (1983a, c) found that third-, fourth- and fifth-year persistent absentees have lower opinions of their teachers than their parents, relatives and other friends. Moreover, the absentees liked fewer school subjects than good attenders drawn from the same forms as the absentees and far fewer subjects than good attenders placed in academic bands. Interestingly, interview data revealed that the persistent absentees claimed that they preferred core subjects like mathematics and English to minority subjects such as religious education.

Two points stand out from Reid's data. First, the persistent absentees saw more relevance in subjects which might help them to gain employment. Subjects which were less relevant to absentees' future needs appeared to be judged on different criteria. Second, the absentees claimed to have fewer friends in their schools and registration forms than both sets of good attenders. This was especially true of the matching controls drawn from the same classes as the absentees. Reid suggests, therefore, that some less able middle- and lower-band pupils may attend school regularly for compensatory social reasons even when they have poor opinions of their teachers and the curriculum than their peers. This may provide a partial explanation of why some disaffected pupils attend school regularly while others withdraw. It also suggests that absenteeism is related to temperamental and personality traits despite work to the contrary (Billington, 1978).

Clearly, much more research into pupils' perceptions of their schools is needed before too many firm conclusions are drawn from one-off surveys. Indeed, there is no reason why schools should not undertake some of their own internal, evaluative work especially as they are being made more accountable for their own outcomes. After all, higher education establishments have for many years evaluated their own courses as one way of monitoring educational standards, keeping in touch with students' opinions and conforming to the changing requirements of validation bodies (Adelman and Alexander, 1982).

PARENTAL PERSPECTIVES

Like work on pupils' perceptions, there have been comparatively few studies into parents' perspectives of their children's learning and behaviour at school, especially the latter. This is surprising considering the credence given to their role on governing bodies. Without such information, teachers are denied crucial insights into parents' values and requirements from the education service. It seems probable that rates of disruption, alienation and absenteeism would all be substantially reduced if teachers were more certain of parental support when dealing with disaffected pupils.

Perhaps the best-known study into parental perspectives of children's behaviour at school in Britain is the work of Newsom and Newsom (1983; 1984). Their longitudinal data derives from a long-term study of child rearing in the East Midlands, based on a social-class-stratified random sample of 700 children. The findings were obtained from semi-structured interviews conducted with the mothers for around three hours each, when the children were aged eleven and sixteen. At sixteen, the children were also interviewed separately. As the implications of this work are so important for an understanding of the relationship between disaffection and schooling, the findings are now presented and discussed in considerable detail in three stages: results at eleven and sixteen followed by overall conclusions.

1) At eleven:

a) Children's disruptive behaviour in school is seen by parents as something which the teacher ought to be able to control. It is also seen as part of a pattern which threatens the child's work and which exemplifies the teacher's inability to interest and persuade the child effectively. Parents have both admiration and sympathy for teachers but they are often critical on specific issues, usually relating to so-called 'new' education.

b) Twenty-six per cent of the mothers in the study were aware that their children were bullied at school; 4 per cent seriously and another 22 per cent bullied in streets on the way to and from school. A few parents admit that their own offspring are inclined to bully other children.

c) One-third of the parents were unhappy about at least one of their child's friendships at school. Working-class mothers were more likely than middle-class mothers to worry about their children being led astray by their friends into delinquency. Aggressive behaviour *per se* was not seen as a serious problem at eleven. Stealing was then the focus of much parental anxiety.

d) Sixty-five per cent of mothers thought regular homework should be given in the final year at junior school. Only 3 per cent of the 11-year-old children received homework from their teachers at this time.

e) The parents were more concerned about teachers' than the children's aggression at eleven. This specifically included shouting by teachers at children in school. The findings show that there is a striking link between pupils' liking a teacher and being 'very happy' at school. Fourteen per cent of Social Class I and II children had specific difficulties with a teacher compared with 7 per cent for all other classes. Overall, 15 per cent of the parents did not like or had strong reservations about their children's J4 class teacher. The findings suggest that middle-class parents are less easy to please than others and may put more pressure on to their children than working-class parents.

f) Some 60 per cent of the parents claimed that they normally react to their children's criticisms of teachers by supporting the member of staff. On the whole, it takes extreme distress on the part of 11-year-olds to make mothers complain to schools or teachers. What parents seem to want from junior schools is 'effective organization applied in a benevolent manner.'

2) At sixteen:

a) Parental emphasis changes from organization to discipline reflecting their offsprings' adolescent, exploratory stage. Parents regard the two worst features of secondary schools as being poor at maintaining discipline and containing pupils, often deviants, who are likely adversely to affect their child. The best things are 'the staff', followed by equal mentions of 'facilities' and 'good discipline or ethos'. The findings show that parents have a natural fear of their children getting into trouble. Working-class mothers fear that their children's friends will involve them in trouble with the law. Parents with high vocational aspirations for their children see the distraction of undisciplined friends and acquaintances as a direct threat to their children's future qualificational needs and employment prospects. Thirty-five per cent of all mothers were unhappy about the 'bad influence' of particular friends on their children; 22 per cent were specifically concerned about the friend's delinquency. More than twice as many mothers from unskilled and semi-skilled as skilled manual and middle-class backgrounds worried about this aspect.

b) Forty-seven per cent of middle-class children (rising to 57 per cent in classes I and II) undertook homework in the evenings compared with only 18 per cent in the working-class (6 per cent in class V) using the Registrar General's (1966) *Classification of Occupations Index*. Fifty-three per cent of working-class children never did any homework compared with only 7 per cent of those in the top two groups (classes I and II). Clearly, these findings are related to pupils' intellectual levels and vocational aspirations. They also confirm how schools reward able pupils at the expense of others (Hargreaves, 1967; Hargreaves et al, 1975). Inevitably, such discrepancies will predjudice pupils' and parents' views of their schools and influence behaviour patterns, levels of alienation and disaffection and home–school links.

c) Social class, sex and family size differences were discerned amongst troublesome children at sixteen. Non-amenability and delinquency showed a strong predictive association. Thus, children who were troublesome in their parents' estimations at eleven tended to remain so, which confirms a trend previously reported in the NCD studies (Davie, 1972). Tense and anxious 11-

year-olds are likely to become troublesome in a more positive way at sixteen. There is a strong association between troublesomeness at sixteen and negative feelings about school at the same age.

3) Overall conclusions:

a) Parents are likely to know a great deal about their child's experience at school, if only because they so often have to deal with its consequences. For example, many children take it out on their families when they arrive home from school angry or depressed. Quite often children will display their real feelings only in front of their parents. Many pupils regularly suppress or modify their conduct and opinions when they are in the presence of more formal authority.

b) The suggestion by teachers that troublesome children misbehave in school because of the way their parents are handling them currently or have handled them in the past is at best an over-simplification, possibly a myth. Children's behaviour at school is much more complicated than that. Most parents are certainly sensitive to potential situational problems. Generally, they endeavour to deal with them before they reach extremes. They are also aware of many of their children's emotional and constitutional difficulties and endeavour to circumvent them as best they can.

c) Early antecedents to troublesomeness at school include children's vulnerability to stress and anxiety and negative attitudes. These findings suggest, when compared with environmental experiences such as family-cohesion and father-participation, that there is an important constitutional component in children which affects their behaviour. This is supported by the fact that many mothers can easily identify particular children as being especially difficult to rear in terms of temperament from a very early age.

d) The child's intellectual competence does have some effect on how well he or she is able to enjoy school. Failure to enjoy school is linked with troublesomeness.

e) Constitutional idiosyncracies, environmental forces and their interaction with the school provide a complex tapestry which in some ways is too difficult to describe. Generalizing behavioural patterns from individual and collective data is an extremely risky business. Schools have experience of children which is not available to parents and vice versa. However, where parents make judgements of their children which go against the grain, these beliefs are likely to be credible because they are often so painful to make. This is one reason why teachers need more regular contact with as many parents as possible. At present, teachers see too few parents, too irregularly and often at the wrong times of the year. Parents' evenings, for instance, are more useful and effective when they are held near the beginning of the academic year rather than the end. Parents and teachers need to forge close partnerships because they are both working towards the same goal – the intellectual and social development of the child.

In another important study, Fogelman (1976) presents the findings obtained from the National Children's Bureau longitudinal data on pupils' rates of absenteeism at the age of sixteen based on pupils', parents' and teachers' perceptions. The results show that on average the parents thought their children attended school more regularly than either the pupils themselves or their teachers. In fact, the pupils admitted far more non-attendance than either of the other two groups which shows the variance which is possible in such work. According to the 16-year-olds, many of them miss the odd day for one reason or another when they feel like it. On balance, Fogelman concluded that the teacher assessments were probably the most accurate of the three, as some parents might have wished to protect their offspring or have been unaware of their children's occasional or persistent absences, whilst some pupils were keen to exaggerate their truancy. What is clear from Fogelman's work is that occasional non-attendance at sixteen is not solely confined to the less able adolescent or to pupils from working-class backgrounds.

THE CURRICULUM

Despite the absence of much work on the relationship between the curriculum and disaffection, writers are in accord that absentees and disruptive pupils often have unsuitable and unfavourable curricula to follow at school. In fact, the literature abounds with adverse comments about the way the curriculum is organized for less-able children especially as so many disaffected pupils tend to experience serious learning difficulties, are backward and/or inclined to underachieve. Falling behind with school work can be one of the initial reasons why some pupils first start to miss school or show disruptive symptoms (Anderson, 1980; Buist, 1980).

Research suggests that there are four ways in which pupils' experiences of the curriculum adversely affect them. These are when they find it irrelevant, too academic, too demanding and, importantly, when it leaves them with a sense of failure (Bird et al, 1980). Undoubtedly, repeated failure in assignments set by teachers in school reduces many pupils' academic self-concepts and tends to lower their general levels of self-esteem as well as raising their degrees of alienation from school (Reid, 1981, 1982a). These points will be referred to again at appropriate times later in the book, notably in Chapter 9.

SCHOOL RULES

All schools have rules of one sort or another for reasons of safety, common sense and need. School rules can be sub-divided into two kinds. General prescriptive rules concern dress, personal decoration and interpersonal relationships – the 'no running down the corridor' or 'do not wear eye make-up in school' ilk. These rules are often perceived by pupils as being petty and can lead to confrontation in school, some of it totally unnecessary.

A second sort of rules take place in classrooms. These relate to behaviour, movement, talk and academic practice. In an important study, Hargreaves et al (1975) analysed the rules which operate within the classrooms and the manner in which routine deviance is expressed by pupils and imputed by teachers. They describe the methods of social typing used by teachers to define certain pupils as potential troublemakers. They also noted the main strategies adopted by teachers to maintain order in the classroom. Hargreaves et al conclude that like rules, teachers can be sub-divided into two sorts – moralists (stringent enforcers) or pragmatists (action geared to the need of the prevailing situation).

Breaking school or class rules may be the first stage in deviant conduct in the eyes of teachers. Some pupils break school rules for fun, or as a challenge; others because of their social circumstances, while others do so maliciously. Most pupils unquestioningly accept the need for rules in primary schools. Challenges to authority in secondary schools appear to increase with age, often as pupils mature and begin to feel that some rules are an unfair imposition upon their maturity.While most pupils in some schools will wear uniform, in others a majority do not or will not. Once some pupils manage to 'get away' with breaking a rule, the evidence suggests that others soon follow. In some schools, especially those located in working-class neighbourhoods, anti-school counter-cultures exist which operate their own group mores. Usually, these working-class groups reject the norms and regulations sought by traditional, academic schooling (Hargreaves, 1967; Willis, 1977; Marsh et al, 1978; Corrigan, 1979) and engage in 'bovver' and aggravation, testing teachers' patience to the limits.

Staff should never underestimate the degree of sophistication which pupils indulge in as they intuitively react to the moods and petty rules of particular teachers. Individual staff foibles, rules, needs and requirements are so complicated that they defy accurate description. In fact, with every class change throughout the day in secondary schools, pupils have to alter their conduct according to different criteria set by different staff. Moreover, some teachers vary their own standards considerably on a daily or hourly basis dependent upon who they are teaching, the needs of the pupils, subject or syllabus and/or inclination. For instance, staff not feeling 100 per cent fit due to a cold or hangover rarely teach as well as when they are fully fit.

It is often reported that disaffection and indiscipline in schools increase with age. This is partly because schools do not always adjust sufficiently to the fact that many pupils are young adults once they reach adolescence. The age of puberty has decreased sharply in the last hundred years while youth has become increasingly more self-confident and assertive, with a culture of its own. Yet, at the same time, the school-leaving age has been progressively raised.There is no doubt that many pupils greatly resent being treated like 'kids' by teachers (Marsh et al, 1978; Tattum, 1982). The fundamental nature of the school, with the demand for compliance and the lack of pupil-power, may cause some older pupils to rebel (Pollard, 1980). This problem can be exacerbated by the fact that some pupils exercise considerable power and freedom in their daily lives outside school. Leading a double life can be just as difficult for pupils as teachers. Many youngsters have to suspend their adult status, power and privileges while at school, which is one reason why sixth-form and tertiary colleges are so popular with the 16–19 age group.

Frude (1984) makes the point that most school 'offences' which constitute disruption in the classroom (making a noise, smoking, making sarcastic comments, daydreaming) are purely situational offences. In adult contexts they would be ignored. Hence certain kinds of disruption may be construed by pupils as merely asserting a freedom which is normally given to adults. By failing to comply with what they perceive as 'petty' rules, some pupils see themselves as resisting the child status assigned them by their institutions. This is why the suggestions for improved internal school management discussed in Chapter 6 are so important because they highlight the need for teachers to defend a limited number of agreed major rather than minor school rules.

TEACHER EXPECTATIONS

Since the beginning of state intervention in education, it has been apparent that working-class children generally achieve lower levels of academic attainment than their peers from more favoured social backgrounds. By common consent, state schools now strive for equality of educational opportunity. Since the 1944 Act, educational legislation has been devised in the hope of achieving this goal. Despite the legislation and subsequent introduction of comprehensive schooling beginning in 1965, many people rightly believe that whilst the main constitutional barriers have been breached, society has found more subtle ways of preserving educational inequalities. Consequently, many working-class children and children of ethnic minority groups still function badly in state educational establishments and remain disadvantaged throughout their lives; a tendency which appears to be passed on through successive generations (Bernstein and Brandis, 1974; Kamin, 1974). Moreover, girls continue to do less well in some subjects at school than boys partly because of sex-stereotyping (Delamont, 1980). This is particularly true in maths, science and computer education.

Rosenthal and Jacobson (1968), Rosenthal (1975), Nash (1976) and Banks (1979) are amongst others who have suggested that one of the main reasons for this state of affairs is teacher (and parent) expectations. For instance, as teachers expect less academic success from deprived, working-class children so they try less hard with classes mainly comprised of less able or middle-band pupils. In any event, comebacks from working-class as opposed to middle-class parents are less likely in schools as these parents generally expect lower attainment levels from their offspring.

Research suggests that differential teacher expectations can exert a strong influence on the academic performance of children in classrooms, although there is little evidence about how these differential expectations are formed or how they are manifested in the classrooms. A survey of the literature engenders the belief that contributory factors encompass sex-stereotyping and the role of women in society, black intelligence quotients and the effect of pupils' physical attractiveness upon teachers (Insell and Jacobson, 1975).

For example, Rist (1974) contends that teachers possess mental images of ideal types of pupils which are based upon social class criteria and subjective evaluations. These ideal typologies are related to individual pupil's intellectual abilities. From these mirror pictures, teachers sub-divide their classes into fast and slow learners. The fast learners are then accorded more of the teacher's attention and are guided to reward-directed behaviour while the slow learners are given less time and guided to more control-orientated behaviour. These patterns of interaction become established and in the child's later school years, teachers no longer have to rely on subjectively interpreted information but utilize data related to past performance. Pupils so treated then perform as they are expected to and these expectations become self-fulfilling prophecies. In this way academic failure can be guaranteed by teachers unwittingly having low expectations and being biased against certain pupils (Labow, 1975).

There is, of course, a corollary to this phenomenon. If adverse teacher expectations can lower achievement in some pupils, it must equally raise it in others. Hence, the vital role of teacher–pupil relationships discussed in the next section. I know from my own experience at school that my early interest in history developed because of lively teaching by someone with whom I could easily identify.

Although many secondary pupils do not experience formal methods of assessment within schools before the fifth year (particularly since the abolition of the eleven-plus in most areas), it is abundantly clear that children receive clear, informal messages about their abilities and attractiveness to teachers in a number of ways. These include: observing the success of their peers in class (undoubtedly mixed-ability situations highlight these differences); through teachers' personal interest, talk and reactions towards them in class; and the degree of subject help they need and receive as well as marks written on books. Most children are bright enough to know when they are not doing very well with their classwork, failing their parents or falling behind their peers.

A lot of teachers probably underestimate the genuine difficulties which some children have in understanding what is required of them in class and in keeping up with new material (Anderson, 1980; Sharp, 1981). Many pupils, too, despise staff who favour 'A' band pupils at the expense of the less able. Sometimes even bright pupils are conscious of this difference. There is a greater emphasis on academic learning in the lessons of able pupils and in their out-of-class teacher conversations compared with the more disciplinary-orientated nature of teaching and discussion in lower-ability bands.

Schools, like teachers, can generate self-fulfilling prophecies. School practices, as well as individual teacher practices, can differentiate between deviants and conformers, the less able and the able. This is especially true in some difficult, disadvantaged schools where the 'truce syndrome' operates. Poorly managed schools in which truce syndromes are manifest tend to be those in which pupil absence is ignored, pupils are sympathetically excluded from certain lessons and bartering takes place in classes for good behaviour by allowing individualized rather than mainstream programmes to be followed (Reynolds, 1975; 1976; Bird et al, 1980). This is all part of 'the anything for peace and quiet' ethos which is apparent in some difficult schools and classrooms. Once teachers break or give in, it is hard for them to pick up the pieces again. It is interesting to note that truce situations are far more widespread in lower-ability than academic bands. Sometimes it seems that many teachers simply do not want to teach low-ability groups. Whether this is because they find it demeaning or harder work is difficult to ascertain. Perhaps their attitudes reflect their own educational experiences. Or perhaps it might have something to do with their lack of training in discipline or remedial education. Whatever the reasons, some teachers who manage very well with 4A seem to struggle with 4X.

TEACHER—PUPIL RELATIONSHIPS

Ensuring that pupils accept the authority of teachers and maintaining order and discipline in schools are of vital importance to the teaching profession. Without such order there would be chaos. Teaching would become twice as difficult, if not impossible.

Teaching is now recognized as such a stressful occupation for heads, deputies and classroom teachers (Dunham, 1977; Kyriacou and Sutcliffe, 1978; Knutton and Mycroft, 1986) that it is near the top of the stress league. Such stress can be exacerbated by teaching large numbers of disillusioned and disaffected pupils, particularly those in their final years at school (Jones, 1980). Despite this, teachers need to remember that there is a subtle difference between authority conferred by institutions and authority earned through good leadership and teacher–pupil relationships. The latter is related to respect; the former to status. Ducking out of confrontation is an easy way of losing pupils' admiration.

Once pupils or classes gain reputations for troublemaking, these are hard to lose as experienced and new teachers alike tend to stereotype the individuals involved. Undoubtedly, deserved or undeserved bad reputations adversely prejudice teacher–pupil relationships both in formal lessons and within schools generally. In fact, it is sometimes difficult for confirmed deviant pupils like absentees and disrupters to convince staff that they have turned over a new leaf, even when it is true (Hargreaves et al, 1975).

Staff-room 'gossip' can establish longstanding and unfavourable reputations for pupils (Delamont, 1976). Many teachers are prone to make hasty and irrational judgements about individuals and groups of pupils based on very little evidence. They can, for example, make assumptions and judgements about likely disrupters on the basis of such little evidence as teacher talk, pupils' appearances, pupils' academic abilities, memories of unpleasant experiences with the pupils' siblings or of one particular incident in class. Such hasty opinions, if they are transmitted to pupils, are likely to be interpreted as 'offences of unfairness' (Marsh et al, 1978).

All pupils test out teachers, especially new teachers, from time to time. This conduct can be seen as a necesary way of establishing each member of staff's particular idiosyncracies and tolerance levels. More than one teacher has earned his nickname from his reaction to such pranks. Such 'messing about' often takes the form of a moderately disruptive subversion of the orderly school routine. I well remember a class whistling quietly at the beginning of a lesson and pretending it was the wind. And another sending a colleague on an urgent, non-existent errand to the far side of the school. Pupils regard this as a natural reaction to boredom and restraint – a bit of fun or a bit of a laugh. In just the same way, class groups try out new members and it is equally as important for pupils as teachers to pass the test.

Peter, for example, was a new boy in class and regarded by his peers as being 'wet behind the ears'. At the start of a maths lesson, his classmates tied him with rope to his chair and desk, turned him round the wrong way and placed him directly in front of the teacher with a gag in his mouth. When the teacher entered the room, he shouted at Peter continuously, eventually freeing him and sending him out of the room for gross misconduct. Peter was later found standing in the corridor by the head of year who then sent him to the headmaster for a thorough talking to and warning about his future conduct. Subsequently, the form was put in detention. Thereafter, Peter was accepted by the whole class because of the way he handled the situation and accepted the blame. Very soon he became one of their chief 'wags'. This story is doubly useful because it shows another common failing in teaching – taking the easy option. In this instance, Peter's teacher picked on him rather than the rest of the class when it was obvious that he was the innocent party. Sometimes, such events lead to justifiable grievances.

Some teachers are better than others at maintaining order in the classroom and in the way they handle and relate to pupils. A few teachers are over-strict in class and tend to over-react to challenges to their authority (Hargreaves et al, 1975). Excessive strictness can provoke adverse reactions from pupils. Pupils particularly appear to dislike being called names, being physically manhandled and constrained too much in class (Shostak, 1982). The literature suggests that most pupils like variety in lessons, they enjoy being taught and being given plenty of encouragement and praise when they do well. They also like acting on their own initiative in class. Fortunately, the evidence suggests that most staff, including new teachers (DES, 1982), appear to maintain order in their classrooms and have good relationships with their pupils. Nevertheless, individual teacher–pupil relationships vary widely as do the quality of these interactions (Delamont, 1976).

Despite disagreement about what constitutes a 'good' teacher and longstanding criticisms of this paradigm, most research suggests that pupils prefer teachers who are strict but fair, approachable and have empathetic attitudes towards them. They dislike teachers who are soft, ineffective, rigid, harsh, uncaring and whose demeanour provokes classroom confrontations (Rutter et al, 1979; Sharp, 1981).

Teachers need to take great care when handling pupils. Many pupils are highly sensitive people. Pupils are notoriously sensitive of their teachers' views of them and will interpret any sign or gesture as indicators of their perceived worth. Frude (1984) states that pupils use signs that their name is known or not known by the teacher, or the fact that they are chosen or left out of various classroom selections, as indicators of their standing with the teacher. This in turn is likely to affect their behaviour. Hence, a child who feels disliked by a particular teacher may live up to such expectations by becoming troublesome.

Inevitably in any classroom some teachers will value and prefer some pupils to others. A teacher who is a keen footballer, for instance, may well enjoy and prefer the company of the captain of the school team rather than someone who detests the game. This is only natural.

Of course, it is always harder to discipline and punish a favoured pupil than another. But ideally, teachers should not have favoured pupils: only some who they know better than others. For this reason, Hargreaves et al (1975) suggest that teachers focus on acts in class rather than on persons. This guarantees equality of approach. Pupils who are rebuked will then tend to define the teachers' actions as impersonal and find it easier to respond normally in the future.

Conversely, few pupils like every teacher to the same extent. Not unnaturally, most prefer some to others. This is even true of disruptive pupils. Galloway et al (1982), for example, found that only a small minority of suspended pupils claimed to dislike the majority of their teachers. Most disliked some and liked others. Interestingly, one-third of the suspended pupils reported an intense dislike or resentment of one particular teacher. Longstanding personality clashes between individual teachers and pupils and/or classes often lie at the heart of problems. Good heads of year should automatically investigate repeated complaints about teachers by pupils and vice versa as a matter of course.

CLASSROOM MANAGEMENT

Research and reviews of research (Docking, 1980; Tattum, 1982; Mortimore et al, 1983) tend to suggest that pupils give two main reasons for disrupting classes. As previously mentioned, these are generally either situations created by poor teaching strategies ('not being treated with respect', 'inconsistency of rule application' and 'poor or non-teaching') or aspects related to the structure and organization of schools ('running down the corridor', 'not wearing school uniform', or 'talking in assembly'). Teachers' expectations of pupils' academic levels can also adversely or favourably influence pupil performance. For instance, a teacher who enthuses about maths and causes the pupils to enjoy his lessons is likely to achieve better performance and conduct in the subject than another who bores the class to tears or is unable to maintain order (see Jason's case in Chapter 10). This is why changing subject or form teachers often has much greater consequences upon individual pupil and class behaviour than many schools seem to realize. Viewed negatively, teachers who expect pupils to display troublesome behaviour probably influence such outcomes, if only unwittingly. Teachers who expect less of pupils get less. Teachers who cannot control classes find they have to combat more misbehaviour than others.

Research suggests that good teachers need to understand some of the lessons from studies into classroom interaction if they are to teach successfully.These show that teaching is far more than standing up in front of a class relating facts to pupils. Teaching is also about understanding individuals and groups of pupils. To achieve this objective, teachers need to spend time finding out what makes their pupil tick. Such time is well spent and will repay them fully. Failure to take an interest in pupils makes the latter feel that their teachers do not care. Thus, understanding is likely to lead to empathy. In turn, this will lead to better pupil–teacher relationships, better lessons, less need for overt control which, in their turn, all lead to a reduction in the possible number of opportunities for disruptive conduct to occur.

Research also shows that pupils dislike four particular traits in teachers. These are:

1) Teachers who are 'inhuman' and interpret their role too literally. Such staff are perceived by pupils as being 'a load of rubbish', 'robots', 'faceless . . .' and 'time servers' (Woods, 1984). Therefore, stand-offish approaches are unlikely to work with pupils.
2) Teachers who treat pupils as anonymous (Rosser and Harré, 1976). Despite current teacher ratios, it is vital that pupils are treated as individuals (Lortie, 1975).

3) Teachers who are soft and/or inconsistent (Marsh et al, 1978).
4) Teachers who are 'unfair' and make unreasonable demands on pupils (Rosser and Harré, 1976).

When pupils regard their schools as having a lot of staff in these categories, it is likely that they will manifest their displeasure by rebelling. Research into pupils' perceptions suggests that when children misbehave under such circumstances, there is a rational basis for the conduct. Consequently, schools with higher than average numbers of disaffected pupils (with all this implies in terms of violence, vandalism, confrontation and large doses of teacher stress) might well be advised to examine their own professional laurels as well as other factors.

Conversely, research suggests that successful schools are characterized by having a majority of their staff in the following categories:

1) Teachers who are able to keep control at all times (*most* important).
2) Teachers who are able to 'have a laugh' with pupils.
3) Teachers who foster warm, empathetic relationships with pupils.
4) Teachers who like and understand children.
5) Teachers who teach their subjects well, with enthusiasm and in interesting ways.
6) Teachers who teach all the time rather than indulging in aimless activities.
7) Teachers who are consistent and fair.
8) Teachers who treat children with respect and as equals.
9) Teachers who create a sense of freedom in class.

MANAGING DISRUPTIVE PUPILS IN CLASSROOMS

Pik (1981) found four distinct phases in incidents of disruptive behaviour in classrooms – the 'build-up', the 'trigger event', the 'escalation' and the 'finale'. He suggests that the first two of these are promoted by either the pupil or the teacher or both. However, the escalation and finale always involve both parties. Likewise, Marsh et al (1978) describe the sequence in disruptive incidents as generally consisting of an offence by the teacher in the eyes of pupils followed by the pupils' consequent retribution.

Examining differences in teachers' abilities to control pupils,

Kounin et al (1966) found that too much activity-change, over-loading pupils with instructions, and interrupting ongoing activities all helped to create opportunities for disruptive behaviour. The micro-analysis of normal lessons by Hargreaves et al (1975) distinguished between the five phases of 'entry', 'settling down', 'lesson proper', 'clearing up' and 'exit'. They suggest that disruption is more likely during some phases than others. Periods of transition from one phase to the next are likely triggers for disruptive behaviour to take place.

The management of control in the classroom has formed part of a number of significant projects including the Teacher Education Project at Nottingham (Wragg and Kerry, 1979; Wragg, 1984), Davie's (1980) special course at Cardiff and Lawrence's (1980) attempts to work with teachers in schools on various strategies likely to reduce disruption. In addition, a number of anecdotal first-hand accounts of teachers successfully controlling potentially disruptive classes have been published (Francis, 1975; Haigh, 1979; Saunders, 1979).

Lawrence (1980) has suggested three ways of training teachers to develop their skills in order to examine and cope with disruptive behaviour. These include the systematic listing by teachers of all the techniques they use for dealing with difficult children. This sensitizes them to the wide range of possible remedial measures which are available in particular situations and helps them to analyse critically their own performance. Lawrence also advises teachers to learn to use and apply Kelly's (1953) repertory grid techniques to measure the difficulty of classes in schools. The results obtained from these grids can provide invaluable information for headteachers on how to deploy staff effectively as well as providing an interesting 'picture' of the school. Finally, Lawrence draws attention to a wide range of behaviour modification techniques which are available. These generally utilize positive reinforcement measures for use by staff with difficult pupils (see also: Harrop, 1984; Yule et al, 1984). Clarke et al (1981) have also reported that teachers can be trained to spot potentially damaging situations in lessons. Their sequence analysis approach shows that critical-choice points can be identified and turned to advantage, thereby reducing the risk of conflict.

By and large, however, much more research is needed into the aetiology and control of disruptive behaviour in classrooms and schools before teachers will be scientifically and intuitively trained to overcome potential and actual misbehaviour. It has to be recognized that disruption in the classroom is and will remain a perennial problem for many years ahead. Its causation is both complex and multi-factorial. In the absence of ideal approaches, researchers and teachers alike will have to employ a variety of perspectives to examine and combat the conduct in schools. In any event, understanding the aetiology of disruption is no guarantee that teachers will be able to control classes or overcome potentially difficult situations (Parry-Jones and Gay, 1984). Moreover, understanding cannot change personality or teachers' innate or acquired managerial skills. This is one reason why Cox (1977) found that teacher-absence is often the result of anxiety about classroom disruption and problems of enforcing discipline. As, or if, discipline in the classroom breaks down, so teacher absences can rise sharply.

BULLYING

The thorny question of bullying in schools has received comparatively little attention in Britain possibly because of the delicate and complex nature of the subject (Olweus, 1978, 1984; Beynon and Delamont, 1984). Evidence is beginning to increase, however, which suggests that some pupils miss school either because they are bullied or because they are the recipients of other clandestine activities such as extortion. Acts of bullying in schools interfere with the mental as well as physical presence of children. In some cases, acts of bullying cause untold misery which is out of all proportion to the event. Alan for example, first began missing school in J3 after some of the other pupils 'pinched' his collection of soccer cards obtained from sweet packets. Winston developed a fear of attending school when older pupils began asking him for twopence a day protection money. If he failed to pay he was bullied – so he began to miss school; too afraid to tell his parents or teachers.

Despite the absence of much research, the literature indicates that bullying poses a greater threat to pupils in some schools and classrooms than others. Particular schools at risk are often situated in deprived, low socio-economic regions with a high proportion of black children on their roll. In the United States, bullying and extortion appear to be much greater problems than in Britain (see Chapter 3).

SUMMARY

While work undertaken within and about schools suggests that each institution is unique, mirroring a miniature society, factors which seem to be related to levels of pupil absenteeism, disruption, underachievement and general levels of malaise and disaffection, include pupils' perceptions of their institutions and teachers, parental attitudes, school organization, the curriculum, school rules, teacher expectations, teacher–pupil relationships, classroom management and bullying in schools. Although further research is necessary before too many firm conclusions are reached on all these matters, it is clear that the quality of staff in schools and the calibre of their teaching is a crucial determinant in the equation. Positive staff attitudes towards teaching, the curriculum and teacher–pupil relationships can undoubtedly reduce alienation and disaffection within schools. Negative attitudes are likely to foster and ferment disaffection giving the conduct a justifiable basis. As Beynon and Delamont (1984) suggest, much more attention needs to be given to pupils' perceptions of schooling if real understanding and progress is to be made. Studying only one side of the coin – teacher's views – may be counter-productive as schools are about pupils as well as teachers. Encouragingly, research shows that schools as institutions have it within their own hands to determine the changes they need to make in order to improve the quality of the educational experience for all their pupils. Pupil-orientated rather than institution-orientated guidelines can be used to implement meaningful and beneficial change for all concerned; a theme which is developed in later chapters. Learning can and should be fun for everybody – not just élite groups. A prime requisite for successful teaching is effective classroom management (Phillips et al, 1985).

8
RESPONDING
TO
DISAFFECTION

This chapter is the first of three which discuss the formal strategies open to schools and local educational authorities for dealing with and combatting disaffection. These chapters not only concentrate on cases of non-attendance and disruption but also on underachievement which is closely related to these phenomena – one of the themes of the book.

The specific issues discussed in this chapter are the pastoral–academic dichotomy in schools, school policies towards deviant and disaffected conduct and identification strategies. The following two chapters focus on initiatives which are open to schools to combat disaffection and the use or otherwise of formal sanctions by schools and local education authorities.

THE PASTORAL–ACADEMIC DICHOTOMY

It is a mistaken proposition to argue that there is a conflict between the intellectual and social or emotional aspects of education for two reasons. First, achieving personal and social growth necessitates a great deal of knowledge. Nobody can fully participate in society if they are ignorant; to know something of a culture is a pre-condition to entering it. Second, both aspects are inextricably linked. All teaching has the unintended consequence of demonstrating concern and regard for pupils' worth. In this respect, time spent marking maths, English or social studies books is no less valuable than participating in a sympathetic discussion of adolescent or primary children's needs. Emotional therapy is an intellectual enterprise.

Prior to the early and mid-1960s, before the teaching and pastoral duties of teachers became artificially divided in state secondary schools, most teachers considered that the welfare of their pupils was an integral part of their vocational responsibilities as teachers. Many probably still do, but the sub-division of academic and pastoral functions often hinders rather than helps the creativity of form and subject tutors in schools.

In many secondary schools today, academic and pastoral dichotomies have been fostered by prevailing career structures within teaching which reward administration and denegrate good classroom teaching. Successful classroom teachers are forced, if they wish to climb the career ladder, to accept more and more routine administration gradually and undertake less teaching contact time. By and large in secondary education, well-qualified post-graduate teachers have tended to follow the academic route from Scale I through to head of department, deputy head and head-teacher. By contrast, college-trained staff often opt for the Scale I teacher, head of year, deputy head route. Within secondary schools the functions and responsibilities of heads of year and heads of department are very different – each has their own chain of command, staff, duties and loyalties.

Whether this two-pronged organizational structure has helped or hindered pupil care in secondary schools is a moot point. Either way, few teachers receive adequate initial or in-service training before taking up their posts of pastoral responsibility. Indeed, many teachers are selected for these positions on the basis of their experience, enthusiasm and organizational skills as form or subject teachers rather than anything else. This is hardly a foolproof system.

In the late 1960s, there was a sudden spirit of enthusiasm for the training and appointment of school counsellors in large secondary schools. Sadly, although these appointments continue to be made in some regions, in others they have declined or been discontinued for a variety of reasons. These include economies being made in local authority budgets, misunderstandings arising about the philosophy of counselling, the low calibre of some of the early and subsequent appointees, and rivalries which have developed between non-qualified pastoral staff and well qualified, professionally trained counsellors. Moreover, some teachers and headteachers have felt uncomfortable about having people in schools who handle as much, if not more, confidential information on delicate matters as they themselves and whose aims are often more in keeping with social workers than educationalists.

Some of these traits are evident in the study by Murgatroyd (cited in Reynolds et al, 1980) which described findings obtained from an in-depth look at the organization of pastoral care in seventy-six secondary schools. The researcher compared schools which had a major problem of truancy with those which did not. Murgatroyd found that high truancy schools tended to make more use of senior and middle management (heads of year, house and counsellors) to co-ordinate information on absence and liaise with education welfare officers than low truancy schools. Interestingly, schools in which middle management posts had proliferated, tended to be those which:

1) had a larger than average number of associated problems, including low rates of attendance and high rates of delinquency;
2) reduced the responsibilities given to form teachers to tackle truancy and truancy-related problems for themselves.

It seems, therefore, that merely creating pastoral posts in schools is no guarantee there will be a corresponding reduction in the number of problems which schools face. Indeed, the reverse can apply. This is hardly surprising. In theory, effective and efficient pastoral provision should prevent and tackle a greater range of problems than non-existent or weak provision. Effective pupil care should aim at discovering, obviating, protecting and preventing pupils' difficulties from becoming insurmountable through good managerial practice in as empathetic manner as possible.

Irrespective of pastoral provision, most schools will or should spot obviously difficult and unhappy children and do their level best to help these pupils. However, identifying pupils who need help and overcoming these difficulties are two entirely different matters. Success rates with persistent absentees are not high, while many underachievers in secondary schools receive no additional daily help on a personal basis. Moreover, many schools are not very successful at dealing with those disaffected pupils who manifest behavioural problems of one kind or another. Schools are often hindered from achieving effective pastoral provision by poor home–school links and inadequate inter-agency liaison. Relationships between schools and social service departments, for example, are notoriously poor in many areas (see Chapter 11).

Unfortunately, some schools fail even to spot obvious candidates for help, probably because of the lack of appropriate training given to staff, the low calibre of appointees or over-demanding workloads. Three of the worst cases of this kind drawn from my own experience are Anthea, Carole and Bill. I came across Anthea when I was asked at short notice to take the place of the normal class teacher who was away ill. Instead of merely keeping the form occupied, I decided to teach a formal lesson which involved setting the pupils some written work. At the end of the lesson the work was handed in. I asked Anthea to stay behind because as I assisted her with her assignment I detected what appeared to me to resemble 'mirror image' writing. She was immediately referred for specialist help. Following 'tests' by an educational psychologist, she was provided with specialist tuition by the local authority in school twice a week.

Unfortunately, my intervention – and the resultant diagnosis that Anthea was dyslexic – occurred much too late for any useful purpose to be served as she left school at the age of sixteen a few weeks later. In other words, no teacher had spotted Anthea's condition in eleven years of compulsory education. This is indicative of the lack of training provided to many entrants to the profession.

Carole's was the reverse situation. She was referred to me for advice at the age of twenty as she wished to train as a teacher but was unable to gain acceptance to an initial course because of her so-called dyslexic condition. Later tests revealed that Carole was not dyslexic but had a complex perceptual problem which affected both her learning and school work when under pressure. Although considered unsuitable for teaching, she eventually went to an art college and now works with mentally handicapped children. Carole claims that she gave up trying in school after one of her teachers had told her she was dyslexic and needed specialist help. To the best of her knowledge, no referral was made by the school; at least she never saw anybody. At the time of writing, Carole is trying to achieve further academic qualifications after years of endeavour by studying in her own time and at her own expense.

Bill's case is tragic. I came across him when I was undertaking a sponsored research project into the interface of medical, social and educational facilities for ESN(S) children and their families in one county in South Wales in the mid-1970s. For ten years, Bill had attended a school for mentally handicapped children. Then, at the age of seventeen, as part of a local authority initiative, he was encouraged to learn bricklaying at a further education college. When I went to visit him in class, the college lecturer called me across and with a smile on his face asked me to try and ascertain Bill's educational handicap. The question was obviously intended to be rhetorical because before I had a chance to do so, the lecturer addressed him. There was no response. He spoke again. 'Notice anything?', he asked jovially. I had to confess that I hadn't, except for the fact that Bill had not responded to either remark. 'Exactly', replied the lecturer who immediately took me to his office to show me Bill's records. It turned out that Bill had been diagnosed mentally handicapped at the age of seven and placed in a special school following the 1970 (Handicapped Children) Act. Even his parents believed him to be mentally handicapped but alert. Following the lecturer's intervention, tests showed that Bill was normal in every way apart from being profoundly deaf. For ten years, therefore, Bill had been educated in the wrong school. Happily, owing to much endeavour and generosity on the part of many people, he is now a successful bricklayer.

These three cases indicate that schools have a long way to go before they achieve effective pastoral provision. For absentee and disruptive pupils for whom there is often little empathy, the gap is sometimes even wider than for their conformist peers.

SCHOOL POLICIES

The aim of most pastoral staff in schools is to enable children with difficulties to overcome them as smoothly and as quickly as possible. In this way the educational consequences for children at risk are minimized. When, however, such intervention fails, especially with deviant children, staff usually resort to more formal sanctions. These include the use of short, sharp shock treatments such as lines and detention; the kind of incidents for which the cane was fashionable in former times. For continued misbehaviour, a series of policies are generally considered dependent upon individual circumstances. These range from the provision of remedial education to more severe options like suspension and court proceedings which are discussed in greater detail in Chapter 10.

Evidence to date suggests that schools vary considerably in the type of responses they make to their pupils, in the level of resources and options open to them, the order in which these options are deployed and the speed at which punitive sanctions replace or are operated instead of welfare-orientated ones. Schools, therefore, tend to be idiosyncratic in their responses to pupils' needs dependent upon their philosophy and assessment of individual situations. One danger of punitive responses is that schools can sometimes reinforce the very behaviour which they are seeking to overcome (Reynolds and Murgatroyd, 1977).

The literature suggests that good schools endeavour and actually achieve a very high proportion of success with pupils. This means arriving at effective solutions for every pupil within their care who has a need. Such lofty but laudable ideals are very hard to achieve without a great deal of dedicated work on the part of staff, especially in schools located in deprived areas or those with an abundance of disaffected or alienated pupils. Absentees, for example, are unlikely to be successfully re-integrated if they are immediately sent home on their return for failing to wear the proper school uniform or if they are 'punished' for falling behind in their school work. What they need is help not victimization. Good schools should aim to identify actual and potential problems at a very early stage in their development, liaise between teachers and parents as and when necessary, link with outside agencies, and provide the right conditions for empathetic support and practical help to be given irrespective of individual circumstances (Clegg and Megson, 1973; Schools Council, 1973).

This is a demanding task which requires consolidated and dedicated support from the entire teaching staff in schools. A few weak links can undo the good work of the majority. To be effective, teachers (especially those in posts of pastoral responsibility) need to be aware of the full range of services which are available to help 'problem' children. Currently, too many professionals on both sides of the fence fail to understand and co-operate fully with one another because of their different professional orientations, training and territorial imperative (see Chapter 11). Fitzherbert

(1977) has written a useful and extensive guide on the services available to teachers for dealing with children 'at risk' based on the premise that schools and teachers provide the crucial first line of defence and have primary responsibility for children's welfare and preventive work. Fitzherbert's book shows the way in which educational welfare, health and psychiatric services, social work and child guidance liaise. More practically, she suggests ways in which schools and teachers can make the best use of these services and promote good inter-agency co-operation. An understanding of all these points would undoubtedly help many teachers in their daily work.

LEA POLICIES

Evidence from the literature suggests that local education authorities vary considerably in their policies for dealing with absenteeism, disruption and underachievement. Authorities differ in the amount of autonomy they give to schools to act as their own first line of defence in coping with disaffected pupils. Therefore, they differ on the extent to which schools are expected to concentrate on teaching, leaving welfare functions to external agencies. In practical terms, this manifests itself in the allocation of LEA resources in determining for example, the balance between schools and external support services, the relative importance attached to education welfare services, child guidance, the school psychological service and special education, and in the degree of support given to the development of pastoral care systems, remedial education and special curricular schemes to deal with and overcome outbreaks of disaffected behaviour.

The evidence suggests that some LEA responses to disruptive behaviour are fairly sophisticated (Young et al, 1979; 1980). Avon, for instance, has a complex six-stage scheme to combat disruptive behaviour within the Authority (Davies, 1980). Stage 1 comes into force when a pupil develops a behaviour pattern which gives rise to serious concern to staff. The parents are notified by a letter written by a senior member of the school's pastoral team. In most cases, Stage 1 suffices and proves to be a useful deterrent. Stage 2 comes into being if the disturbing behaviour pattern persists. The parents receive a warning letter from the headteacher advising them that detailed records of incidents involving the pupil will be kept and the family is warned of the imminence of Stage 3.

In Stage 3, information about the behaviour of the pupil is passed to the local education officer. Thereafter, a dossier is kept of incidents with details such as dates, witnesses, and the pupil's and parents' response to disciplinary measures. The pupil is automatically placed on the Authority's 'at risk' register.

In Stage 4, the pupil is suspended from school at the head-teacher's discretion. The pupil is escorted home by a member of staff and set work to be completed at home during the period of suspension. The parents are summoned to a specially convened hearing of their case at the education offices. The committee is chaired by the chief education officer and includes advisers, the principal education welfare officer, senior personnel from the social services, headteachers and appropriate teaching staff. Unknown to the parents, it is clearly understood that all schools will re-admit the offending pupils at Stage 4, although parents will have been warned previously that the dossier of offences held by the Authority may be presented to a juvenile court to support a claim that the pupil is beyond control. Clearly defined conditions are made by the hearing committee for re-admission of the pupil to his or her former school. Detailed records of proceedings are kept for future reference.

If the pupil reaches Stage 5, he or she is automatically expelled for serious further breaches. The parents are invited by the chief education officer to apply for the child's admission to another school in the Authority subject to clearly defined conditions being met. Davies considers that these transfers are generally effective as they remove pupils' peers group support.

If a pupil fails to comply with the conditions specified in stages 4 and 5, the pupil is transferred to a special school for disruptive pupils. Davies believes the scheme to be very successful. He cites the experience of one headteacher of a comprehensive school with 1400 pupils in the Authority who estimated that at any point in time thirty to thirty-five of his pupils would be subject to Stage 1, approximately twenty to thirty to Stage 2 and only three or four to Stage 3. None of his pupils had reached stages 5 and 6.

The Avon scheme takes account of major misdemeanours by pupils in the classroom and/or on the school premises committed either by suspended or by pre-suspended pupils through one all-embracing policy. Other authorities have their own schemes for dealing with large-scale misbehaviour such as assisting schools through the modification of the curriculum or the appointment of school counsellors as well as policies for handling suspended or pre-suspended pupils like the provision of off- or on-site units (see 'Further Reading Lists' on p. 247).

Rather less attention appears to have been given by local education authorities towards co-ordinated policies aimed at preventing and overcoming absenteeism. Existing reports stress the need to improve inter-departmental communication, instigate effective school practices which record and identify persistent absentees at early stages and plan viable local policies which strengthen and support the Education Welfare Service (Strathclyde, 1977; West Glamorgan, 1980).

Information on policies for dealing with underachieving pupils is less readily available possibly because of the complexity of the topic. Generally speaking, most authorities expect schools to make their own arrangements for underachieving pupils after consulting advisory teachers and others on appropriate remedies. Some authorities do provide specialist teachers for particular groups of children within their boundaries who are known to suffer from specific learning difficulties. These include the appointment of officers for work with gypsy and black pupils who may, for example, have remedial, reading or speech difficulties.

IDENTIFICATION

Absenteeism

Measures taken to identify and prevent absenteeism should begin in primary schools. This is particularly true because once pupils pluck up the courage to miss school for the first time, the behaviour tends to persist and escalate (Davie, 1972) especially as they progress through their secondary schools.

There are a few case studies in the literature of persistent absentees and truants being successfully re-integrated back into their schools. There is also comparatively sparse evidence of schools implementing special schemes to detect and prevent non-attendance. Two exceptions are the Vauxhall Manor School operation (Jones, 1980) and the three-tier Bicester scheme (Reid, 1982d).

In the Bicester plan, absenteeism is counteracted by registers being taken at the start of each formal lesson as well as at registration. Any pupil found absent from a class who is not on the class monitors' daily absence list is immediately investigated. This reduces specific-lesson absence. All causes of absence for pupils on the daily absence list are systematically checked and regular feedback reports given to staff. Although this process is time consuming, it has substantially reduced absenteeism at Bicester and, as a by-product, shown pupils that their attendance matters and is a cause of concern to staff. A key to the success of the Bicester scheme is the unity and coordinated effort on the part of the entire staff. Without such unity, schemes are doomed to failure.

Early identification and 'treatment' of initial and persistent absenteeism is arguably one measure of the effectiveness of pastoral care teams in schools; more especially of the speed of schools and education welfare officers to respond to the conduct. Clearly, this is less easy in large than small schools and in schools with high rather than low rates of truancy and absenteeism. Occasional and irregular absence is often less easy to detect and check without a great deal of diligence on the part of staff. Both occasional unjustified non-attendance and specific lesson absence, however, are fairly easy to detect and respond to in the Bicester scheme. Unfortunately, too few schools are probably prepared to be as conscientious as the Bicester staff because of the disproportionate amount of time needed to operate the scheme as well as the loss of teaching time.

Research shows that some teachers and their institutions wittingly or unwittingly connive at the non-attendance of some of their least favoured pupils (Sullivan and Riches, 1976; Bird et al, 1980), especially those in their final year at school. After all, teachers are only human and many would prefer to find twenty large fifth formers in class rather than thirty.

Some persistent absentees, particularly disruptive absentees, are liable to spend their final years of compulsory education in special on-site units in schools. These are often deliberately separated from the main school setting, perhaps across a yard, at the end of a school drive or on the far side of playing fields (Jones and Forrest, 1977). Some disruptive absentees complete their formal education in any one of a number of kinds of off-site units which are currently in vogue (Robinson, 1974; BIOSS, 1976; Ball and Ball, 1980; Grunsell, 1980).

Short- or long-term placement in on- or off-site units are used in attempts to re-establish good attendance habits and, when necessary, to provide remedial education (Palfrey, 1979; Taylor et al, 1979). Unfortunately, research shows that successful reintegration in schools is rarely achieved in such cases, especially after pupils have spent time in the less formal atmosphere of some off-site units or alternative schools.

Other truants and absentees end up making court appearances and being put on care and supervision orders (see Chapter 10). This is especially true of truant delinquents (May, 1975). Schools differ in their policies for taking persistent absentees to court. Some schools take their more ebullient and older absentees (in their final years of schooling) to court more readily as a means of combatting the worst features of their behaviour in schools. By contrast, other schools see little point in punishing older pupils and prefer to reserve such action for use with younger absentees on whom court outcomes may have greater effect.

Once again, evidence shows that schools differ substantially in their policies towards absenteeism and truancy. Much depends on the standpoints and workloads of education welfare officers and senior staff (Milner, 1982). My own research (Reid, 1985a) suggests that some persistent absentees are sophisticated enough to detect the within-school differences which occur in cases of non-attendance. Bob, for instance, felt very aggrieved that he and his parents had been taken to court twice when Mark, another absentee in the same class, had never been. Bob attributed this to the 'boardy-man's' prejudice against him, spiteful staff, bad luck and Mark's unfortunate home background. He was probably right.

Disruption

Serious disruptive behaviour in schools and classrooms poses immediate threats to teachers. These threats are even more serious when groups of disruptive pupils gang-up in groups. As mentioned in Chapter 7, staff who confront disruptive pupils on a daily basis, often for several lessons or hours a day, can suffer from severe stress or psychological exhaustion. These personnel can include form teachers and heads of year as well as subject teachers. Continually being disobeyed or insulted by pupils is never easy, even for experienced members of staff. A great deal depends on the temperament of individual teachers in high-confrontation schools. Sometimes a calm exterior in the staff-room can hide the fact that the person is on 'Valium' daily.

The presence of a large number of disruptive pupils in schools can lower morale amongst staff, especially when some disrupters appear to be getting away with too much non-conformist conduct. Strong, firm leadership by headteachers, deputies and heads of year to combat disruptive behaviour is essential if anarchy is not to prevail. Likewise, chronic disruptive behaviour in classrooms can lower the morale of conformist pupils and lead to a reduction in academic attainment.

School responses to disruptive behaviour are dependent upon the seriousness and longevity of the conduct, the age of the pupils, the attitudes of the staff and the resources available to the school. Possibilities open to schools include: coping with disrupters in their original class through successful intervention; a change of form; excluding the disrupters from certain troublesome lessons; appointing special tutors for disrupters within the school with full responsibility for their academic and behavioural welfare (report cards, daily bulletin sheets etc.); attempts at curriculum innovation (special timetables etc.); referral on a short-term basis to an on- or off-site centre; short-term exclusion; suspension, special educational placement or specialist remedial teaching initiatives; involving social workers in and out of school hours; referral to the educational psychology service or child guidance; school transfers and various combinations of all these options.

School responses to disruptive behaviour are complicated by the fact that:

a) Certain schools and teachers are predisposed to recommend that the majority of disruptive children should be educated outside the mainstream, and make their referrals to the educational psychologist accordingly (Liverpool, 1974; Galloway and Goodwin, 1979).

b) Schools often feel or have a pressing need to remove the child from the institution or classroom as soon as possible and make him somebody else's responsibility – even if only for breathing space.

c) Some authorities have a greater number of places available for special education than others including 'maladjusted' (disruptive and absentee) pupils. This situation affects diagnosis, assessment and provision; it also influences school reports.

Underachievement

The measurement of achievement in secondary schools is ascertained from pupils' work in class, oral and written tests, homework, examinations, teachers' assessments, school reports and a variety of out-of-class activities such as games, music and drama. Marks awarded to pupils are not everything. Assessments and teachers' comments from primary school days and the results of verbal and non-verbal intelligence tests are a helpful guide. Generally speaking, however, it is difficult to be precise about exactly what a particular pupil should or could achieve as so many interwoven factors are involved. These include a pupil's motivation, subject interest, 'natural' ability, parental encouragement and teachers' skills.

Sometimes children underachieve even though they have not been identified as underachievers by teachers because in all other ways their progress and behaviour is regarded as 'normal'. Consequently, these needy pupils lie 'hidden' amongst the masses continuing to progress less well than they should. Some educationalists (Boyson, 1974) believe that these circumstances apply to a large proportion of pupils in the low-ability bands in comprehensive schools. Unfortunately, as large-scale underachievement is so hard to measure, it is difficult to be certain precisely what leads to and constitutes an underachieving school. Various suggestions to explain this phenomenon have been postulated on this matter in the literature. These include: poor primary education; schools located in unfavourable and deprived catchment areas; the lack of coherent structure in the secondary school curriculum; irrelevant and unsuitable curricular for the age and aptitude of pupils; bad teaching; lower teacher expectations and effort from staff teaching less able lower- and middle-academic bands; unfavourable school climate; schools with a high staff turnover; schools which have very high teacher–pupil ratios; schools which have too few resources and schools where the morale of teachers and/or pupils is very low (Welsh Office, 1984).

Options open to teachers to boost underachievers include: personal tuition/tutor schemes; extra work being given in school and at home; additional help in lunch-times and out-of-school-time, hours; the provision of extra tuition by peripatetic staff; and the systematic use of positive reinforcement measures (Harrop, 1984). Too often large classes, onerous teacher responsibilities and the shortages of resources forestall much endeavour with under-achievers. In practice, this means that specialist 'booster' schemes tend to be reserved or given to a few of the most deserving cases; only a proportion of those that need them. Often these 'booster' schemes are reserved for those in the remedial or special units attached to the school. This may mean that some pupils leave school without any CSE's or 'O' levels who, with more concerted attention, could have achieved a reasonable number of passes.

UNDERACHIEVEMENT AND DISRUPTION

The extent to which underachievement precipitates absenteeism and/or disruption is never easy to gauge. Reynolds (1982b) and Reynolds and Murgatroyd (1981) argue that secondary education in Wales tends to generate underachievement amongst its pupils partly because of an over-concentration upon the higher-ability child. In 1979–80, for example, 25.1 per cent of pupils left schools in Wales with no formal qualifications compared with 12.2 per cent in England.

When making their own internal assessments, schools should attempt to discover the underlying 'causes' of each pupil's problems, whether it is related to behaviour or learning or both. Schools have to decide whether individual disrupters misbehave for reasons of psychological disturbance, social factors within the family or neighbourhood, because of happenings within school, or various combinations of all three possibilities.

Cases of underachievement and disruption pose severe difficulties for teachers. Staff have to make judgements about whether the underachievement or the misbehaviour is the most pressing need. They have to ensure that one course of action does not conflict with another, especially when writing their reports to external agencies.

A variety of evidence is available to show that teachers are quick, sometimes perhaps too quick, to assign labels to non-conformist underachievers. Using pre-Warnock categories, some teachers assign labels like 'maladjusted' or 'ESN' to pupils without really being sure of their meaning. Other more emotional labels are frequently assigned to some non-conformist underachievers in everyday staffroom talk. These include terms like 'thick', 'stupid', 'moronic', 'hopeless' and 'spastic'. Great care should always be taken by teachers to ensure that they do not inadvertently use emotional or technical labels about pupils in front of their classes or other pupils – irrespective of whether the terms have been correctly used. Such generalizations are unhelpful at the best of times and liable to make pupils draw their own conclusion. As John once said to me during an interview in a large comprehensive school in South Wales, 'If he calls Rhys thick what does he say about me behind my back?'

There is no single solution or panacea which will overcome underachievement. This is because of the complexity of the factors which 'cause' the phenomenon (see Chapter 4).

According to Mortimore (1982), teachers can best help in the following ways:

1) Monitor the progress of all groups of pupils so that differences in achievement can be identified early, and appropriate remedial action be taken.
2) Consciously strive to raise teachers' expectations of the achievement of pupils from working-class homes, of girls in some subjects and of ethnic minorities, in order to reduce the influence of negative stereotypes.
3) Select books and learning materials which are suitable for *all* pupils.
4) Critically evaluate classroom practices so that any unintended biases can be eliminated.
5) Achieve closer co-operation between specialist and remedial teachers so that joint approaches to learning problems can be developed.
6) Draw on the new technology to provide individual learning programmes where these seem appropriate.
7) Capitalize on parental influence by showing how pupils can be helped at home.
8) Provide extra learning opportunities such as homework clubs and revision courses to help pupils who have poor facilities for study at home.
9) With regard to sex differences:
   a) implement a school policy on equal opportunities;
   b) include at least one physical science in the compulsory core of fourth- and fifth-year work;
   c) hold special parents' evenings, prior to option choices, in order to focus on the importance of maths, science and technology for girls.
10) With regard to ethnic groups:
   a) have a language policy that caters for individual needs and takes account of the literary heritage of other cultures;
   b) accept and build upon the diversity of cultures in the school;

c) have an agreed school policy on racism. Provide a forum for discussion of this difficult subject for older pupils within the security of the school.

Mortimore considers that these changes will not eliminate underachievement. They will, however, make school life more profitable and acceptable for many pupils and, indirectly, make life more worthwhile for many teachers. Like Hargreaves (1984), Mortimore believes that the real educational answer to under-achievement lies in the reform of the curriculum, the examination system and the internal organization of secondary schools. The latter aspect is often forgotten. Few secondary schools, for example, provide pupils with an opportunity to 'catch up' once they fall behind with their class work either because of illness, personal difficulties or for any number of other reasons. Quite often, once a pupil begins to fall behind, he or she tends to fall further and further behind his or her peers and may give up altogether.

SUMMARY

Although local authorities and schools follow a range of diverse policies for dealing with and identifying disaffected conduct in schools, in practice there is probably a great deal of similarity between the schemes which operate owing to the limited number of options which are available. Absenteeism and disruption are far easier to identify than underachievement *per se*. Many absentees and disrupters however, are also underachievers. Identifying absenteeism, disruption and underachievement is far less difficult than curing or preventing the conduct from continuing. Based on the limited evidence which is available, it seems that some schools do better than others in coping with their disaffected pupils.

9
SCHOOL
INITIATIVES

This chapter concentrates on initiatives which schools can take for coping with and combatting disaffected behaviour. In particular, the chapter is concerned with the diversity and effectiveness of pastoral care provision, the role and options open to form tutors and subject teachers, pupils' perceptions of pastoral care and counselling, school-based social work, alternative school-based schemes, and external referrals. The chapter is concluded by taking an in-depth look at the case of Vince in relation to his and the staff's experiences at St David's, a large comprehensive in South Wales.

PASTORAL CARE SYSTEMS

Pastoral care systems can be defined as the functions of guidance, support, discipline and administration that schools perform in relation to pupils (Skinner et al, 1983). Schools act in an *in loco parentis* capacity when pupils attend them, thereby acting in the same manner as careful parents.

Schools differ considerably in the way in which they organize their pastoral care systems, depending upon such factors as size, need, the wishes of the local education authority, the attitude and capabilities of staff and the preference of the headteacher, governors and parents. Consequently, the range of staff involved in pastoral care teams includes form and subject teachers, specialist pastoral care staff (deputy head – pastoral and/or girl's welfare; heads of year, house or year sub-groups) and, in some schools, trained counsellors.

The philosophy and emphases of pastoral care teams in schools are very dependent on the interests and calibre of the staff concerned, particularly key personnel such as deputies, heads of year, counsellors and, of course, the headteacher. It is probably fair to say that only a minority of pastoral staff are trained for their work, although some attend short in-service courses or cover the subject in postgraduate courses for higher degrees and diplomas. Likewise, the quality of postholders is probably equally variable.

Theoretically, pastoral care teams provide a coherent framework within schools to support all pupils. Inevitably, the nature of their work brings certain pupils to their attention more than others. These include pupils with major behavioural problems, learning difficulties and those who manifest disaffected tendencies through their non-attendance, lack of effort in class and poor peer-group relationships (Bird et al, 1980; Johnson et al, 1980).

Pastoral care teams also exist to support form tutors and subject teachers in their work by advising them of difficulties being experienced by pupils in their charge and helping them to overcome administrative, behavioural and learning difficulties. Inevitably, some teachers liaise better with colleagues than others and in large schools communication and co-ordination can pose difficulties. Moreover, some teachers prefer academic rather than pastoral duties and resent the amount of paper work which good pastoral care often engenders (Lewis and Murgatroyd, 1976).

Finally, staff in middle management posts frequently act as the link between parents and schools, not only by organizing parents' evenings but also by writing to and seeing parents in times of need on such matters as pupils' non-attendance or minor behavioural problems. More serious behavioural offences or problems of a personal nature are usually dealt with by headteachers, deputies or qualified school counsellors.

The literature is full of case studies which cite good practice in primary and secondary schools (Murgatroyd, 1980b; Galloway,

1981; Jones, 1980; 1981). These usually illustrate important themes in pastoral care including: the school's disciplinary policy; liaison with and support for teachers, parents and outside agencies; handling disruptive behaviour within classrooms and schools and providing apposite remedial education as well as giving descriptions of favourable outcomes with extreme cases (Covill et al, 1984). Conversely, the literature is deficient in systematic evaluations of the effectiveness of pastoral care systems and school counselling in meeting the needs of both ordinary and disaffected pupils. By and large only general statements about effective and efficient pastoral care systems seem to be made in the literature such as those in the school differences studies previously referred to in chapters 6 and 7. These suggest that successful schools stress academic rather than pastoral goals.

Research shows that schools differ considerably in the way they react and relate to the behaviour problems and personal difficulties manifested by pupils. Some are more successful than others. The continuum ranges from apathy and laxness through to over-concern and over-reaction on the part of pastoral staff. Bird et al (1980) found in schools they studied that at one end of the spectrum were systematic monitoring and action taken at the first sign of disturbance. At the other were teams who only reacted to severe symptoms of distress or dissent.

A number of writers are openly critical and cynical of pastoral care work in schools as it is currently practised. Some authors believe that too many teams devote far too much of their time to disciplinary matters and administration rather than welfare (Best et al, 1980; Johnson et al, 1980). The Teachers' Action Collective (1976) go even further. They argue that the provision of pastoral staff and special units does a considerable disservice to schooling. They contend that the very existence of pastoral care teams means that appointed staff have to justify their scaled posts which, ultimately, are untenable. Hence, they believe that large pastoral care teams are partially responsible for diverting financial resources away from basic education and removing responsibility from the classroom teacher which is not to the benefit of pupils in schools.

FORM TUTORS

It is often forgotten that pastoral care systems in secondary schools begin with the work of the form tutor who is arguably the most important link in the chain. Similarly, in primary schools, the classroom teacher is the vital cog in the wheel. Without proficient work from form tutors, pastoral teams are unlikely to succeed. After all, every team is only as strong as its weakest player.

Form tutors have more opportunities than most teachers to get to know their charges very well. Ideally, good form tutors will endeavour to learn something about their pupils' personal interests, strengths and weaknesses, home backgrounds, fears and aspirations. Such information is vital in preventative work and can be invaluable when dealing with disruptive and underachieving pupils. Obviously, in non-attendance cases, particularly those of the persistent kind, form tutors get fewer opportunities to develop worthwhile relationships with pupils.

It has always been my own view that form tutors should rotate with their classes in secondary schools. Not everybody shares this view, partly because pupils with poor form tutors can suffer considerably. Nevertheless, the continuity of form tutors moving up the age range from first to fifth year with their class far outweighs any disadvantages. In this system, form tutors learn much more about the temperament, personality, academic ability, behaviour and home backgrounds of their pupils and also gain crucial insights into their motivation and maturational processes. In pastoral work, these insights are invaluable. Moreover, the continuity achieved by good long-term pupil–tutor relationships can engender confidence in parents, pupils and year tutors alike and lead to greater consistency in approach over a number of years.

When form tutor–pupil relationships break down, the consequences can be devastating. Pupils, for instance, often feel there is no one to whom they can turn in times of trouble. This means that problems which teachers should know something about lie undetected.

Form teachers have to strive hard to get to know their disaffected pupils very well. Persistent absentees, for example, often fail to give their form teachers the same benefit of the doubt as their parents. This is sometimes true even in cases of parental neglect (Reid, 1983c) due, presumably, to natural ties and loyalties. In my own research into persistent school absenteeism, some of the absentees expressed their disappointment and lack of confidence in many of the staff, including their form tutors. In one sense, this is again only natural as pupils like absentees inevitably come into more actual and potential conflict situations than good attenders because of their deviant behaviour. Dealing with absentees therefore, requires considerable tact on the part of form tutors and pastoral staff.

An increasing amount of interest has been shown in recent years in making the role of the form tutor more active and effective, especially in secondary schools (Hamblin, 1978; Baldwin and Wells, 1979; 1980; 1981; Button, 1981; 1982). In one small-scale project, Raymond (1982) investigated how seventy-one form tutors in secondary schools in South Wales perceived their role and how their perceptions differed from their actual responsibilities. Four-fifths (80.3 per cent) of them were happy to have been appointed form tutors. Roughly two-thirds (64.8 per cent) considered they had been given a clear idea of the tasks which they were expected to fulfil by senior staff before they commenced their duties. A similar number (67.6 per cent) thought they were given enough support by colleagues in their schools. Perhaps significantly in the light of recent developments in teacher training (Hopkins and Reid, 1985), only one in ten of the form tutors (9 per cent) considered they had been given enough training for their duties as form tutors in their initial course.

According to the respondents, their major functions as form tutors were in order: 'administrative duties'; 'acting as a source of discipline'; 'giving out school notices'; 'developing close personal relationships with pupils'; 'developing positive attitudes in pupils towards school'; 'providing individual counselling to pupils'; 'developing good study habits in pupils'; 'fostering good peer-group relationships amongst pupils'; developing interdependence and maturity in pupils'; 'developing a thorough understanding of the school as an institution'; 'ensuring no serious problems arise in the future by encouraging good coping strategies'; 'developing coping strategies that can be used outside the school environment'.

This survey uncovered a number of interesting views on the part of the respondents. The form tutors thought they should be less involved in activities which endangered their chances of acting as successful class counsellors. These included giving out school notices and acting as major disciplinarians. The tutors felt sceptical about being able to fulfil every part of their role. Explicitly, the form tutors considered that some of the ethereal aspects of their work were unattainable. These included: 'ensuring that no serious problems arise in the future by encouraging good coping strategies', 'helping pupils develop problem-solving skills', 'developing self-awareness amongst pupils' and 'developing interdependence and maturity in pupils'.

A slight majority of the tutors (56.3 per cent) felt that there was a need for a pastoral curriculum to be developed for use in schools like the Baldwin and Wells (1979; 1980; 1981) packages. Roughly three-fifths of the tutors (59.2 per cent) indicated that they would welcome the chance to develop their role if an opportunity arose. Asked how this could be achieved, the most popular answers were through 'regular discussions with colleagues' (47.9 per cent), 'school-based in-service training' (31 per cent), 'curriculum planning with colleagues' (25.4 per cent), 'in-service training' (21 per cent), 'curriculum planning with colleagues and psychologists' (18.3 per cent) and 'individual help from psychologists' (7 per cent).

Raymond's study suffered from a low response rate which probably meant that her questionnaires were answered by some of the keenest tutors. However, the significance of the work lies not so much in its individual findings but in the fact that it is one of the first studies to investigate how form tutors perceive and undertake their role. This is surely an area where further research is necessary, especially studies of form teachers in action. These may reveal differences between effective and ineffective work and how good tutors enhance pastoral care both with conformist and disaffected pupils.

Galloway et al (1982) found considerable variations in practice in Sheffield's pastoral care systems. They reported that some pastoral care systems appeared to succeed in allowing class teachers to consult with colleagues informally and receive advice on how to handle difficult pupils, thereby helping to defuse potentially volatile situations. By contrast, other school systems were found to divert the problem from the source by requiring form tutors to refer incidents to specialist middle management staff from the onset. Galloway et al concluded that the latter style is less successful than the former as it carries with it a greater danger of turning minor incidents into major confrontations. They also found that the latter style increased the possibility of suspension being used with disruptive pupils. Presumably it also lowered pupil confidence in the work of the form tutors.

The extent to which form tutors and heads of year liaise over pupils' problems and difficulties is always a matter of judgement and style. Certainly, such consultation should always be handled with discretion. Great care should be taken not to break pupils' confidences in case work. Too often, this does not happen. It is not uncommon, for instance, for middle management to walk into form periods and openly discuss the problems of individual pupils with teachers or the pupils' peers. Sometimes teachers inform pupils of the finer details of problems which either they or their peers would rather not know. Such situations can lead to pupils withdrawing from school, becoming disenchanted or bitter; occasionally understandably so.

When classmates see that one of their peers is embarrassed by teacher-initiated actions or talk, they, too, draw their own conclusions. Once a form tutor is perceived by the class as a mere extension of authority or as someone incapable of retaining confidences, his or her capacity for effective pastoral work is much reduced. Form teachers should start from the basis that the quality of their relationship with their pupils is all-important. Nothing should be allowed to lower or interfere with the trust which this work requires and engenders between pupils and form teachers. In reality, form teachers and pupils need one another. After all, when things go wrong, middle management are not going to stand by and admit it was their fault for interfering. More likely, they will suggest to headteachers that unfortunate consequences are the result of poor work by form or subject teachers, or because they were called into a situation too late or were given too little or inadequate information. After all, people do have feelings.

PUPILS' PERCEPTIONS OF PASTORAL CARE AND COUNSELLING

There have been comparatively few studies which have utilized pupils' perceptions of pastoral care systems and counselling in schools. Based on the evidence which does exist, there appears to be some conflict between the findings.

Johnson et al (1980) report on their work in two outer-London boroughs in which, amongst other things, they investigated models of school counselling and pastoral care systems. They found that:

1) Most pupils in the study regarded their school counsellors as approachable.
2) Most pupils tend to develop close relationships with at least one individual teacher who may or may not have pastoral responsi-

bility for them. In this respect, empathy seems as important as position.

3) Some pupils thought there were too many personnel in schools interested in finding out about their particular problems.

4 Pastoral care systems in schools did not affect pupils' problems outside school. Whether they should is, of course, a matter of opinion.

The latter point is worthy of further discussion. Very often pupils' school problems cannot be resolved without an understanding of complications in their home or social backgrounds or vice versa. A sick mother, for example, is likely to worry a child in school. So is an unemployed father, a house move to another area or a gang conflict in the neighbourhood. Likewise, being punished in school, falling behind in class work or tension between a teacher and pupil can lead to anxiety at home.

Murgatroyd (1977) undertook a survey of pupils' perceptions in a comprehensive school in South Wales which had a highly developed and admired counselling service. He reported that counsellors were regarded by pupils as senior teachers with considerable administrative duties. Two of their main tasks were perceived as checking on attendance registers for truancy and reporting truants to education welfare officers. They were not seen as major sources of help by pupils with personal problems.

By contrast, Hooper (1978) analysed pupils' perceptions of counsellors in a school in South-West England. He found that the pupils were quite willing to approach counsellors with their personal problems in school. He suggests that variations between the two studies can be accounted for by differences in counsellor's styles: whether counsellors are client- or institution-centred. It seems, therefore, that much depends on a counsellor's ability, personality and the ethos of particular schools. The same may well be true of pastoral care systems.

THE PREVENTION OF DISRUPTIVE BEHAVIOUR

In chapters 6 and 7, the relationship between school and classroom management and disruptive behaviour were discussed. In this section, consideration is given to ways in which pastoral care teams, subject and form tutors can prevent disruptive behaviour from occurring in the first place. Inevitably, some of the same points recur which reinforces their fundamental importance.

There are probably very few teachers who escape encounters with unruly pupils and troublesome classes from time to time. How teachers handle these situations is usually a matter of judgement and experience. There are no ready-made panaceas which will embrace every occurrence of disruptive or deviant behaviour. Different solutions will work for different teachers, just as some teachers require greater moral support from middle management than others.

There is a great deal of contrasting opinion in the literature about the best way for teachers to cope with disaffected and troublesome children in the classroom and in special units. The following paragraphs summarize the consensus from those publications which are included in the relevant 'Further Reading Lists' on pp. 252–4.

1) A key factor in maintaining control in the classroom is to provide plenty of work and vary the activities and tasks. With difficult groups early control is essential. It is often a good idea to start the lesson with a short piece of desk work – perhaps something from the blackboard or from pre-prepared work sheets. This avoids unnecessary movement and minimizes opportunities for disturbance.

In earlier times, many teachers used to sharpen classes up by giving them five minutes or so of mental arithmetic or spelling or other quick 'tests' under 'examination' conditions which sufficed for more than one purpose. These measures ensured that all the pupils sat in their places with their books and materials, thus minimizing later opportunities for disturbance. Nowadays, in mixed-ability situations, there is often a need to keep the momentum going throughout a lesson, especially with the most able (fast finishers) or those who cannot cope with the theme of the main lesson. Sometimes flexible or alternative worksheets, text books, schemes of work or additional tasks for early finishers need to be resorted to and all have their merits in particular circumstances. Hard work is what all children need and actually like although this is not always apparent from their comments or teachers' lesson plans.

2) It is very important that commands in class are given clearly and precisely. Transitions need to be kept as brief as possible. At the outset of a lesson it is sometimes helpful to summarize a lesson's content so that the moans and groans are overcome straight away.

Class rules and teachers' expectations of the pupils should be consistently applied and made explicit. If an exception is made, a clear and fair reason for the exemption should be stated. As in soccer, once a 'yellow card' is shown, teachers, like referees, must respond positively in similar circumstances. Failure to do so can escalate disturbances. Pupils need to know where they stand at all times. Teachers should take opportunities to praise good classroom performances as well as highlighting naughtiness. Generally speaking, just as animals like to please their owners so children prefer to please their teachers given a free choice.

3) Within the classroom, teachers need to be vigilant at all times and show that they are in control and aware of what is going on by developing their intuition and powers of perception (eyes in the back as well as the front of their heads). Despite the advice given by researchers in earlier chapters, my own view is that banishing children from the classroom should always be avoided except as a last resort. Banishment merely reinforces the fact that a teacher has failed. It also reduces pupils' self-worth and hardens their attitudes against teachers.

4) During unpleasant confrontations it is important that teachers restrain their tongues and keep their innermost thoughts to themselves. Otherwise, a difficult situation is likely to be made worse. Teachers must never lose their tempers with or in front of pupils. Teachers have to learn to 'manage' and overcome difficult situations rather than over-reacting, passing the buck to someone else or liberally handing out punishment. To be effective the latter should always be used sparingly as a last resort. Once again, consistency is all important. Children find great difficulty in rationalizing love and rejection, empathy and abuse, encouragement and criticism, pleasantness and nastiness from the same teacher.

Amongst other qualities which teachers need for coping with disaffected and underachieving pupils, those most frequently mentioned include: stability, compassion, sensitivity, intelligence, resilience, humour, maturity, stamina, patience, empathy and flexibility. Who said that teaching is easy?

SCHOOL IMPROVEMENT

In recent years there has been an increasing literature on school improvement which concentrates on the ways in which teachers can raise the performance and management of their institutions (Hopkins and Wideen, 1984). One of the most influential pieces of work in this field in Britain is the Report produced by the Hargreaves Committee (1984) entitled *Improving Secondary Schools*. As with most things with which David Hargreaves is connected, this report is worth reading in full. The Committee's terms of reference were to consider the curriculum and organization of secondary schools in Inner London as they affected pupils mainly in the 11–16 age range. The Committee gave special attention to pupils who are underachieving, including those taking few or no public examinations, and those who show dissatisfaction with school by absenting themselves or through their unco-operative behaviour. The Committee made no fewer than 104 specific recommendations which are aimed at the Authority, governors and secondary headteachers, heads of department, teachers, the Chief Inspector, the Inspectorate/Advisory service, divisional education officers, primary headteachers and the Central Advisory Committee on Induction and In-Service Training. The Report suggests that substantial changes in the organization and structure of schools by local education authorities, headteachers, teachers and other educational personnel will be necessary if underachievement and disaffection are to be combatted successfully. In order to improve schools, the Committee feels that specific changes and innovations must be introduced in: the teacher–parent partnership; school attendance; the transition from primary to secondary school; the whole curriculum; pupil grouping; pupils with particular needs and aptitudes; pupils for whom English is a second language (ESL) and bilingual (or multilingual) pupils; skills for independent learning; activities within the fourth and fifth years related to core and option subjects, active learning roles and curriculum organization and assessment; pupil involvement and participation; learning out of school; links between the school and community and between schools, industry and the trades unions; and improved alternative provision for disruptive pupils.

For example, the Report suggests that governors and secondary headteachers should ensure each school has an effective attendance policy. The Committee believes good practice is associated with:

1) a senior teacher being charged with specific responsibility for pupil attendance;
2) a list of absentees being produced quickly, ideally by morning

break, for use by appropriate teaching and office staff (see Reid, 1982d);

3) the school devising a sensitive scheme for the immediate follow-up of absentees either, for example, by telephoning home or sending out letters to parents/guardians;

4) form tutors ensuring that records of attendance are as accurate as possible and explanations for absence are produced when pupils return to school;

5) heads of year/house monitoring the work of form tutors;

6) heads of year/house and teachers with responsibility for pupil attendance having regular meetings with Education Welfare officers, perhaps once a month;

7) regular 'spot checks' for specific-lesson truancy and for pupils leaving schools before the end of the school day, being enacted at intervals;

8) rewards introduced for individual pupils or classes with an excellent attendance record in the form of praise or prizes;

9) penalties being introduced for pupils who are persistently late;

10) absentees and truants being quietly welcomed back to school upon their return and efforts made to re-integrate them socially and academically.

The Report urges advisers/inspectors to encourage schools with good records of attendance to report their practices to an innovation exchange within the authority. Meanwhile, local education authorities should phase in schemes to attach education welfare officers to every school throughout the secondary sector and devise suitable career and promotion structures for EWOs in the field.

For disruptive pupils, the Committee propose substantial and significant changes in the provision of alternative education and pastoral care. They recommend the creation of a school inspector for pastoral care who, amongst other things, should be given responsibility for the dissemination of good practice in relation to suspension. In addition, headteachers should ensure that all newly appointed pastoral staff make personal visits to local off-site support units and include a visit to an off-site support unit in their induction programmes for probationary teachers. The staff of off-site support units should be invited to make contributions to courses on classroom management for use by teachers in ordinary schools. Finally, governors and other members of appointment committees should regard experience of work in a support unit as advantageous to a teacher seeking promotion.

For underachieving and disaffected pupils, the Hargreaves Committee wish to see a radical change in the secondary curriculum by providing pupils with a distinctive vocational education. On school and industrial links and work experience programmes, the Report recommends that headteachers establish their own liaison committees comprised of teachers in charge of personal and social education. These within school committees should include teachers of science, craft, design and technology (CDT), careers, geography, history and the social sciences to review and co-ordinate school policy on this matter. Furthermore, the Inspectorate should establish a committee of the ten divisional industry/school co-ordinators in the Authority (Inner London) and the staff inspectors for careers, science, CDT, careers, geography, history and social science to review present practice and to disseminate good practice.

Like previous reports and research studies (Bullock, 1975; HMI, 1977b; 1979; 1980; 1981; DES, 1981; ILEA, 1981; 1983; Schools Council, 1981; Cockroft, 1982; Galton and Willcocks, 1983; Reid, 1985a), the Hargreaves Report is right to acknowledge the unsatisfactory nature of much of the secondary school curriculum and its potential and/or actual effects upon pupil learning and behaviour in schools. At present, far too many pupils in our secondary schools are bored and confused by aspects of their curriculum; a situation which urgently needs rectifying. Despite the fact that the central importance of the curriculum in combatting and reducing absenteeism, disaffection and disruption in secondary schools is well documented in the literature, too little is known about how this can be achieved. The Hargreaves Committee is one of the first which attempts to redress the balance. In their report, the Committee stress the need for choice, coherence, breadth, balance and structure throughout the whole secondary curriculum and the important parts played by pupil grouping, teaching styles, the requirements of pupils with particular needs and aptitudes as well as the need for pupils to acquire appropriate study skills.

Perhaps the most interesting idea to emerge from the Hargreaves Report is the need to change the curriculum for fourth- and fifth-year pupils, especially for the betterment of underachievers. The Committee considers that there should be a compulsory curriculum for all fourth- and fifth-year pupils which contains six elements and comprises 62.5 per cent of total teaching time. This is made up of English language and literature (12.5 per cent), mathematics (12.5 per cent), science (10 per cent), personal, social and religious education (7.5 per cent), at least one 'aesthetic' (art, music etc.) subject (10 per cent),and at least one 'technical' (craft, design, technology (CDT) or computer studies) subject (10 per cent). The remaining 37.5 per cent of school time should be devoted to *either* additional periods in compulsory subjects *or* the free options *or* some of each. Pupils would therefore be able to select from among classical and modern languages, history, geography, economics, commercial and business studies, physical education, additional science subjects, additional 'aesthetic' subjects, additional 'technical' subjects and additional English and mathematics.

As so many fourth- and fifth-year pupils are disappointed with their secondary school experience and feel that the curriculum-as-it-is-taught is inappropriate to their abilities, interests and aptitudes, the Report suggests and/or recommends that heads of department of all curriculum subjects should ensure that:

a) pupils exercise all communication skills – talking, listening, reading and writing – in equal amounts, with the same value ascribed to each;
b) topics and relevant issues are raised in classes which stimulate pupils to express opinions, argue, explain and negotiate for a consensus;
c) the assessment of oral skills is seen as equally important as the assessment of other skills;
d) teachers ensure there is an oral component in any assessment procedure they devise, and pressure external examination bodies to do the same.

To achieve this, Hargreaves suggests making radical changes in the organization, assessment and teaching of the fourth and fifth year by: implementing formal reviews of schools' existing curriculum programmes; encouraging the development of systems of units and unit credits and leaving certificate and pupil profile schemes; promoting opportunities for creative timetabling; and reducing the pressure on pupils caused by external examinations and existing and outmoded assessment procedures. Moreover, headteachers should ensure that structures exist to provide pupils with experience of taking responsibility and participating in decision-making at various levels (individual, class, year, whole school) and of various kinds in the life of the school (cf. Rutter et al, 1979). Heads should also make provision for all pupils to have structured out-of-school (off-site) learning experiences throughout the school year, as part of a planned school policy. This could be achieved by the establishment of Urban (and Rural) Studies Centres, Easter and Whitsun revision centres.

The acquisition of good study skills is central to the Report's plans to tackle underachievement. In this respect the Committee recommend that:

a) Headteachers, in consultation with the whole teaching staff, instigate a clear homework policy and introduce measures by which its implementation is regularly monitored.
b) District inspectors/advisers provide headteachers with support and advice on the matter of homework policy and practice.
c) Headteachers ensure that the school fully informs parents about the homework policy and takes measures to enlist their support.
d) Headteachers seek to provide opportunities for pupils to complete their homework on the school premises.
e) The Authority, in the longer term, investigates the extent to which additional resources are needed for supervised 'extended study' by pupils and meet these vital needs.
f) Headteachers and teachers ensure the school has a study skills policy and helps pupils both to acquire independent learning skills and to pass examinations. In this latter context, schools and districts within local authorites can make a major contribution by:
  i) devising INSET programmes with the aim of creating a body of expertise within each subject area of the curricula;
  ii) preparing study skills booklets for pupils;
  iii) introducing a teachers' guide which provides ideas and examples of good practice within schools; and
  iv) devising a booklet for teachers comprising supplementary papers on specific topics such as the ILEA (1983) package on *Effective Learning Skills*.

Finally, Hargreaves and his team recognize the key roles played by teachers and adequate resource levels throughout the educational process. Consequently, some of the recommendations made by the Committee include:

1) The Authority advising governors to take account of appropriate experience when considering staff for promotion.
2) The improvement of induction and probationary year schemes.
3) Headteachers ensuring that all heads of department have clear job specifications.
4) Inspectors, when their help is sought by headteachers, giving high priority to improving the effectiveness of heads of department.
5) The Authority providing courses on basic classroom management and in dealing with disruptive pupils, especially for teachers in professional difficulties.
6) Heads of department ensuring that members of their subject teams participate in meaningful self-evaluation exercises.
7) Heads of department adopting policies of using classroom observation and co-teaching methods to ensure and/or raise the quality of teaching as appropriate.
8) Schools pioneering self-evaluation, quinquennial reviews and staff appraisal and course monitoring schemes (see ILEA, 1977; 1982).
9) Headteachers designating a deputy as staff tutor with overall responsibility for staff development within the school.
10) Headteachers establishing a representative staff development committee to advise them and the staff tutor on the school's INSET programme.
11) The Inspectorate including a component on staff development and INSET in all management courses for headteachers and senior staff.
12) The Authority giving greater priority to school-focused INSET to meet increasing demand.
13) The Authority giving higher priority and better financial allocation to the in-service education of teachers (INSET) which extends opportunities for teachers to observe and learn from the work of colleagues in other schools.
14) The Authority making financial provision to enable teachers to visit schools outside the ILEA (perhaps along the lines of the West Glamorgan Teacher Fellowship Scheme – see Reid, 1985b).
15) The Inspector for pastoral care work co-ordinating with a committee the promotion and development of the pastoral curriculum through INSET.
16) The Authority making provision for more local and central

courses on the pastoral curriculum and personal and social education a high INSET priority.

17) Headteachers ensuring that all information about the school's INSET programme is on the innovation exchange information sheets.

18) Divisional educational officers enabling schools to replace satisfactorily teachers away on INSET courses.

19) The Authority providing schools with substantially increased administrative assistance.

20) The Authority granting a half-term sabbatical leave every five years to headteachers.

Through all these means, and others, Hargreaves seeks to improve the management and organization of schools, making them more meaningful to the wide range of pupils within them. The Committee emphasize the need for curriculum change, appropriate and better staff development and in-service schemes, involving pupils in decision-making and the vital role of community and parental liaison. The Report is not only innovative, but worthy of discussion by every secondary school and local education authority in Britain. It provides a clear lead for others to follow. The pity of this far-sighted and clear-thinking document is that it has been produced in an era of economic restraint in education, cut-backs, falling rolls and low staff morale. It will be a great tragedy for pupils and teachers alike if its lessons go unheeded and the experiments remain untried. As with the case of falling rolls, a great opportunity to innovate will have been missed (Reid, 1983d).

TOWARDS EDUCATIONAL CHANGE

By the 1990s education is likely to have changed in a number of ways. In a White Paper published in March, 1985, the Education Secretary, Sir Keith Joseph, produced his ideas for changing schooling which are meant to 'equip children for the 21st century' by promoting 'the nation's ability to seize the challenging opportunities of a technological and competitive world.' In the White Paper, Joseph sidetracked such important quantitative questions as 'Do we want small or large schools?' or 'Do we want comprehensive schools?' in favour of qualitative issues. In doing so, he attempted to tackle problems which many employers, universities, parents, politicians and teachers themselves have complained about for at least a quarter of a century but which are not universally popular. His proposals include:

a) Examination reform to reduce sixth-form specialization, more realistic targets for pupils who will not enter higher education, and new exams for 16-, 17- and 18-year-olds by 1990.

b) A different kind of initial teacher training which will make courses more practical and school-focused with penalties for those who fail to comply.

c) More and better in-service training to combat the trend whereby money intended for in-service was diverted elsewhere by local authorities. Joseph has introduced legislation enabling him to earmark grants for particular in-service schemes.

d) Stronger emphasis on practical, rather than academic learning in schools. Official concern about schools' remoteness from industry and commerce, and about the lack of esteem given to technical work, dates from 1976, when the Labour Prime Minister, James Callaghan, made his famous Ruskin College speech. As part of these plans, Joseph previously introduced a technical and vocational educational initiative for 14 to 18 year-olds (TVEI) funded through the Manpower Services Commission. He also insisted that the 16-plus exams give a high proportion of marks in all subjects to practical applications.

e) A better deal for less able children. Since the school-leaving age was raised to sixteen in 1972, teachers have struggled to hold the interest of the bottom 40 per cent. The 16-plus exam was designed so that it can be taken by children of all abilities. Similarly, the graded tests (in specific areas like swimming and music) and records of achievement (pupil profiles) are meant to provide targets for children across the whole ability range.

f) More public accountability in schools. Measures designed to publish HMI reports on schools, give parents more power on governing bodies, as well as the introduction of teacher-assessment procedures are three initiatives Joseph has pioneered along this difficult and controversial path.

g) More common ground between school curricula. Parents, for instance, have long been baffled by a system which, theoretically, allows a head to devote the entire week to gardening, cooking, religious education and physical education lessons. Those who move house may find their children repeating work or switching to a completely different exam syllabus. During the first year of secondary education, teachers may have to cope with children from twenty or thirty different primary schools, with as many different work schemes. The result is that one in three children regress during that year (Wilby, 1985). Thus, Joseph issued a series of policy statements on such subjects as science and English, which specified the common ground which pupils should follow at each stage of their schooling. Moreover, syllabuses for the 16-plus exams have to conform to a common framework.

Sir Keith's White Paper criticized schools for 'the mistaken belief that a concentration on basic skills is enough to improve achievement in literacy and numeracy' and for 'excessive direction by the teacher of the pupil's work'. It adds: 'pupils need more opportunities to learn for themselves, to express their own views and to develop their ideas through discussion.'

In many ways the White Paper was highly innovative and, in some respects, adapts ideas from suggestions and findings made and reported by such groups as the Hargreaves Committee and Rutter and his colleagues. In fact, the 1985 document is the most wide-ranging since its equivalent – the forerunner to the 1944 Education Act. It is coherent, and provides a consistent programme that tackles some of the major weaknesses in the educational system. The contents contained in this document fired the first shots in a long drawn out battle which will continue into the twenty-first century. As the White Paper specifically accused teachers of poor planning, lack of vigour and 'inadequate knowledge and under-standing', its early reception was far from favourable in some quarters. Only time will tell how successful Sir Keith has been in changing standards within the teaching profession and improving schooling. The extent to which the new measures will reduce or increase absenteeism, disruption, disaffection and underachieve-ment is another vexed question. As Dame Mary Warnock's Dimbleby lecture in March 1985 indicated, many educationalists accept the need for change and applaud moves towards making teaching a high-quality profession. But it is *how* change is achieved that present and future debates will be about. Throughout these professional debates, it is most important to remember that in the final analysis schools are about educating children as efficiently and effectively as possible. *All* children – irrespective of age, aptitude, ability or social background.

ST DAVID'S SCHOOL

The chapter is concluded by illustrating how one school copes with its own problems of absenteeism and disruption. This is achieved by approaching events from the perception of Vince followed by the views of staff who know him well and who have assisted in the remediation strategies adopted by the school. Vince represents the large number of pupils whose behaviour causes concern to staff but is not so severe as to warrant exclusion or suspension. He is a semi-disruptive truant; the kind most teachers meet from time to time on a daily basis. By presenting the case in this manner, some of the managerial practices adopted by the school will be highlighted. These include pastoral intervention policies and links between middle management and form and subject tutors. The data reveals the kind of human dimensions and difficulties under which many teachers and senior teachers operate. Before discussing the perceptions of Vince and the staff in detail, the circumstances surrounding the case are put into their proper context by: a) outlining relevant information on the school; and b) providing details on Vince's home, social and educational background.

St David's contains approximately 1000 pupils. It has sixty-two full-time members of staff, a seven-form entry and 110 sixth-form pupils. The official number of pupils who attended the school fell from approximately 1250 to 1000 between 1980 and 1985.

St David's is located in a deprived neighbourhood in the northern suburbs of a large town somewhere in South West Wales. Owing to its denominational status and foundation, the school is unusual in several ways. First, the school is a genuine comprehensive containing large numbers of pupils from different socio-economic backgrounds. Second, some pupils travel up to twenty miles each way daily in order to attend the school because of their religious backgrounds. Third, there has been little staff mobility for many years with the result that the school contains very few young teachers and a high proportion of experienced teachers in non-managerial positions.

Consequently, the school has a special difficulty. As the school roll includes so few pupils from the immediate working-class neighbourhood, the local population do not identify with it. This may be one of the reasons why the school is repeatedly vandalized by local youths. Indeed, according to the headteacher, three break-ins or serious acts of vandalism a night are commonplace.

Moreover, graffiti is rife on the outside of the school buildings. However, considering that the school was last painted some eighteen years ago, the interior decoration is remarkably well preserved which is probably indicative of the high standards set by staff. One incident in particular highlights St David's alienation from the local population. On Guy Fawkes night, a gang of youths who attended other schools in the neighbourhood, built a bonfire against some of St David's buildings and burnt them down. After being detained by the police, one of the ringleaders claimed he felt no shame as he considered the school fair game because it did nothing for the local community.

According to the headteacher, St David's is 'slightly under-provided' for with resources by the local education authority. He thinks staff morale is suffering 'for the usual external reasons, although camaraderie amongst colleagues is good. Although I have an ageing staff, the fact is that many of them would not even leave for promotion. Falling rolls may be affecting the curriculum but so far the detrimental consequences have been limited. What I really need is to be able to find ways of keeping staff morale high because their opportunities for internal promotion, in-service work and staff development are so limited. Recently, I have tried to counteract the effects of this through a limited job rotation policy but this is not the long-term answer.'

St David's average daily attendance rate is approximately 88 to 90 per cent; worse in the fifth than other years. For a short period between 1984–85, attendance rates fell to about 83 per cent daily after the local authority reduced its bus service to pupils at the school because of cut-backs in expenditure. This resulted in the formation of a parents' action committee followed by a local publicity campaign which eventually led to the local authority re-introducing all its original bus services.

During my visits, I found that the staff was in the process of introducing new policies for dealing with non-attenders. These measures differed in some ways from the county guidelines because the school has found these to be bureaucratic, unworkable and unsuccessful in obtaining positive results. Under the old policy, the education welfare officer did not sift through registers, rather responded only to referrals from staff and/or the social services. Parental visits were then made. If the parents were out and failed to respond to the appropriate forms which were left through their letter boxes, the staff felt there was too little follow-up action.

Hence, certain absentees and persistent absentees continued their non-attendance almost unchecked. Eventually the staff pressurized the head to take more positive action. They resolved that the education welfare officer should be asked to provide reliable information to staff on pupils' reasons for missing school and outline what measures were being taken and/or being considered to ensure that non-attenders returned.

The new policy is as follows. On the third day of a pupils' absence without reason, a form tutor has to complete a pre-prepared letter to parents (form NA1) about their child's non-attendance and address an envelope. This is sent via the head of school and office to the pupil's home. At the same time the absentee is referred to the education welfare officer. No immediate action is taken by the EWO until he or she receives a reply from the parents. If none is forthcoming, the EWO then makes a home visit which means that he may have to travel a considerable distance because of the school's catchment area. If, however, parents respond positively to form NA1 and the pupil returns to school, the matter is dropped although the form is retained by the EWO and can be referred to again in subsequent action.

For non-attenders who take the odd day off a week, the same procedure applies after the third occasion, but the wording on the letter to the parents is different. Once again, the EWO attempts to ascertain the reasons for the child's absence from the parents. For both kinds of absenteeism, the parents respond on form NA2.

If and when parents fail to respond positively to the school's initiative, either condoning or turning a blind eye to their child's absence, then the EWO is empowered to complete another circular (form NA3) which invites the parents to the school to explain the reasons for their child's non-attendance. Refusal or failure to do so may result in the EWO instigating court proceedings.

In practice, instigating court proceedings is not quite as simple as it sounds for a variety of reasons (see Reid, 1985a). First, the EWO must inform the social services of his intentions. In theory, the latter should then respond to the EWO to let him have their views within ten days. Quite often, however, there are delays owing to staff shortages, pressure of social workers' workloads, bureaucracy and any number of other reasons dependent upon individual circumstances.

Second, disagreements between the EWO and teachers at St David's and between the EWO/school and social services abound, especially in cases where there is often a conflict of interest between pupils' social and educational circumstances. Usually, when the social services openly come out against court proceedings, their will prevails. In these situations, the EWO normally loses interest in the case because of his own workload and passes the buck onto the social services department. Thereafter, senior staff at St David's consider that few serious cases of non-attendance ever improve.

Third, irrespective of his personal views, the EWO is limited in the numbers of absentees he can refer to the courts because of the amount of administration involved, number of cases which courts can reasonably cope with, teachers' judgements, parental circumstances, educational factors and, in extreme circumstances, reports written by educational psychologists and psychiatrists. In addition, as the EWO tends to be overloaded with requests for home visits to be made, it sometimes happens that by the time these visits are made, the pupils have graduated from occasional absenteeism to the persistent stage. As a result, truant fifth formers at St David's no longer receive priority from the school or EWO in non-attendance cases. In the headteacher's words they are 'left to rot'.

Internal investigations revealed that absenteeism amongst fifth formers has increased substantially in recent years probably due to the lack of local work and job prospects for unskilled or semi-skilled youngsters in the region apart from those afforded by Youth Training Schemes. In 1985, St David's had thirty-five persistent absentees in the fifth form out of 200 pupils. In addition, there were a number of occasional or specific-lesson truants. One deputy head commented that the increase in absenteeism in the fifth year 'is caused by a general disenchantment amongst less-able and average-ability fifth formers towards the educational system as a whole, particularly what they perceive as an irrelevant curriculum and bleak job prospects in the area.' By way of retribution, the headteacher refuses to enter the names of persistent absentees in the fifth form for public examinations. This is a more effective threat than it seems because the school's policy is to enter all pupils for public examinations, including those in the remedial department.

Finally, the school EWO is restricted in his work by circumstances peculiar to himself and St David's. These include his own ill health, variable help from staff, parents, pupils and social workers, as well as the need to differentiate between serious and lesser cases. According to staff, the new policy is only a partial success. It still seems that many new referrals are not being acted upon quickly enough. Return to school rates for occasional and persistent absentees remain much too low.

In practice, therefore, the new policy at St David's means that the EWO selects his own cases for action once form NA1 has been completed. He is also empowered to make evening as well as day-time visits. Owing to the need to be cost effective he is allowed to plan his own daily work schedules in order to concentrate on specific districts rather than selecting cases from the entire catchment area. Senior staff at the school rigorously support the EWO by following up and interviewing those staff who fail to complete form NA1 within the stipulated time limits.

The headteacher justified his new policy by saying: 'I decided to act before, quite frankly, truancy got out of hand. The whole staff felt cases of non-attendance were rising. Too much time was being wasted on persistent offenders in the fifth year. Both my staff and the Education Welfare Officer were disillusioned by the lack of success in integrating absentees back into school. We had to do something. Frankly, I foresaw a likely escalation of absenteeism because of the diabolical local job situation, especially for young school leavers. I only hope the scheme is successful. At the moment, it is too early to tell.'

The changes in policy towards non-attendance at St David's mean:

1) The whole staff are involved in the prevention and detection policies on pupil absenteeism (Reid, 1982a).
2) The quality of the interaction between the EWO and the school has improved.
3) The parents are also involved in the entire remedial, consultation and referral stages from the very beginning. Bringing them into the school (as and when necessary) to explain their child's non-attendance with senior staff is proving very effective and most unpopular with both occasional absentees and persistent truants. Failure to comply with the school's reasonable request can lead to court action being taken or pupil exclusion or both. Therefore this measure is a genuine threat to parents.
4) A change in the role of the EWO to give him earlier warning, more backing and greater and more effective authority.
5) A deliberate concentration on younger truants and absentees, especially those in the first three years.

As with their policy on absenteeism, St David's has recently changed its pastoral structure. There are now four heads of school: head of lower school; head of middle school; head of senior school (fifth year); and head of sixth form. Formerly there were four heads of house.

The role of the form tutor is very important and is regarded as the first line of defence in pastoral work. In addition to form periods, pupils are allocated to seminar groups for weekly discussions with a nominated staff member on mutual topics of interest. There is no school social worker or school counsellor on the staff. However, St David's is supported by an active chaplain and other clergy.

The school has a clear policy for disruptive conduct. Serious cases of abuse to members of staff are dealt with by the headmaster or his senior deputy. These always result in immediate exclusion followed by a formal interview with the parents at the school. On average, the headmaster considers that the school suspends some five or six pupils a year for short periods. Over the last few years, pupils have been excluded for such reasons as bullying, extortion, persistent internal truancy and gross disruptive conduct. The evidence shows that periods of exclusion and suspension often involve the same pupils on different occasions.

Generally speaking, St David's is well controlled in school hours. Naturally enough, some staff have more disciplinary problems than others. My visits revealed that few pupils wander aimlessly around the corridors in lesson time. Like many other large schools, there is a 'smokers' union' and a few minor disturbances in the playground at breaks.

A particular grievance of pastoral staff lies in the perceived failure of links between the caring agencies in cases of need especially between the school and the social services. Multi-disciplinary case conferences are generally considered a waste of time. A deputy head reported that many of the case conferences which he attended had failed because particular social workers or educational psychologists did not turn up at designated times, even when the social services had initiated proceedings. The deputy thought that the time spent attending these case conferences was usually wasted and led to few positive outcomes for either the pupils or the school.

Senior staff felt that the relationship between the school and the social services needed improving. They considered that the locally poor education–social service links were caused by unnecessary professional delays, incompetence and prejudice on the part of individual social workers. The hierarchy stated that certain actions taken by individual social workers had led some absentees and their parents to believe that their behaviour was being condoned and understood. Consequently, some staff at the school had concluded that a social worker's only real value lay in treating particular cases to which they had been referred by the courts or other agencies such as those involving care orders, theft or ill treatment at home.

VINCE

Vince is fourteen. He is in the fourth-year remedial unit at St David's. He is exceedingly small and light for his age, about four-and-a-half feet tall.

Vince is the youngest of three children, a married sister and a brother aged sixteen. Technically, Vince's brother, Mike, also attends St David's. However, he has been persistently absent from the school since the beginning of the academic year and has no intention of returning. In fact, Mike is legally allowed to leave school in two months' time.

The family live on a council estate, approximately four miles from the school. Vince's father is a skilled furnace worker; his mother a post office clerk.

Vince spends much of his free time in his evenings on his own as 'my parents enjoy a drink and going out to night clubs'. Sometimes his cousin spends the evening with him playing snooker, watching videos, practising dancing and going to the local youth club.

Vince's major hobbies include break dancing (with his cousin he came third in the county final of the pairs tournament); boxing in which he has won three of his four fights on stoppages ('I have a good punch, see'); snooker ('I have my own six-foot table') and watching videos ('so far I have thirty-two of my own mostly with good fights in them'). By nature, Vince is pugnacious, ebullient, puerile, brash and hyperactive.

Vince's brother Mike is a very good boxer indeed. At fifteen, he became the Welsh champion for his weight and only lost the British championship final on points. Mike also plays soccer for the town's schoolboy team and has had a professional trial.

Vince has considerable admiration for his brother. It is a matter of some regret to him that he cannot emulate his brother by getting into the school soccer team. 'I'm skilful enough but I'm too small.' He also misses his brother's presence at school. 'When Mike was here no one dared touch me. Once two boys hit me in the playground. My brother found out and chased them across the yard. He nearly killed them when he caught up with them. No one ever hit me again until he left. Now I have to fight back. Usually though, I tell my brother when I get home and he says he'll get them back for me.'

This is Vince's version of events told in his own words in response to specific questions.

My primary school was the best school there ever was. It was quite a way from here. I liked everything about it especially the games, football, teachers and all the lessons. They used to help you all the time. The only time I was ever in trouble was just before I left because I was the only boy going to a different school. The other kids tied me to a railing and hit me.

I hated it when I first came here. I didn't like my timetable, particularly the moving between lessons. The school was too big and the teachers didn't know you. Some of them never gave me any help.

In the first year I got poor reports. I was fooling about in too many lessons. My behaviour in the second year was better. In the third year, I really improved. My mother said my report this time last year was the best Christmas present she had ever had. This year things have gone down-hill again. I got suspended for two days for throwing objects in the playground. It wasn't fair because I didn't do it. The teacher picked on me and my friend because we're always in trouble. My parents were so disgusted that they smacked me. I was furious especially as I didn't do it – I really didn't.

Next year I hope to take some exams (CSEs). I want to take religious education, English, maths, physical education and woodwork. I don't want to take social studies, economics, environmental studies and music.

My best subject is PE, my worst maths. Mr Harper, the PE teacher, is my favourite teacher. He's got a real sense of humour. Also, he teaches the only subject I really like. You can tell he's good, the girls like him as much as the boys.

I also like Mrs Watkins, the history teacher. She too has got a great sense of humour; used to make us laugh a lot in class. I'm sorry we haven't had her take us any more since the third year. Mr Giles, my seminar teacher and my woodwork teacher is also very kind.

I really dislike Mr Isaac, the RE teacher. He has a dreadful temper. Sometimes he flares up and shouts at you for no reason at all.

But most of all I hate Mrs Snook. I try to come to school now on most days. But I hate Thursdays. On Thursdays, we get Mrs Snook for five hours a day. She starts on me from the beginning of the day 'til the end. She's always picking on me. She takes me for economics, environmental studies, maths, social studies and English. She used to take me all Wednesday afternoons as well so I used to miss those classes. Recently my timetable has been changed. But I still only get two teachers on Wednesday afternoons and Thursdays.

We also get Mrs Snook too often on a Friday. It's not fair – other kids get different teachers. We don't. That's why I mitch now – because we get Mrs Snook too much.She's a good teacher really but I can't get on with her. She's always shouting and treats the class badly. She makes the lessons boring and the kids unhappy. She says she doesn't like teaching us.

Usually when I'm on my own in her class I'm all right but when I'm with my friend, Alan, I'm always joking and talking. Alan is my one really good friend. I'm friendly with the others including the girls but Alan's my mate. He's the best thing about the class. He's very good to me.

My classmates are fine. We get on well. Sometimes, however, there's a lot of arguing outside and inside lessons. Some of the boys bully the others. But not me. I can take care of myself. Some of the older boys in another class bullied me in the yard last term. They picked on me for nothing. They threw me up in the air and then let go. They could have broken my back. The only reason they picked on me is because I'm small. They wouldn't have dared if my brother was still here.

I had a real fight the other day. I went to support Alan because some kids were bullying him. I punched one of them in the face. He won't touch us again.

I don't get homework very often. Our class gets homework from one teacher occasionally. I'm glad we don't get any more. Even once a week is too much.

I'd like to change some things about this school. First, I'd like to get rid of school uniform. Then, I'd change some of the school rules. I hate smoking but I'd let my mates smoke if they wanted to. The school should have a sports and disco hall. Now, I have to practise my break dancing in the yard. Sometimes it's too cold for the other kids to watch the practice when they'd really like to learn from me. I'm the best in this school, you see.

The food here is far too expensive. My parents give me a pound a day for food. You can only buy three rolls and a drink for that.

I'd like to move to another class – only to get away from Mrs Snook. Also, I'd like Friday's off. Coming to school for five days a week is too much. Last week, my mother gave me permission to miss Friday. She said I was too tired. I go to bed at about 10.30 p.m. most nights, but not before midnight at the weekends. Sometimes I wait up until my parents get back from their night club. Now they let me watch their videos with them – soft porn, the funny kind. They don't like videos with swearing in them.

In the summer I go swimming in the sea and in the baths. I hate surfers. Some surfers beat my cousin up last year because he's a 'trendy'.

My behaviour can be good, mostly it's good and bad. It depends on the teacher and the mood I'm in. If it's Mrs Snook and Alan and I feel like it, we really misbehave. She deserves it. I really wish we could have someone else. I need a teacher who will help me, not shout all the time. It gets me down.

MRS SNOOK'S VERSION

Mrs Snook is a teacher of remedial subjects at St David's and Vince's form tutor, but not his seminar teacher. She is middle-aged and in her eleventh year at the school. Owing to diminishing opportunities, she is still on Scale 1. Currently, she teaches Vince for 50 per cent of his timetable for the second year running. This is her version of events also told in response to specific questions.

Vince's main problem is his lack of interest in his work. He couldn't care less. He was demoted to the remedial class at the end of the second year. Originally, he was placed in a higher band because of his favourable primary school report. For a while after his transfer he made very good progress. This time last year, his mother said that his school report was the best Christmas present she'd ever had. During the last year, however, there has been a slow deterioration. At one time he would do some work. Now he normally does nothing. You won't believe this, but he can disrupt a class just by being there.

Alan, his best friend, is a real troublemaker. When the two of them are together there is a real undercurrent, sometimes culminating in an eruption. Alan is the worst of the two, the catalyst. Vince can be serene for a while. Then he erupts, either shouting, throwing books or being generally defiant.

Conversely, he can be extremely kind. One day a colleague told one of the girls off for her behaviour and said she'd write to her parents. At the end of the lesson Vince remained behind to tell my colleague that Mandy is an orphan. He asked Mrs Williams not to mention the fact to anyone.

On other occasions, he can be spiteful – even deliberately hurtful. He disrupts lessons just for the pleasure of it, particularly when Alan's in the mood. Basically, however, he's just immature and very small for his age. For example, he often forgets his pencils, rubber and books, even his coat. He frequently comes to school wearing another coat because he's forgotten his other one from the day before. He's very thoughtless. He never tidies up. I have to do it for him all the time.

His truancy varies. Sometimes its a hundred per cent, other times intermittent. There's no real pattern at all. He often takes time off on Wednesday afternoons and Thursdays, probably to miss some of my lessons. But you have to remember that he began to truant in the first year. His attendance is so erratic its surprising he's never been to court and never had a social worker. Most times, Mr Richards, the Head of the Remedial Department, phones his mother and she seems to make him come back. She usually says she didn't know he'd been away. He misses things he doesn't like, or stays away if its fine and hot. In some ways I think he follows his brother, although Mike's truancy and behaviour were much worse.

I think that his trouble started because he got bullied in years one an two, probably because he is so exceptionally small. When I first taught him in the second year he had to kneel on his chair in order to get enough pressure on his desk so that he could write.

Generally speaking, his work is neat and tidy; what there is of it. In some lessons he appears busy all the time and then you find he's written nothing. At the moment he's on course to take nine CSE examinations but there's no final decision. Much depends on him and his truancy. In the Remedial Unit we encourage all our pupils to sit examinations. I suppose he has an Intelligence Quotient of 85, so he could pass some.

When he's troublesome, I prefer to inform Mr Richards. He either phones his parents or puts him in detention in the summer months. Unfortunately, detention rarely works, the pupils simply don't attend. We've tried essays on truancy and on bad behaviour but he rarely does those either. My own view is that if Alan and Vince were separated, the class would improve overnight. The trouble is there's no other class in which to place them. At first, I think he behaved because he wanted to get back with his former classmates. Once he'd adjusted to the mores of the new class, his behaviour immediately deteriorated.

On extreme occasions, I refer Vince to Mr Appleyard the head of year. This is not very easy for me because there's a longstanding personality clash between the two of us. Let me tell you what happened on the last occasion I did so. Vince and Alan were playing truant after coming to some of the earlier lessons. They were walking home when it started to rain. As school was nearer, they returned to my lesson mid-way through. Immediately, they were insolent to me and I had no option but to report them. Mr Appleyard decided to sympathetically exclude them from my lessons. He said they were not to come to my lessons for three days. Instead, they were sent on messages and errands. Vince really enjoyed himself and openly laughed at me. Not much later he was excluded from school at Mr Appleyard's request for urinating on another pupil in the yard.

As I see it, the other pupils in the class are fed up with both Vince and Alan. When they were suspended, some of them openly said 'thank goodness'. At least there was peace in the class for a while. Strangely enough, none of the parents of the other children have ever complained to the school, although a few have spoken privately to me about the influence of Vince and Alan on their offspring when I've seen them out shopping.

There's not much more I can say. Vince needs to calm down and apply himself. He's too puerile. He has little hope in the future. His parents are really very caring, or that's what I've been led to believe.

Some of the other staff feel like me. The harder you try, the more likely it is to lead to confrontation with him. He loves the chance to grab the limelight. Perhaps none of the disruption would have started if he'd been correctly placed in the remedial class in the first place.

Truthfully, I feel a little sorry for him. He can be a most loveable little boy. He can also be a right so and so. . . . When he's in the mood, nothing is ever right. The school needs to find some way of making a breakthrough. So far we've all failed.

Deep down, I believe Vince wants to be good. I think that he believes a boy has to be hard. If not, he's a sissy. He's determined to show he's hard because of his size. He's desperate to show Alan that he is as tough as him when truthfully he isn't. Alan is much the more evil of the two.

Looking to the future, if I had to hazard a guess, I'd say he'll end up taking only one exam – English. But even this depends upon him starting to do some work. At the moment he does none at all.

MR APPLEYARD'S VERSION

Mr Appleyard is Vince's head of year. Formerly, Mr Appleyard was a head of house. Consequently, he has only been consistently dealing with Vince for a term but he already has some profound views on the case. This is his version of events.

First, let me state my policy as a head of year for dealing with pupils like Vince. I always try to have a fallback situation without having too many specific stages. I try to handle situations myself whenever I can. This means you have to make judgements on particular incidents or a series of incidents. I suppose I weigh up the seriousness of an incident against a pupil's previous background then ask myself what are the consequences of my action for all concerned. I try to avoid bringing in the head unless its absolutely necessary such as a case of possible suspension. This is the ultimate sanction. Options for heads of year are strictly limited. Sometimes one solution leads to an escalation of conflict, another to decrease. For example, if you remove a pupil from a class you may inadvertently be rewarding the deviant conduct or vice versa. Even in the old days, in my experience the cane was ineffective.

Because I deal with Vince, let me give you a few home truths as I see them. Education welfare officers don't do their job well enough. They don't want to take cases like Vince to court. They prefer the most extreme cases; it's easier to get sympathetic verdicts. Because of the amount of administration involved, we've not really got an effective welfare service. Its very much a long-term decision for EWOs to take court action. EWOs are too readily satisfied with parental responses or a warning. In this school its ironic that our own EWO's attendance is not very good, although I must say this is mainly due to sickness.

Now let me turn to Vince's case. I had to threaten him with suspension near the beginning of term; a consequence of several minor things accumulating – mainly subject teacher complaints, being disruptive and offensive. One teacher took his conduct personally due to a longstanding personality clash between Vince and Alan and her. I suppose this was partially due to the disadvantages of having one teacher for such a large proportion of school time. But there were other incidents. For instance, Vince threatened another fourth-year boy without reason, another longstanding feud. He borrowed money from the lad and then failed to pay him back – deliberately. There again, there is his truancy and specific-lesson absenteeism. His pattern of non-attendance is most difficult to deal with legally.

In the end, I wrote to the parents warning them that he might soon have to be excluded. Then I had to withdraw him from Mrs Snook's classes for a while, a kind of cooling-off period. I took this action partly to give Mrs Snook some relief but also for punitive reasons. During this time, he did odd jobs for me and Mrs Snook set him some work which he did under my supervision. Unfortunately, Mrs Snook didn't concur with my action but I'd rather say no more on this subject.

Not long afterwards, he was excluded. He threw urine or a substance which looked like urine (cloudy water) at some fourth-year kids in the playground. Either way, he claimed it was urine and really upset the pupils. Whether it was urine or not is a moot point but he deliberately gave this impression and this ultimately led to his exclusion. Incidentally, round about the same time he had been reported for fighting in a lesson. Also, he was truanting a lot which compounded the situation. The parents were invited to the school to see me but in the event preferred to deal with the matter on the telephone.

Summarizing, I would make the following points about and as a consequence of Vince's case. First, another teacher apart from Mrs Snook might have fewer problems with Vince. Second, heads of year and other teachers have too little time for casework. Vince's case should have been sorted out long ago. Third, Vince is a sad commentary on the failure of existing procedures for dealing with non-attenders. The education welfare officer should have taken positive action instead of leaving the matter to others. As things now stand, I am doing my best in difficult circumstances by responding at a fairly late stage in the proceedings. All I have to offer is a fresh face and approach to a perennial problem – one of many.

Apart from its denominational foundation, St David's is typical of many medium-sized comprehensives in Britain. It has a hard core of truants and a comparatively small number of disruptive pupils. It is fortunate in having a stable, experienced staff but is beginning to suffer from the disadvantages of falling rolls and resource shortages in an era of decline and change (Reid, 1983e).

Vince is not a particularly serious disruptive truant. Rather, he represents the kind of troublesome pupil who many teachers have to deal with and handle on a daily basis; some with more success than others. In the final analysis, effective teacher–pupil relationships depend so much on teachers' charisma, personality and resourcefulness, especially when coping with disenchanted pupils.

Vince's case highlights several features. These include:

1) The importance of implementing remedial treatment for intellectual and/or behavioural needs as early as possible in pupils' school careers.
2) The onus on schools to have viable, flexible but consistent policies for dealing with minor as well as major instances of disruption and truancy.
3) The crucial importance of placing potential or actual disrupters in classes taught by experienced, competent and firm staff.
4) The different perceptions and versions often held by major participants in the same case which can themselves complicate and cloud issues.
5) The bad influence which one or two disruptive truants can have upon the rest of a class.

In Vince's case, Mr Appleyard – the head of year – was in much the same position as the education welfare officer whose policies he criticized. He was being judged on his results by Mrs Snook. As Vince's behaviour had not significantly improved following his intervention, Mrs Snook believed that the head of year had failed. As the EWO had not responded punitively to Vince's truancy, presumably due to his heavy workload, Mr. Appleyard considered him blameworthy. Perhaps Vince's case highlights some of the inherent difficulties faced by middle management and EWOs in coping with referrals. It also shows the dangers of colleagues jumping to hasty and unfavourable conclusions when, if they were in the same position, they would have little choice but to make the same kind of decisions and face similar consequences.

In most schools there are a minority of pupils who are unlikely to respond to their teachers' interventions, although these often effect short- rather than long-term cures. Pastoral staff and education welfare officers normally do the best they can on limited time and resources. Considering their lack of initial and in-service training and the large numbers of disaffected pupils, it is not surprising that some pupils like Vince either baffle or fail to respond to initiatives to resolve their difficulties. Finally, whether the right or best solutions were implemented in Vince's case must remain a matter of conjecture and some doubt. But this is always a matter of opinion and judgement. In the long run, the real loser is Vince himself.

SUMMARY

Schools vary considerably in the organization and ethos of their pastoral care systems. Far more school-based research is needed into studies of pastoral care in action in order to identify good practice with disaffected pupils. At the present time, some disaffected pupils are treated more empathetically than others owing to disparities between teachers' attitudes and school policies. A number of disaffected pupils probably receive very little sympathetic or remedial treatment either from qualified or un-qualified pastoral staff or professionals in other welfare agencies. As a consequence, some schools appear to rely too heavily on overt punitive measures to control and combat disaffected behaviour in schools. Regrettably, ill-conceived punishment schemes often exacerbate rather than ease tension in particular situations. Some pastoral care teams and form teachers are too identified with authoritarian rather than welfare work by their pupils to be successful in both areas. Far more imagination is needed by school personnel before disaffected behaviour will be significantly checked and overcome. When conventional pastoral care fails, schools are forced to rely on the use of more formal sanctions and referrals to external agencies. These two themes are discussed in fuller detail in chapters 10 and 11.

Therefore, the prognosis for disaffected pupils continues to be bleak. Substantial changes in school policies towards disaffected behaviour are needed. In the first instance, schools should set themselves some reasonable and attainable targets. In their first year of secondary education they could, for example, identify certain pupils as being at risk and thereafter concentrate much of their existing resources and time upon these pupils. Unless disaffection is attacked at source, later remedial measures will have little chance of success. Prevention is often better than cure.

10
FORMAL
SANCTIONS

This chapter concentrates on the use and application of formal sanctions by schools and local education authorities for dealing with non-attendance and disruption. The first part of the chapter is concerned with the regulations governing non-attendance and subsequent court proceedings. The second half deals with the use of suspension and exclusion with disruptive pupils. The final section concentrates on two serious cases of disaffection – Craig and Jason.

Schools normally initiate formal sanctions against pupils when everything else has failed; both school-based approaches and early liaison with external welfare agencies. In one sense schools are openly admitting they are unable to cope or unwilling to tolerate certain aspects of the pupils' behaviour. Generally speaking, formal sanctions are a final option taken with extreme cases. Formal sanctions usually include court proceedings against non-attenders or their parents or the suspension or exclusion of disruptive pupils. Occasionally, some pupils are suspended for absenteeism although such a procedure is often counter-productive.

ABSENTEEISM AND THE LAW

The operation of current legislation and court proceedings for non-attendance is a complex and thorny topic (Berg, 1980; Reid, 1985a). The laws on school attendance are mainly governed by the 1944 Education Act, the Children and Young Persons' Act, 1969, as amended by the School Leaving Age Regulations and the 1981 Education Act. Some legal and practical variations pertain in both Scotland and Northern Ireland when compared with England and Wales (Reid, 1985a).

The 1944 Act states that 'it is a parent's duty to cause a child of compulsory school age to receive efficient full-time education suitable to his age, ability and aptitude, either by attendance at school, or otherwise'. Parents in England and Wales can be prosecuted under Section 39 of the 1944 Education Act for failing to ensure their child's attendance at school, or under Section 37 for failure to comply with a school attendance order. Section 40 of the Act enables magistrates to fine (or, on third conviction, imprison) the parent. They may also, or instead, direct the local education authority to bring the child before the juvenile court under Section 1 of the 1969 Children and Young Persons Act. Alternatively or additionally, before deciding whether to prosecute, the local education authority must decide whether it is appropriate to bring independent proceedings under Section 1(2)e of the 1969 Act. The LEA has sole responsibility for initiating care proceedings in respect of school non-attendance if the child is thought to be in need of care and control which he is unlikely to receive unless the court makes an order. In practice, however, local education authorities generally liaise very closely with local social service departments which have responsibility for initiating care proceedings on other grounds. Existing legislation ensures that no parent or parents have the right to deprive their offspring of the advantages of full-time education provided by the state. Under very special circumstances, suitable home tuition may be permitted but this practice is not widespread and acceptable excuses for non-attendance are kept to a minimum (Reid, 1985a).

Court action for non-attendance is normally a last option, although school policies differ on this matter. Usually, court action is preceded by a series of intense efforts on the part of schools and education welfare officers to encourage better attendance. In the final analysis, court proceedings can be brought against either the parent or child, normally not both simultaneously.

The laws governing non-attendance in Northern Ireland are roughly similar to those operating in England and Wales. However, the Black Committee Report of the Children and Young Persons Review Group (HSMO, 1979) includes recommendations on the legal sanctions available in the case of school absentees. The Committee suggested a new juvenile court model with the separation of care and criminal proceedings. The Committee took the view that voluntary supervision by an education welfare officer should be the first stage in cases of school non-attendance and if this proved unsuccessful, a supervision order could be requested from the juvenile court under care proceedings. The nominated supervisor would usually be the education welfare officer. Finally, school non-attendance would not of itself be grounds for seeking a care order, although it is when a supervision order is broken.

The law in Scotland pertaining to non-attendance cases is different from England and Wales. Section 35(1) of the Education (Scotland) Act of 1962 states that 'where a child of school age who has attended a public school on one or more occasions fails without reasonable excuse to attend regularly at the said school, then, unless the education authority have consented to the withdrawal of the child from school . . . his parents shall be guilty of an offence against this section'. A certificate from the headteacher of the school is sufficient evidence of the child's record of attendance for the purposes of prosecution.

Recent research has consistently shown substantial variations in practice between the ways in which schools, local education authorities and education welfare officers use their discretion in bringing about court proceedings (Green, 1980; West Glamorgan, 1980; Galloway et al, 1981a,b). Prosecution for non-attendance appears to be more likely in cases where children have committed additional offences and are known to be persistent troublemakers (Taylor et al, 1979; Galloway et al, 1981c). Factors which impinge on these decision-making processes seem to include: the amount of non-attendance in the area; attempts to avoid swarming the courts, and the kind and availability of local alternative provision (residential schools, special units, home tuition); the individual judgements of education welfare officers, headteachers, pastoral care teams and local education authorities on legal and administrative sanctions; socio-economic and familial aspects; and the views of the social services.

Taking pupils and parents to court in non-attendance cases is a contentious process generally more 'popular' with teachers than social workers given their respective standpoints. Criticisms of court procedures abound for a variety of reasons. These include: the long delays which often occur in non-attendance cases; the ineffectiveness and reluctance of some social workers to co-operate in court processes and with verdicts reached by magistrates; the failure of social workers to ensure that children placed under their supervision attend school regularly; the inadequacy of existing options open to courts for dealing with non-attendance cases including the inadequacy of existing fines; the unfavourable long-term effects of court outcomes upon non-attenders; and the injustices and inequalities of existing procedures. For instance, Green (1980) notes that a high proportion of pupils routinely absent themselves from school with relative impunity. At the other end of the continuum, some pupils are taken to court for first offences in the hope that this will provide a sharp deterrent. Moreover, absentee pupils placed into care tend to come into contact with more serious offenders which often exacerbates rather than eases their social problems and can lead to increased criminality.

Inevitably the numbers of children and parents brought before the courts for non-attendance are small. In a national survey undertaken in 1980, Thomas (1982) reported that there were approximately 4000 prosecutions of parents in England and Wales under the 1944 Education Act. In the same year, 2230 children in England and Wales were brought before the juvenile court on care proceedings under Section 1(2)(e) of the 1969 Children and Young Persons Act on the grounds of their non-attendance at school. This was one per cent of all juvenile court cases; the remainder being criminal prosecutions.

Local statistics confirm the small numbers involved. Berg et al (1977) found that 0.014 per cent of the total school roll in Leeds was taken before the juvenile court in 1972–3. In 1976–7 prosecutions of parents and children represented about 0.15 per cent of all pupils on school rolls in Sheffield, (Galloway et al, 1981b).

For whatever reason, Martin et al's (1981) authoritative study of the Children's Hearing system indicates that national statistics on prosecutions for non-attendance in Scotland are higher than for England and Wales. These again provide further evidence of variance between regions in implementing policies concerned with non-attendance cases. They report that in 1979 there were in excess of 2500 cases referred to the Reporter on the grounds of truancy. This figure constituted 10 per cent of all referrals for all grounds including offences. Martin et al found that the reporters dealt with some 15 per cent of the cases themselves. The remaining 85 per cent were referred to the Children's Hearing. Thus, the latter were dealing with about the same number of truancy cases as juvenile courts throughout England and Wales which cover a population approximately ten times greater.

Published statistics on court outcomes also suggest that different policies appertain in different regions. Thomas (1982) reports that of the 4000 parents prosecuted under the Education Act in 1980, 3670 were found guilty. Of these, 83 per cent were fined. Fifteen per cent received absolute or conditional discharges. Galloway et al (1981a) found that 78 per cent of parents appearing before magistrates' courts in Sheffield between 1976 and 1978 were fined. Eight per cent were conditionally discharged.

For juvenile court truancy cases in England and Wales, Thomas (1982) ascertained that of the 2230 in 1980, the magistrates made no order in 15 per cent of the cases. Of the rest, about half received supervision orders and half care orders. In Sheffield between 1976 and 1978, Galloway et al (1981a) found that of the 126 juvenile court cases, 11 per cent were withdrawn or dismissed, 14 per cent adjourned *sine die*, 51 per cent received supervision orders and 24 per cent care orders. In Scotland, Martin et al (1981) discovered that the Children's Hearing discharged just under a quarter of the truancy cases, made supervision orders in 70 per cent of cases and residential care orders for 6 per cent.

The issuing of care orders for pupils involved in non-attendance cases is a highly emotive and controversial subject, partially because these outcomes often depend upon places being available. Considerable concern, however, is frequently expressed about children's short- and long-term experiences when in care. Casburn (1979), for example, suggests that care orders are frequently invoked in non-attendance cases as a way for courts to exercise control over the behaviour of girls who deviate too far from the accepted female norm.

In two revealing and successive projects, Berg et al (1977; 1978a) studied pupils whose cases had been adjourned. They found that these children subsequently attended their schools more frequently than those who had been placed on supervision orders. They also committed fewer criminal offences.

In another experiment undertaken in Sheffield, Galloway et al (1981b) ascertained that some court procedures appear to lead to better outcomes than others. For instance, pupils whose parents had been taken before the School Attendance Section and the magistrates' court subsequently made better attendance at school than those children who had been taken before the juvenile court; both in the short- and long-term. Interestingly, children for whom no formal intervention was made also made reasonable improvements in their attendance, although these were not as good as those whose parents had been brought before Sheffield's own School Attendance Section and the magistrates' court. Whilst the subsequent attendance levels of this group did not reach those achieved by the other two, they were higher than the levels obtained by the juvenile court group. On a related theme, Galloway et al also found that school transfers stimulated better attendance in some cases.

Another thorny aspect is the liaison between courts and schools in non-attendance and other juvenile cases prior to court proceedings, especially the amount and quality of information provided and the use made by magistrates of school reports prepared for the courts. Ball (1981) notes that unsatisfactory school records as revealed by school reports are a major factor influencing the court's decisions when making care orders. Similar results were obtained in Scotland where Martin et al (1981) concluded that discussion of school reports often took up a large proportion of the available time in individual cases. They noted however, that details on some reports are often incomplete, concentrating solely on specific aspects such as attendance, behaviour and educational ability and attainment.

In a follow-up paper, Ball (1983) argues that the amount of discretion allowed to headteachers when making their school reports to courts and the extent of collusion which exists between some juvenile benches and schools is tantamount to the administration of secret justice. In fact, secrecy surrounding the contents of school reports to courts is an issue in itself. Ball found in a survey that 59 per cent of school reports are not shown to panels. The remainder are. Her paper outlines the idiosyncratic factors which impinge upon open and closed justice in this respect. These include magistrates' styles and preferences, the attitude of the court clerk and the relationship between local headteachers and magistrates. It seems that headteachers are more reluctant to provide courts with full reports if they are likely to be read out to the offenders and their families. In cases where confidence is assured, court reports tend to be less restrained.

Millham (1981) suggests that school reports carry greater weight with magistrates than social workers' reports. Cryptically, her reasons for making this assertion include the fact that magistrates seem to understand and sympathize more with the language and tone of educational reports. This may be because school reports concentrate rather less on justifying the child's behaviour. Millham wonders whether all schools are aware of the enormous impact which their recommendations are likely to make upon a child's subsequent career in attendance cases. Of course, Millham's views differ and contradict the opinions of many headteachers and education welfare officers who believe that courts are often too soft when dealing with non-attendance cases. It seems, therefore, that magistrate's courts frequently displease one or both sides in individual cases. This often places magistrates in an invidious no-win situation as they cannot hope to please everybody and should not try to do so.

Discrepancies between reports written by social workers and teachers are another occupational hazard for magistrates. Social workers appear to value school reports rather less than familial and/or social issues. Moreover, some social workers are inclined to be unsympathetic to school traditions and policies, often regarding them as precipitating or contributing to pupils' non-conformist conduct (Giller and Morris, 1981: see also Chapter 11).

FORMAL SANCTIONS AND DISRUPTIVE BEHAVIOUR

When exceptional outbursts of disruptive behaviour occur in schools, headteachers have three major 'weapons' at their disposal. The first of these is expulsion which is the ultimate sanction and is used very sparingly indeed. Although expulsion is legally permissible, some local education authorities forbid headteachers to use this option (Jennings, 1980). Expulsion means expelling pupils and removing their names from the official school roll which can create an administrative headache for LEAs in making alternative, often short-term, educational provision (Galloway et al, 1982).

Expulsion remains the ultimate sanction of fee-paying public schools with whom it is more commonly associated. Expelling pupils from private schools is a much easier process and sometimes invoked for comparatively minor offences such as smoking or drinking because of its deterrent effect upon the conforming majority. It will be seen later in the chapter, that Craig was expelled much more readily than Jason.

Suspension is a procedure which operates closely to expulsion and has a similar effect upon recipients. Suspending pupils means that they are forbidden to return to school or enter the school premises until the sanction has been lifted. Moreover, there is little possibility of a pupil being readmitted in the short term until the headteacher and LEA are satisfied that readmission will not interfere or endanger staff or other pupils or normal school life.

Headteachers are obliged to notify parents, the chief education officer and school governors that suspension proceedings against a pupil have been implemented. The formal act of suspension is incorporated in Schools' Articles of Government, subject to safeguards contained in the 1959 School Regulations that pupils can only be excluded or refused admission on reasonable grounds. Appeal procedures against suspension are available (Taylor, 1980; ACE, 1981).

The kind of situation which warrants suspension is shown in the following extract:

Jane was participating in a fourth year French conversation class being taken by Miss D. When the teacher turned to write a few words on the blackboard, Jane sneaked forward and emptied the contents of Miss D.'s handbag on to the floor. The teacher turned round and ordered Jane to pick them up. She refused and repeatedly used foul language to Miss D. After the teacher had retrieved her own handbag, she was suddenly and unexpectedly attacked by Jane and knocked to the floor. In the ensuing struggle, Miss D. had her arm broken. Jane was pulled off the teacher by other members of the form and subsequently suspended; a long-drawn-out process to remedy the immediate situation and redress the harm done to Miss D. was started.

Assuming that expulsion is practised by LEAs, the third option open to headteachers is exclusion which enables schools to debar pupils on a temporary basis. Exclusion is normally used to provide a cooling-off period. It also gives schools time to plan new strategies for dealing with particularly difficult pupils.

Headteachers are empowered to use exclusion under conditions laid down by the 1944 Education Act and the 1936 Public Health Act. The average length of time for which exclusion operates varies by authority and school ranging from, say, one day to several weeks, although the latter is rare. Three days is an average amount of time (ACE, 1981).

Ronald rarely attends school. When he does, he often remains on the premises but out of the classroom. At morning break and lunch-time, he persistently picks on younger pupils in the playground. This has led to a number of confrontations with staff on duty, a deputy head and other pupils. During one of the deliberations, he repeatedly swore at a female teacher. After she had returned to her own classroom to take a lesson on home economics, Ronald appeared outside the room on the grass verge and threw a stone through the window. He was immediately excluded. A letter was then sent to his parents inviting them to see the headteacher to discuss his behaviour and the conditions for his readmittance to the school.

A few pupils graduate from periods of exclusion to formal suspension and/or expulsion. Frequently, however, a bout of exclusion is sufficient warning, especially in cases where the parents co-operate with the school. In extreme cases, exclusion has little effect upon pupils and/or parents as, for instance, in Ronald's case. He returned to school a week after being excluded, remained for four days before his absenteeism re-commenced.

Exclusions and suspensions are not merely penalties against pupils and warnings to parents. They can be used by some headteachers as ploys to obtain renewed interest in a case as these measures indicate to LEAs, parents and outside agencies the seriousness with which the school regards the pupils' conduct.

Reasons for suspension often include assault on teachers and pupils and serious acts of vandalism against school property. Reasons for exclusion can include verbal abuse and insolence, persistent disobedience or breaches of the peace in school, perpetual or isolated instances of disruptive behaviour, refusal to accept and/or obey school rules and major breaches of school discipline.

According to headteachers, their reasons for suspending pupils include the safety of staff and pupils, the deterrent effect on other pupils and in order to make the LEA provide an alternative form of education for the pupil (Galloway et al, 1982). Some headteachers have been accused of being too willing to suspend children living in care in the belief that the social services will make alternative provision for them (Davis, 1977).

Violence towards staff in schools is rare, despite considerable media coverage on this topic. Between 1975 and 1979, twelve out of 266 suspensions or exclusions of pupils in Sheffield were for acts of violence towards staff (Galloway et al, 1982). In one London borough between 1975 and 1978, violence towards staff accounted for only five cases out of eighty-five (Grunsell, 1980).

Teachers' unions rightly show the greatest concern in instances of violence towards their members. Under certain conditions, teachers can take court proceedings against pupils for assault (NAS/UWT, 1974; AAM, 1975; NUT, 1976). One association says that teachers who have been assaulted by pupils should not accept them back into their classes without their specific consent being given prior to the re-entry (AMA, 1978).

Statistics on suspension and exclusion emanating from LEAs are notoriously unreliable. Such figures are often imprecise and can fail to distinguish accurately between suspension and exclusion, while other occurrences appear to go unreported. Some cynics believe that LEA's have a vested interest in keeping these statistics as low as possible. Otherwise, the general public may get the impression that there is a greater breakdown of law and order in local schools than actually exists (ACE, 1981).

In 1977–8, Grunsell (1980) found that suspension and exclusion amounted to 0.73 per cent of the total secondary school population in one London borough. In 1967–9, York et al (1972) reported that 0.023 per cent of the school population in Edinburgh were so involved. Galloway et al's (1982) statistics on children suspended and excluded for at least three weeks in Sheffield between 1975 and 1979 were never higher than 0.38 of the total on roll in any age group. Of these, two-thirds were boys and one-third girls.

Periods when pupils are suspended or excluded have given rise to a number of legal and educational complexities and anomalies. A child who is absent from school because of exclusion or suspension, for example, is technically guilty of an offence and the parents liable for prosecution (Jennings, 1980). When cases are reviewed or appeals held, the outcomes usually favour or support the action of the school and local education authority (Taylor, 1980; ACE, 1981; Galloway et al, 1982).

During periods of suspension, pupils are in a state of limbo and are often liable to get into further trouble or seek employment illegally. Galloway et al (1982) found that 70 per cent of excluded or suspended pupils receive alternative educational provision or returned to their original schools within an eight-week period. By contrast, Grunsell (1980) reports that periods of suspension may operate for much longer. His research in one London borough ascertained that the average delay before any kind of part- or full-time provision was made for suspended pupils amounted to three to four months and for nearly a quarter of the cases took six months or longer. Delaying tactics are a useful weapon in the armoury of local education authorities.

Home tuition can be given to suspended or excluded pupils under conditions laid down in the 1944 Education Act but is used very sparingly (Reid, 1985a). Grunsell found that about half of his sample of suspended pupils received home tuition either alone or in groups. However, this only applied to 12 per cent of Galloway et al's sample of suspended and excluded pupils.

Statistics on outcomes for suspended and excluded pupils are fairly revealing. Half of Grunsell's suspended pupils did not receive any further full-time educational provision again before they were legally entitled to leave school. This was partly due to their age at the time of suspension and suggests that some headteachers are more liable to use this sanction as pupils enter their mid-teens. It is probably also attributable to the fact that some pupils become bolder in their disruptive behaviour at school as they mature. Galloway et al's research into excluded and suspended pupils reported that a quarter were eventually readmitted to their original school, 18 per cent never received any formal education again, while the remainder were transferred to other schools including special schools and a centre for disruptive pupils.

Explanations for disruptive conduct have normally centred on family and personal factors, although the search for school aspects is beginning to gain momentum. York et al (1972) studied forty-one children excluded from schools in Edinburgh in the late 1960s. They examined the personal characteristics of the children, their family backgrounds, IQs and behaviour as measured by standardized tests. They found that excluded children tend to come from lower class origins; live in homes which experience or have experienced marital discord; manifest personality disorders and are less able intellectually. York et al suggest that exclusion is the culmination of a series of aggressive acts by seriously disturbed children from stressful and socially deprived familial backgrounds.

Galloway et al (1982) examined fifty-eight pupils suspended from schools in Sheffield. They found that both pupils and their parents had histories of illness. The children were likely to have been in care at one time or another, to have low IQs and to be seriously backward in reading. Contrary to York et al's work, and cases of absenteeism, Galloway et al concluded that social class and socio-economic disadvantage were not reliable predictors of suspension rates.

Longworth-Dames (1977) compared the personality and behaviour of children excluded from school with their peers who were not. She found that there were no significant personality differences between the groups as measured by standardized tests. Excluded children, however, did score higher on certain tests which measured malajusted behaviour. She suggests that some disruptive pupils' behaviour in schools is more influenced by their desire to maintain their position in their local sub-culture rather than by anything else.

Research into school factors relating to exclusion and suspension is scarce. Both Galloway et al (1982) and Grunsell (1980) found higher rates in comprehensives which had been former grammar schools. This may suggest that some experienced staff in these schools are trying to maintain traditional standards dating back to the grammar school era. Galloway (1980) reported that a third of his sample of suspended pupils had longstanding differences with particular teachers. He also noted the tendency for minor acts of disruption to escalate in schools leading to suspension. Both Longworth-Dames (1977) and Galloway et al (1982) have reported that the behaviour of some suspended pupils improves following school transfers.

Research into school differences has so far excluded suspension or exclusion rates as measures. The evidence which is available from the literature suggests that differences between schools in their policies and rates of suspension and exclusion do exist. Accurate information and statistics on these matters, however, might well prove difficult to obtain.

Some schools frequently use their own internal measures rather than formal sanctions for coping and/or dealing with their potential suspended or excluded pupils. One such practice is personal tutor schemes. This often operates by technically removing or suspending disruptive pupils from all or certain lessons and giving them a special or separate timetable, room and member/s of staff to look after them. These schemes can sometimes last for days, weeks or a whole term. Very little is known about these measures and their effectiveness.

When teaching, I once had a pupil attached to me for the entire day for a period of several weeks. He attended every lesson I taught acting as a kind of co-helper. He was given his own special assignments which, naturally, were different from those undertaken by my regular classes. We stuck so close together during this period that he even wore my cricket cap in net practice at lunch-times and followed me around when I was on duty at breaks. Unfortunately, within two days of the practice ceasing, he was suspended for threatening behaviour towards another member of staff.

Like so many innovative schemes, it is hard to know when to return a deviant to the fold. Sometimes schools have no option but to try their own measures with difficult pupils as the demand for placement in special units, both off- and on-site, generally greatly exceeds the supply.

COMPARISONS BETWEEN NON-ATTENDERS AND DISRUPTERS

A number of comparisons between formal sanctions used with non-attenders and disruptive pupils can be made.

1) Formal sanctions for dealing with both absentees and disrupters are marked by conflicts of interest between caring and punitive actions. This is why such pupils so often find it hard to relate to their teachers and social workers as professionals have to castigate and help non-conformers at differing times. Some pupils must become very confused by these two extremes.

2) Sanctions aimed at overcoming severe disruptive conduct normally seek to remove offenders from classrooms and/or schools in order to give teachers and other pupils some respite. By contrast, legal proceedings for truancy have the reverse object.

3) Suspension and exclusion for disruptive behaviour are carried out at the discretion and instigation of the school. Conversely,

the outcome for truancy is entirely in the hands of the courts.

4) Decision-making processes in formal proceedings used against truants and disrupters are both characterized by their variance, an idiosyncrasy which often borders on arbitrariness to the eyes of untrained observers (Reid, 1985a).

5) Non-attendance cases usually rely heavily on school and home background reports. Generally speaking, adverse familial backgrounds, social deprivation and poor educational attainment are three features which stand out in truancy cases. The evidence in instances of suspension and exclusion, however, is mixed. Some research suggests that suspended and excluded pupils have similar social and home backgrounds to absentees and truants. By contrast, Galloway (1980) reports that pupils' chances of suspension or exclusion owe at least as much relationship, if not more, to the schools they attend, as any familial, stress or constitutional factors within the pupils themselves. Further research is needed from larger and more representative studies before too many firm conclusions are reached on this latter point.

THE END OF THE LINE

The two cases of Craig and Jason are fairly extreme. They depict pupils whom teachers and schools find difficult to contain, who require skilled specialist help from external agencies, and who have graduated from the disruptive truant stage to delinquency and young offender status. Craig is atypical. He comes from an affluent family background, attended a private fee-paying day school and only really started displaying disaffected and disruptive behaviour at home and at school at the age of fifteen, partially in response to a specific discovery.

Jason is more typical of cases described in the literature. He is the eldest son of a chronically disabled father. He comes from a poor and deprived home and social background; a member of a disadvantaged working-class family with its inevitable bickering and arguments and usual crop of misunderstandings born of strife and struggle for human survival. The family live in a small council home dependent upon social security and a war disablement pension for support. Unlike Craig, Jason has openly shown his hostility towards schooling from the age of eleven onwards.

CRAIG

Craig is nineteen. He is a young offender. He is a tall, well spoken boy with a faint moustache. Before entering prison, his main interests were cars and rugby. Since starting his sentence, he has taken up body building. At the time of writing, he has served seven months of a two-year sentence after being caught in possession of a stolen motor bike. Originally, Craig was stopped on suspicion by a police officer for displaying false number plates. After being cautioned, Craig reacted so badly and violently that he attacked the officer causing him actual grievous bodily harm. In fact, the officer was taken by ambulance to hospital where he was detained for a considerable period while his injuries healed and he overcame the shock caused by the ferocity of the attack.

This is Craig's story told in his own words in response to a series of questions.

CRAIG: I suppose I first got into trouble, real bother at the age of fifteen. One night when I was at home my mother called me into the kitchen to have a chat with me. For some reason, I can't understand why, she told me that I was adopted, that my brothers and sisters were really foster brothers and sisters and I was a foster child. I don't know why but I couldn't take it. I was really angry. Fancy being told at fifteen that you haven't got any real parents and no one knows who your real parents are. It blew my mind. I couldn't grasp the situation.

After that everything changed. I couldn't speak or look at my father. Well, sort of father. I decided to get my own back on them. They should have told me the truth from the very beginning, when I was 5 or something. How would you feel if you discovered that your two younger brothers and sisters belonged to your parents and you didn't like?

RESEARCHER: What happened then?

CRAIG: For a while I couldn't believe the news. It left me cold. It numbed my mind. I didn't know what to do. At first, I didn't do anything too stupid apart from starting to truant. I couldn't face school any longer. Then when I went back, I began cheeking the teachers and disrupting their classes. One day the deputy head called me into his office and told me off for my lack of enthusiasm. Things went from bad to worse from there. I got suspended from school for truanting and being disruptive in class. The school couldn't understand it. I was due to sit nine mock 'O' levels that term and there I was being suspended. My father was furious. We had some terrible rows at home – really unpleasant. One day I decided I'd had enough. I told my parents I was going to run away. My father said that if I ran away I shouldn't ever come back. So that's what happened.

RESEARCHER: How long did this phase last?

CRAIG: About three or four weeks. Later, I got in touch with my grandparents to see if they could help me. I was fed up of living rough. They put me in touch with a social worker. She managed to get my parents to agree to a trial reconciliation so I went back home. This only lasted for three days. I couldn't stand it. The atmosphere was awful. My father ignored me. He pretended not to hear when I spoke to him. So I left home again. Then I went into care.

RESEARCHER: What happened then?

CRAIG: After that my social worker arranged for me to be transferred to a state school. I didn't mind this. I went there to take my exams but never did. When I left school I went on to the dole.

RESEARCHER: How did you find your new school?

CRAIG: The school was all right, I suppose. I knew most of the boys there from playing rugby. I used to get on with all the lads from my first school because of sport, rugby like. I was a good wing forward and in the school first fifteen by the fourth year. But I had other problems at the time.

RESEARCHER: What were these?

CRAIG: I kept getting transferred from one home to another.

RESEARCHER: Why?

CRAIG: Mainly because I couldn't settle and I kept on getting into trouble. This carried on until I was aged eighteen. Then I left care. Dr Barnardo's agreed to help me out and set me up in a bed-sit where I stayed for one year.

RESEARCHER: Is this when you started getting into a lot of trouble?

CRAIG: No. It began before this. When I was in care I got prosecuted for trespassing. Honestly, I really didn't know I was trespassing at the time.

RESEARCHER: So what happened when you were in your bed sit?

CRAIG: Well I had to make a living. I wanted to take my 'O' and 'A' levels and join either the Air Force or the Army but no one would take a criminal, would they? So I began to look after myself.

RESEARCHER: What did you do?

CRAIG: I stole and handled stolen goods.

RESEARCHER: Such as?

CRAIG: Crates of beer, cassettes – you name it.

RESEARCHER: Is this what led you to being in here?

CRAIG: Yes. I saw the bike. I liked it and wanted it for my own. Then I decided I had to have it, so I stole it.

RESEARCHER: Did you ever try contacting your parents for advice or help?

CRAIG: One day I rang my parents from a coin box. My father answered the phone. I spoke to him but he never answered once. He knew it was me. I kept trying to speak to him for five minutes but it was no use so eventually I put the phone down again.

RESEARCHER: Did your schools try to help you?

CRAIG: Neither of them cared. They were only worried about how I affected the other boys. After the deputy head at my first school found out that I began running a protection racket he gave up on me. The other school didn't really know me, did they? They were only helping my social worker out.

RESEARCHER: Looking back, how do you think your circumstances could have been improved for you?

CRAIG: What do you mean?

RESEARCHER: If you started life all over again, what would you like to be different?

CRAIG: I'd have liked a better relationship with my father. He isolated himself from me. He never took me out anywhere. He always left me behind when the family visited my grandparents. I wasn't like a son to him. When I was eleven and twelve my mother and I had a lot of problems with my father. They nearly got divorced because of it. She took me away with her, leaving my two younger brothers and two younger sisters behind. We went and stayed in a hotel for a while. Then we went back. But it was never the same for me after that.

RESEARCHER: Is there anything else you would change?

CRAIG: I wish my father could say 'sorry' to me and I had it in me to say 'sorry' to him. But neither of us have. The social worker says its a classic breakdown of a family situation. She says it happens all the time.

RESEARCHER: What do you think the future holds for you?

CRAIG: Not much, I suppose. I'm hoping to start work on a new project soon with motor bikes. My probation officer said he'd try and fix it for me when I get out. I also hope to pass my test so I can get a licence.

RESEARCHER: Will you go back and see your parents or continue your education.

CRAIG: I won't go and see my parents. You have to understand. It was my father who put the clamps on me. He wanted me to grow up to help him in his business. When I worked for him he didn't pay me much. I suppose I could go back as an employee provided he didn't want me as a son and I lived away. If I don't get parole I'll ask to be transferred from here and take my City and Guilds in Mechanics. That should come in handy.

RESEARCHER: Do you miss your brothers and sisters?

CRAIG: No, they're mostly too young. My eldest brother is very different from me. I like sport and cars. He hates sport and cars. He likes sitting around doing nothing except watching television.

RESEARCHER: Who do you blame for what has happened to you – yourself, your parents or your school?

CRAIG: In a way everybody. Mostly me I suppose. I couldn't handle finding out that I was illegitimate. But my father is also to blame. He should have told me the truth from the very beginning instead of acting differently to me from the rest all the time.

RESEARCHER: What about your school?

CRAIG: I just took it out on them. It wasn't their fault. I wanted revenge on my parents, especially my father. It was easier to take it out on people at school than anywhere else.

RESEARCHER: Do you regret this now?

CRAIG: I suppose so. But you'd have to be me to understand. Everything could have been so different.

RESEARCHER: Do you think it's too late now?

CRAIG: Maybe. Who knows? I expect so.

JASON

Jason is eighteen. He is also a young offender. He is currently on remand awaiting sentence for shoplifting. He is asking the magistrate for community work but fears he may get another six months as he has already served one sentence of twelve months in prison for burglary.

Jason is one of life's born losers, repeatedly in trouble, weak and with little chance of breaking the trend. His pimpled face and soft-spoken voice belie his well-developed criminal brain. This is his story. It is a tale of disaffection eventually turning sour.

Jason has three younger sisters and one younger brother. The family live in a council house on a notorious housing estate somewhere in South Wales. Jason's father is disabled following a serious war wound which severely affects his mobility. His father has never worked since the war and the family rely on a war disablement pension and social security for their means of support. His mother has never worked.

At the age of ten, Jason was referred to the social services for the first time because he was unable to get on with the rest of his family, especially his father. For him, domestic life was nothing but a series of quarrels and bickering.

Between the age of ten and fifteen, he had a succession of some seven or eight social workers. Some left his case after a short while to take up new posts but others asked to be taken off his case because of his repeated insults towards them. 'I was too much for them. Anyway, they weren't a lot of help,' he stated proudly.

For the last three years, he has had the same male social worker. 'He's much better. He doesn't do much for me really, except find out about things.'

Jason began truanting at the age of eleven. He never adjusted to life at his local comprehensive.

> Things didn't seem to work out for me. The school put me in the wrong class straight away. I was made to go into a class with a lot of dumbos – kids who were much duller than me. That didn't give me a chance, did it?

At first, Jason enjoyed the thrill of missing school. Then boredom crept in and he returned to school occasionally, sometimes for the odd lesson, day or week. But these instances became increasingly rare.

When present at school, he was always in trouble for not wearing school uniform or having the requisite sports kit but mainly for disrupting nearly every class he attended.

> I didn't like the teachers, the lessons, going to school – anything. I never got on with any of the teachers. I got caned a few times but it had no effect. What did I care. One day I told the deputy head to — off and shove his cane.

This was the cause of his first suspension but not his last. In five short years of secondary education, Jason was expelled for twelve months and sent to three other schools, none of which could handle him. Eventually, he always returned to his first school.

I had one decent form teacher who taught me about maths. I still love maths today. Maths is much better than English. One year I turned up for my maths exam at school but none of the rest. The other teachers taught me what I learnt in junior school – kids stuff. It used to make me sick. So I decided to pay them back. I used to walk into a lesson, sit down and then walk out again. Sometimes I'd walk into the middle of a lesson, shout out and then leave.

Some of the teachers I really hated. I told one woman to piss off and mind her — business. I remember that because she never gave me any cheek again.

I used to go and sit at the back of the class and talk to my mates. If any teachers said anything to me I'd give them hell. If they called out 'shut up' or 'be quiet', I'd tell them where to go. It was great. Some of them got fed up and ignored me. Then I'd talk louder and fool around even more. I was never quiet.

Not surprisingly, Jason's turbulent school history was a succession of truancy and suspension. Ironically, however, it was not his truancy which first brought him to the attention of the courts.

I started shoplifting on my own. Then a group of us started pinching things together. It began as something to do, a kind of dare. Later, I found I couldn't stop it and it has become a way of life.

Jason left school at sixteen. Since then, he has had two short periods of employment.

I got my first job through the MSC government scheme. It didn't last long. I got sacked. My next full-time job was as a sales assistant for — (a well known double glazing firm). I got sacked after I robbed the manager's house of his video . . .

Jason himself believes it will be difficult to change his life-style and sees little prospect of betterment in the years which lie ahead.

I went to the juvenile court about forty or fifty times for shoplifting. Since leaving school, I've been to the magistrate's court for shoplifting and burglary twice. Its become my way of life. You have to survive, don't you?

In fact, when out of prison Jason does not fare very well. He mainly lives rough in bed and breakfast establishments, flats, empty houses or with his 'mates' whenever he can.

I never go home. I might do one day. I'm too much trouble for my parents. After my brother was sent to Borstal for shoplifting, it was the end. They never want to see me again. I think my parents got fed up of the police calling back and forth to the house all the time.

Jason has adjusted well to prison life. In his first term of imprisonment he obtained a distinction in his maths City and Guilds 1 examination. He is very proud of this achievement.

It's just as good as any 'O' or 'A' level. I might take my City and Guilds 2 in maths if the magistrate sends me down again.

Inside prison, Jason mainly watches television in his leisure time. He plays the odd game of 'pool' or table tennis to occupy his mind. He has strong views about education and his parents.

I didn't get on with people at school – teachers, that is. And I couldn't stand my parents. So I decided for spite to get them back, to get them fined. That's why I started truanting. My best friend felt the same. He got his parents much bigger fines than me. I could never get taken to court for truancy but he did.

Education is a waste of time. In the prison all we do is rubbish. There's nothing formally organized. We don't have any normal lessons like maths and English. I wish I could do more maths. One hour a week is not enough. We need more relief from our cells. We don't learn enough.

In fact, under the terms of their sentences, young offenders convicted by courts receive one hour a day of compulsory education. Those awaiting sentence also receive one hour a day. Young offenders on remand are not obliged to take education classes but in practice most elect to do so. This helps to break up their daily routines which are normally comprised of physical education and education in the mornings, workshops in the afternoons (sewing mail bags etc.) followed by a period in the cells. In the evening there is supper and association (recreation with inmates within the prison wings) followed by return to cells at 8.30 p.m. The educational programme for young offenders at Jason's prison has three objectives: to improve cognitive clarity and communication skills and achieve better personal relationships. A varied curriculum includes modules on such options as life skills and remedial education. The education officer attempts to make the curriculum as enjoyable and meaningful as possible and as different from the school environment as common sense allows. He acknowledges that young offenders in prison can be as bloody-minded as pupils in schools. Hence, his staff use attitudinal, verbal and material rewards whenever possible. One such reward for good motivation and achievement is the showing of the latest videos on Friday evenings.

Jason's education officer accepted some of his criticisms about the curriculum. However, he pointed out that his hands were tied because of an acute shortage of resources, difficulties arising out of coping with untrained part- and full-time staff, differences between the perceptions and demands of educational programmes on the part of prison and educational staff as well as the individual needs of constantly changing inmates. In reality, being a prison education officer is not easy as the intellectual levels of young offenders covers people with several 'O' and 'A' levels as well as those who are innumerate and illiterate.

Jason gets on well with his peers in prison.

Most of them I knew at school or from my first term in jail. They're a good lot – understand the ropes. Some of us used to work together flogging our stolen goods. It was easy money.

Nevertheless, he is far from optimistic about his future.

Last time when I was out I had five interviews for a job. I never got anywhere. They always gave them to someone else. They're not prepared to give people second chances. I'll never go for another interview again. I'd rather just sign on the dole.

Jason was quite forthcoming in his views about why pupils truant from school and disrupt lessons.

Kids miss school either because they want to spite their parents, or because they hate their teachers, or because they get bored Some kids truant because they're afraid of getting bullied. You should know what school is like. A lot of the teachers don't teach and what they teach is rubbish. Most teachers are stuck up and don't understand their pupils. That's why we truant and misbehave. Honestly, I never did anything wrong in my maths lessons when I had a decent teacher.

No school could keep me for long. Any teacher who spoke to me I ignored. It went in one ear and out the other. I couldn't be bothered with teachers. Now I can't be bothered with work. Why should I when obtaining money is so easy . . . .

IMPLICATIONS

These two detailed extracts from Craig and Jason's case histories warrant further discussion. Craig is an example of a complete over-reaction following the receipt of ill-timed and badly handled news on the part of his parents; crucial information which was always likely to have a devastating impact on the rest of his life. How much thought had his parents really given to the likely effect upon Craig of discovering that he was an adopted, probably illegitimate child? Why tell him at fifteen prior to taking his mock 'O' levels? Why not have left the information until after the exams were over or even until he was much older? After all, if they had left the news until later, perhaps delaying the announcement to around his eighteenth or twenty-first birthday, surely, his increased emotional maturity might have enabled him to cope far better with the shock. Who knows, by then Craig might even have been grateful to his parents for their care and concern throughout his childhood.

But perhaps the cracks had begun to take place much earlier, before or after Craig and his mother left home for a while when he was twelve. Perhaps the father wanted to get back at his successful adopted son – nine possible 'O' levels and already a place in the first fifteen. Perhaps Craig was achieving too much and making his father jealous, especially as his own offspring showed less natural talent.

Alternatively, had Craig's father ever loved him? Or, had the father rejected Craig in favour of his own offspring many years earlier? Was Craig really born to his mother before she had married Craig's father? Unfortunately, the case files do not answer any of these possibilities. What they do show is an over-concentration on the outcome of Craig's actions rather than on the real motives or reasons for his misbehaviour. Therefore, educationalists and social workers alike had been treating the consequences of the distress rather than the root cause. The files also show that Craig had crammed eighteen years' misery into three since the discovery that he was an adopted child. And these three short years had probably ruined his future career and in the process ensured that he carried a scar for life.

Jason's case is less complex. He was born into a disadvantaged home; a home in which his father's physical and mental state, as well as poverty, were all-consuming.

Alas, Jason's case is typical of many of his generation – pupils from deprived home and social backgrounds who underachieve and whose life-styles magnify their own disadvantage through the folly of missing school and, later, indulging in criminal activities. Retrospectively, there is little doubt that Jason's intellectual ability was greater than his achievements at school indicate. There can also be no doubt that his downward spiral will continue unless chance or good fortune intervene. He is probably destined to spend much of his life in prison as a compulsive shoplifter and burglar.

Few teachers will probably have much sympathy for Jason when they read his history of teacher-baiting and disruption at school. Nevertheless, staff at his schools can take little credit for their work with him. They failed to control him at any time, understand his genuine difficulties or really tried to get to know him. It seems that only one teacher really got through to him. The fact that this one maths teacher made such an impression on Jason in a comparatively short period is indicative of what might have been achieved. In some ways, Jason is an unwitting victim of an educational system which ensures minimal individual treatment for many lower- and middle-band pupils from disadvantaged backgrounds.

It is ludicrous that so much credence is given to pastoral care in schools and social work when so little is sometimes achieved. If we truly live in a caring society, surely much more should be done for pupils like Jason before it is too late: hard though this work might be. Surely it was elementary for staff to spot that much of his attention-seeking behaviour was really a plea for help. A plea to ensure that he had the opportunity for upward social mobility in later life, rather than a stark recognition that he faced a struggle in life similar to that of his own parents. Surely this is really why being placed in an unfavourable group of less able and similarly disadvantaged pupils concerned him so much. What would have happened if staff had taken the trouble to relocate him in another and more demanding form in that crucial first year of secondary education? Might he have made normal or better progress? Of this, no one can be sure. What both he and his records do indicate however, is that his attendance and achievement up to the age of eleven were both quite satisfactory, despite his home difficulties.

Craig and Jason's cases also suggest that some disaffected truants and disrupters deliberately and wilfully plan their own self-destruction in the mistaken belief that they are really hurting others; in these cases parents and teachers. Unless teachers and social workers are trained to spot these tell-tale signs and learn how to handle such difficult cases, the opportunity for society to prevent such wanton self-destruction is strictly limited.

Craig and Jason represent aspects of some of the worst features of disruptive absentees (Reid, 1984c) and chronic cases of disruption (Beynon and Delamont, 1984; Covill et al, 1984). It is a tragic fact that some of the traits they show are far from uncommon which is an indictment of much pastoral care and social work. Many truants and disrupters absent themselves from school or misbehave because they have anxieties and concerns which remain unsolved. For all these pupils, the end of the line is never far away unless wise, properly trained professionals intervene and respond correctly. Craig and Jason received no such wise counselling, only a great deal of corrective work designed to smooth away the rough edges rather than tackling the major problems. In Jason's case the real cause for his misbehaviour lay either undetected or was misunderstood even though he was prepared to tell all and sundry of the real reason for his aggressive behaviour; his fear of following in his parent's footsteps. In Craig's case, the receipt of crucial information that he was an adopted child was bungled by parents and teachers alike. Indeed, the school was only concerned about Craig's behaviour affecting the other pupils, thereby passing the buck on to the social services. Both cases reinforce the points made in earlier chapters about the lack of cohesion and agreement between educationalists and social workers on following unified schemes to tackle serious cases of need. Partly because of these faults Craig and Jason both reached the end of the line before some of their less able, disadvantaged and unfortunate peers. No doubt they will be endlessly punished for their misfortunes for the rest of their lives – if only psychologically.

SUMMARY

Despite complex legal, school and local authority policies for dealing with cases of truancy and disruption, the evidence suggests that there is widespread variation in the implementation, use and outcomes of formal sanctions. Whatever measures are used, they all too rarely achieve their objectives – ensuring that non-attenders return to school regularly or that disrupters cease their misdemeanours.

11
MULTIDISCIPLINARY APPROACHES

This chapter specifically concentrates on four aspects which hinder multidisciplinary initiatives. These are: school-based social work; alternative education schemes; external referrals from schools; and territorial imperatives. The text focuses upon a number of interdisciplinary schemes which have been attempted between social and educational agencies in endeavours to counteract the effects of disaffection. Some of these schemes have met with more success than others.

Professional goodwill is frequently expressed in the literature towards interdisciplinary and multidisciplinary co-operation (Davie, 1977; Kahan, 1977). Unfortunately, these ventures continue to be blighted by poor links between agencies, personality differences, shortages of resources, problems relating to confidentiality and territory, and differential professional philosophies and training backgrounds. Nevertheless, the potential for preventive and remedial work with disaffected youngsters from good interdisciplinary and multidisciplinary teamwork remains high.

SCHOOL-BASED SOCIAL WORK

Some schools have specialist welfare officers or social workers appointed to their staff under interagency agreements reached between local education authorities and social service departments. These school-based social workers are appointed in addition to or instead of school counsellors.

School-based social workers can be appointed in numerous ways. For example, they can either be on the permanent or temporary establishment. Their conditions of appointment vary considerably. Sometimes social services employees attached to schools are only consulted in particular cases such as truancy or in a limited number of different kinds of cases previously agreed between the education and social service departments. Alternatively, appointees are only used in circumstances which lie outside the scope of educational personnel to handle and/or to provide requisite social and familial reports in routine or specialized work. Then again, some school-based social workers form part of multidisciplinary experimental teams working on joint ventures of mutual interest in schools or local communities such as improving home–school liaison, vandalism or child drug abuse.

A number of complex variations on this theme exist. These include part- or full-time appointments, combined teacher–social worker roles, liaison teachers, teachers performing social work roles in schools, teacher–social worker exchanges and many more besides. Either way, these school-based social work schemes provide institutions with added options in cases of disaffection or disruption – especially in complex cases which require family rather than school-orientated approaches.

School-based social workers can be valuable acquisitions to schools, especially in social priority areas or conflict-orientated or underachieving schools. Experiments conducted on interagency social work/education projects report limited, mixed or a great deal of success dependent upon a number of local factors including proper pre-planning, mutual understanding and suitable appointments being made. Private professional conflicts and jealousies, interagency and role rivalry and problems concerned with confidentiality appear to be some of the main difficulties associated with these schemes.

Marshall and Rose (1975), for example, report on the findings obtained from the Central Lancashire Family and Community

Project. Five workers with varying social work, youth work, medical and counselling backgrounds were placed in schools with the brief to help children and their families solve or adjust to personal and social problems. Their aim was to determine experimentally the value of social work undertaken in secondary schools. Children referred to social workers in school showed sustained improvement in behaviour and in test measures of social adjustment when compared with peers referred for court action. This scheme however, was not helped by teacher–social worker rivalries.

ALTERNATIVE EDUCATION

Apart from school-based social work schemes, a number of alternative social or teacher-based schemes exist to provide collective or individual help for older, usually non-examination pupils. These generally promote the use of positive, alternative learning experiences to the traditional school curriculum with selected chronically disaffected pupils. Many of these programmes were introduced in the wake of the raising of the school leaving age in the early 1970s and have suffered a variety of fates (Grunsell, 1980).

Alternative-education schemes have a variety of aims. Some are provided as part of the educational provision for the secondary age group in the often erstwhile hope that improved attendance and behaviour will take place. Others are specifically designed for individually referred pupils who have special needs, sometimes as alternatives to home tuition. These experiments can take place either within existing school buildings or on alternative sites, on a full- or part-time basis.

There are numerous examples of the variations and innovatory work undertaken as part of this provision in the literature. Drinkwater (1981), for example, describes an initiative in which fifth-form boys and girls from a school in Wales who might otherwise have been truanting, acted as tutors to primary school children in a nearby school providing help with reading and writing. Marshall (1981) used fourth-year pupils with learning difficulties and associated behaviour and personality problems in a 'tutor mothering' venture. In this scheme individual pupils spent one day a week with volunteer mothers who had young children at home. The pupils shared in the running of the home and care of the family.

Another popular type of approach utilizes intermediate treatment (IT) groups. These groups often meet in school time either on or off the premises, as an agreed part of the curriculum for pupils who may be referred for behavioural or attendance problems. In IT schemes, school and social service staff co-operate together in mutually agreed programmes. Bietzk (1982) describes a typical six-week IT programme in a school in Northamptonshire in which an education welfare officer, two social workers and a teacher worked together with fifth-form pupils who had underachieved during their school career, exhibited disruptive behaviour in class and were at risk of being suspended. The social education programme was centred around a discussion of the pupils' problems during their school careers using self-assessment questionnaires, role-play exercises and modelling.

A fourth set of alternative education programmes includes using weekly community placement schemes outside school (White and Brockington, 1978) in places like hospitals, factories, shops and offices. These ventures provide attractive social and work experience for otherwise disillusioned youngsters. Along with a former colleague, I introduced similar weekly placement schemes with less able pupils in my fourth- and fifth-year social studies groups at Bicester and found them very beneficial; although not all staff were united in this view. In a few cases, pupils continued to make hospital and other social visits to see particular elderly and chronic sufferers long after the scheme ended. In my opinion such programmes can be invaluable in a number of ways. First, they broaden pupils' experiences. Second, they often bring out the best in adolescents. For instance, the empathy which can exist between old and young sometimes has to be seen to be believed. Third, they are a useful appendage to careers programmes providing pupils with valuable insights into life at work in different occupations.

Notwithstanding all these short-term programmes, the best known alternative education schemes remain the 'free' or experimental schools, truancy and/or disruptive centres or workshops catering for a host of drop-outs (Grunsell, 1980; Davies, 1982). When added to the literature on specialist short- or long-term on or off-site centres they form a considerable volume of knowledge about the pros and cons of alternative education schemes. This body of literature on 'experimental' education is frequently highly enthusiastic about the work. Writers tend to stress the benefits and informality of the relationships which develop between staff and pupils. Only rarely do they highlight the disadvantages. Nevertheless, doubts about the value of these programmes remain. Some educationalists, for example, are disenchanted at the thought of non-conformers being educated outside the mainstream or given preferential or different treatment within it. Others think that the long- and short-term benefits to the pupils far outweigh any educational considerations. The degree to which pastoral care staff and/or counsellors assist in the aforementioned alternative schemes also varies enormously. Some are specifically organized by school personnel while others fall completely outside their aegis or areas of interest.

Features of many of these alternative education schemes include having: different aims and philosophies from conventional schools; specific curricular, often non-traditional and pupil-centred rather than academically orientated programmes; relaxed peer-group and staff–student relationships; and flexible hours of operating including daily, weekly, evening and weekend opening dependent upon regulations.

Finally, the list of achievements of alternative education schemes is hard to discern with accuracy. One point however, does stand out. The students usually like the 'schools', not least their freer ideals. How much the pupils learn, however, is a vexed question. Nevertheless, it should be noted that some absentees attend alternative centres far more regularly and willingly than their comprehensive schools.

EXTERNAL REFERRALS

School assessments of disaffected pupils tend to place the problems firmly on the child rather than on the teachers or the institutions. Consequently, most school initiatives are directed towards making deviant pupils conform to the rules and regulations of the institution by promoting regular attendance and good behaviour. The opposite approach – schools changing and conforming to the needs and demands of their pupils – is rarely tried.

Apart from formulating their own policies to overcome disaffected conduct, schools have the option of consulting a number of outside agencies to assist them in their diagnosis and treatment of 'abnormal' behaviour. These include the Education Welfare Service,

School Psychological Service, Child Guidance Service and the Social Services. Normally, the Education Welfare Service is only involved in non-attendance cases, although the complexity of these cases varies considerably. The School Psychological Service, Child Guidance Service and Social Services Departments can all be involved, collectively or individually, in cases involving non-attendance, disruptive behaviour and underachievement dependent upon circumstances.

Although these services exist to help schools, resources for implementing their full potential (including ştaff) are distributed unevenly across Britain which sometimes leads to delays in diagnosis and treatment. Hence, some non-conformist pupils tend to experience longer periods of 'institutional hassle' than others before their cases are investigated by the appropriate service in a complex welfare circuit (Fitzherbert, 1977). What this means in practice is that some deviants tend to be dealt with only punitively by schools whereas others, in different areas, are subjected to a host of highly imaginative schemes under the aegis of well qualified and skilled professional staff. A great deal depends upon need, individual circumstances, staff availability and local resources.

The Education Welfare (Social Work) Service is a much misunderstood profession. Currently, the service is administered by local education authorities. Some recent publications however, have suggested that the profession would be better located within the social services (Ralphs, 1974; Macmillan, 1977; Webb, 1980; Wood, 1981).

The service is also much maligned by pupils (the 'boardy-man' image), parents, educationalists and social workers for different reasons. Pupils, especially non-conformers, dislike the deterrent role of Education Welfare Officers. Parents of disaffected children tend to object to the punitive aspects of EWOs role such as their involvement in court proceedings. Regrettably, some teachers look down on EWOs whom they regard as being less well qualified and intellectually informed than they themselves. Finally, some social workers often see EWOs and rivals operating different codes of practice to themselves with different aims and objectives. In one sense all these views are understandable as the main functions of EWOs include checking on pupils' non- or irregular attendance, instigating court proceedings for non-attendance, checking on child employment, investigating neglect and advising on clothing and free school meals (Davies, 1976). It can be seen, therefore, that the nature of EWOs' role often places them in invidious positions as they attempt to reconcile their dual functions of welfare and control (Pedley, 1975).

The operation of EWOs in schools is dependent upon a number of factors. These include the personality, preferences, determination and ability of postholders, their previous backround, experience and training (if any), as well as the school's policy for referring and dealing with cases of non-attendance; all of which vary considerably. Non-attendance cases are generally referred to EWOs by head-teachers, deputies, heads of year, school counsellors, form tutors, parents and a host of other sources dependent upon individual circumstances such as the age and needs of the pupils. In many schools, EWOs do their own 'checking' in registers and thereafter make their own decisions about which pupils to follow up (Wood, 1981).

Strategies adopted by EWOs for dealing with non-attendance cases also tend to differ by school and authority. Some schools, for example, instigate early court proceedings as deterrents; others see them as the final option.

The normal daily routine of EWOs includes checking on registers, liaising with appropriate teaching, education, social service and other welfare personnel, 'roaming' the school, the school's perimeter and local neighbourhood (including well-known 'sciving' dens such as cafés and public recreation facilities) in search of non-attenders and making home visits. The latter are a crucial part of the EWOs' role although, once again, their value has been questioned (Gregory et al, 1981). The main reason for this is that accurate statistics on return-to-school rates following home visits are not known. Moreover, some home visits appear not to work in many of the most persistent and difficult cases; a process which can backfire on EWOs themselves as school personnel lose confidence in their persuasive powers and bemoan the lack of progress which these home visits sometimes engender.

Through home visits, EWOs attempt to gain clear or clearer pictures of reasons for pupils' non-attendance, ascertain the interaction of social and educational facets of the case and effect strategies which are designed to improve pupils' attendance habits. These include writing reports for pastoral staff, making referrals to social services, summoning parents to attend school attendance committees and instigating court appearances dependent upon the need and severity of cases.

Ideally, EWOs require tough exteriors. They can be frequently abused by disenchanted pupils and parents when making home visits and neighbourhood checks. They have to deal with and overcome parents who condone or partially condone their children's absences and who often manifest anti-education feelings. Another problem is that court outcomes can fail to meet the aspirations of schools and EWOs which not only undermines their authority but sometimes their confidence.

Contrary to the Education Welfare Service, the School Psychological Service is regarded in awe by many pupils (the 'shrink man'), parents, teachers and social workers. Nevertheless, conclusions reached by educational psychologists do not always find favour with every party and are often misunderstood by teachers (Topping, 1978; Wright and Payne, 1979).

The role of the educational psychology service has also become increasingly contentious because many schools seek instant diagnoses and 'cures' for their difficult and underachieving pupils. This is often nigh impossible for educational psychologists to achieve given their terms and conditions of employment, caseloads and lack of refined and precise instruments for use with pupils. Teachers sometimes fail to comprehend that educational psychologists are not solely employed to give further backing to schools' own internal assessments and requirements. Educational psychologists have to stand back and take a broader view of the problem. This frequently means making judgements on the quality of parental–child relationships, parental–teacher relationships, pupil–pupil and teacher–pupil relationships as well as the social, psychological and educational circumstances surrounding each case.

The School Psychological Service is normally staffed by 'qualified' educational psychologists, although, once again, regional variations in organization abound nationwide (Wedell and Lambourne, 1980), including those concerned with channels of communication between schools and the SPS. The traditional role of the educational psychologist is one of accepting referrals from schools and, thereafter, undertaking cognitive and personality assessments of children's emotional and educational needs. Based on results obtained from standardized 'tests', reports supplied by other professionals, their own observations, pupil interviews and school performance records, educational psychologists generally make recommendations concerning the future handling or placement of children.

More recently, a considerable debate within the profession has begun as many psychologists increasingly question the wisdom of their conventional role. Many psychologists now believe that they would achieve greater success and recognition if they were encouraged to undertake more school-based therapeutic work alongside teachers and pupils both in and out of the classroom, more along the lines of community and clinical psychologists (Ravenette, 1972; Upton and Gobell, 1980).

Owing to time delays between initial referrals and assessments taking place, some disaffected pupils leave school before their problems are resolved. Moreover, some reporting-back procedures to schools take so long that their conclusions arrive after other remedies have been implemented; the latter improving or worsening the behaviour.

The Child Guidance Service is little understood by many teachers and parents. Leaving regional variations to one side (BIOSS, 1977; CRC, 1980), the CGS is often comprised of interdisciplinary teams made up of psychiatrists, psychiatric social workers, non-medical psychotherapists and educational psychologists.

The value of the CGS is difficult to gauge accurately as no national survey of its role and school liaison policies exists. Nevertheless, it is clear that the CGS is a contentious service. Criticisms of its operating processes, effectiveness and quality abound in the literature. The CGS has been criticized for irrelevance, professional distance, ineffectiveness, understaffing, poor communication, sending incomprehensible reports and over-use of technical language. Others have vigorously defended its work and achievements, given its function within the welfare network (Davie et al, 1973; Tizard, 1973; Mead and Mead, 1975; Fawcett, 1979).

According to the little evidence which exists on the interaction of the CGS with schools, it appears that the service mainly concentrates on the diagnosis and treatment of disturbed children and their families, often focusing on younger, primary school age pupils. Treating cases of school refusal is one speciality. In general, typical cases of absenteeism, disruptive behaviour and under-achievement rarely require the intervention of the CGS unless there are extenuating or difficult family circumstances surrounding the case which warrants referral.

Social service departments are frequently involved in casework with families of schoolchildren without the knowledge of schools owing to particular domestic circumstances such as unemployment, deprivation and other social needs. Schools normally refer needy or disaffected pupils to social service departments because their personal, social or home backgrounds warrant it or because specialist provision is required as in the case of pupils with handicaps. Inevitably, a high proportion of social workers are involved in cases of persistent school absenteeism (Reid, 1982c) because of the adverse home backgrounds of these pupils.

TERRITORIAL IMPERATIVES

There is a great deal of professional goodwill towards interagency co-operation for improving services towards disaffected and deviant pupils (Davies, 1977; Kahan, 1977). The smooth operation of this system requires some degree of effective communication between teachers and the other welfare agencies involved. Unfortunately, however, there is not always a consensus among professionals as to what procedures should be invoked and whether the care or control of the child is the primary aim. Reports about worker perceptions and interagency liaison indicate that conflicts of value or interest may prevent or hold up certain processes which one party to the relationship feels are desirable. Sometimes it seems that territorial imperatives are more important than the needs or views of the young, for whose benefit the changes have really been proposed. Multidisciplinary schemes demand close teamwork but often suffer from the lack of it.

Surveys of how school staff perceive 'professionals' in other agencies show that their judgement is governed by three aspects: the professionalism of the group concerned including their expertise and competence; their style of work and the helpfulness of this to teachers; and their value to young people.

These findings also suggest that:

1) Teachers tend to value the work of police and probation officers very highly; more so than professionals in other disciplines.
2) Teachers and headteachers have mixed views on education welfare officers. There are wide regional variations between teachers and headteachers in the value they place on the work of education welfare officers.
3) Teachers respect educational psychologists but do not always find either them or their work very helpful and regret the time

delays between initial consultations and reports back to schools.
4) Social workers traditionally attract most criticism from teachers because of their perceived lack of professionalism, poor communication and feedback, rapid staff turnover, slowness, and ineffectiveness in casework, as well as philosophical differences between the aims of the two professions.

The work of Wolstenholme and Kolvin (1980) helps to shed light on some of the reasons behind the territorial disputes which exist between social workers and teachers in what is rapidly becoming a perennial fight. They undertook a survey of teachers who participated in a school-based social work scheme. Their findings revealed that these teachers were not impressed by the social workers' identification, managerial or remedial skills with the schoolchildren. Nevertheless, the teachers did find the extended case reports written by social workers very helpful in giving them insights into the pupils' difficulties at home and at school. In particular, the teachers welcomed the additional information on pupils' family backgrounds. This latter result shows the considerable potential which exists when teachers and social workers do pull together for the sake of children.

Apart from social workers, research shows that professionals in other disciplines also criticize teachers for their narrowness of approach, for misunderstanding their roles, powers and/or methods of work. These problems are sometimes exacerbated due to: poor interdisciplinary communication; differences in agency structures, procedures, levels of decision-making and territorial boundaries; ignorance of one anothers' roles, priorities, methods of work and professional language and the values associated with these professional 'secrets'; teachers' tendencies to emphasize professional distinctions rather than similarities; teachers withholding professional assessments and reports from other services (and vice versa); and differences in status, pay and conditions of service.

Education welfare officers sometimes feel that their role in schools is too restricted, being related only to non-attendance rather than social work. Moreover, some EWOs feel they are too much at the beck and call of headteachers in schools, carrying out school policies rather than their own (Macmillan, 1977; Johnson et al, 1980). Likewise, educational psychologists can feel constrained by the pressures exerted on them by school staff for supportive assessments and pre-conceived treatment schemes which are sometimes encouraged at the expense of preventative or longer-term approaches (Topping, 1977; Gillham, 1978). In other words, some schools sometimes expect too much from other professionals; expectations which these personnel are often unable or unwilling to fulfil.

The gulf between social workers and teachers which occurs in many areas is repeatedly stressed in the literature. Initial differences in recruitment are greatly enlarged by separate professional training with its own particular aims and objectives, the evolution of distinctive styles of work and having different professional goals. The situation is often made worse because some teachers think they could do social workers' jobs better and vice versa.

Skinner et al (1983) have endeavoured to encapsulate the key distinctions which exist between the everyday experiences of social workers and teachers. These show:

1) Schools represent social authority displayed in bricks and mortar, whereas social workers have to cope with society's ambivalent attitudes towards the groups they attempt to help.

2) Social workers are more likely than teachers to see themselves as agents of change trying to promote fairer distributions of resources in society.

3) Teachers are primarily concerned with cognitive development and the acquisition of knowledge. Social workers are more committed to the intangible and global goals of personal well-being and social functioning.

4) Teachers, especially in secondary schools, generally relate principally to the child or young person. Social workers deal more with the family as a whole, perhaps in a wider community context.

5) Teachers work mainly in large-group settings, with all that implies for management and control. Social workers focus on individuals or very small groups. Teachers' contacts with children are more frequent but less personal than social workers'. Teachers are often sensitive to group needs; social workers to individual problems.

6) Teachers' relationships with young people are heavily influenced by the institutional setting. They have to be aware of the collective sense of purpose within the school, yet have a high degree of autonomy in their everyday work, which is largely

unsupervised. Social workers generally operate in the field outside the safer haven of the office. While they are bound by agency purposes and mandates, they have considerable autonomy and discretion, even affecting clients' liberty, though this is subject to formal supervision.

7) Teachers in mainstream schools are likely to have a strong belief in the importance of education to the child's personal and social development: hence their efforts to involve other agencies in trying to ensure that a child attends school and can benefit from it; hence, too, their concern that the classroom behaviour of a few can jeopardize the educational progress of the majority. Social workers are also likely to place high value on education and learning, but are less likely to see the school as the only possible setting for these. Their concern about the school experiences of individual children can lead them to discount the all-embracing demands of the school and its staff.

Despite these major territorial, practical and philosophical differences, teachers and social workers do share one thing in common. They are both equally powerless to promote change in large welfare bureaucracies (Davies, 1976).

THE WAY FORWARD

Effective promotional levels of coping with disaffection will never be achieved until good and better links exist between the respective welfare agencies. Fortunately, there are growing signs that individual agencies, professionals and counties are keen to collaborate in finding ways of overcoming existing obstacles. Some of the ideas for implementing better interagency and interprofessional collaboration include:

a) corporate planning to review and co-ordinate policies, operations and resources;

b) making agency boundaries co-terminous;

c) local monitoring to identify blocks in communication and the development of local communication systems for sharing basic information;

d) careful analysis of working situations in their organizational context, to identify points of friction;

e) joint in-service training;

f) opportunities to learn and practise the skills of interprofessional work;

g) reduction of anomalies in pay and conditions of service;

h) the development of interdisciplinary teams and cross-placement of workers, joint projects and better co-ordination of casework;

i) combined efforts by professionals in different agencies to change their own bureaucracies and make them more responsive to consumers;

j) adequate resourcing of services.

From all the literature on multidisciplinary approaches, two major areas of interagency and interprofessional collaboration in relation to disaffected children can be discerned (Davies, 1977). The first area concerns routine procedures and processes. In practice today, children who come to the attention of schools and other agencies may be assessed by one service, referred to another for treatment or made subject to court procedures (see Chapter 10). The smooth operation of this system requires some degree of effective communication between teachers and other welfare professionals involved in individual cases. As there is not always a consensus among the workers involved as to what procedures should be invoked and whether the care or control of the child is the primary aim, reports indicate that conflicts of value or interest may prevent or hold up certain processes which one party to the relationship feels are desirable. If this is a regular experience it may counteract and denegrate the various endeavours which are being made on behalf of the child. In such instances, there are bound to be important concerns felt by participants related to the ultimate purposes of interprofessional liaison. Good multidisciplinary practice should result in more imaginative and effective outcomes for young people in trouble or in need of help. If the end result is merely a smoother transfer between various agencies then this is a secondary rather than primary gain. Children not institutional needs should always come first.

A related concern is the extent to which young people can make their own views known to multidisciplinary teams who may, after all, be deciding their future. The question of child and parent representation at interdisciplinary case conferences is a complex and vexed issue affecting all kinds of situations. Once again, research shows wide variations in practice throughout Britain over this matter.

A second issue revolves around the collaboration of the various agencies in determining local policy on major issues such as coping with and handling disaffected youngsters. Skinner et al (1983) ask whether concern over troublesome adolescents must inevitably be the *raison d'être* of such groups, or whether a desire to co-ordinate policy on adolescent provision in general, in which the management of problematic behaviour would be one element, might on occasion be the prime motivating force. Once again, collaborative policy groups must be seen to work rather than merely to function in order to be judged effective. Otherwise, they can become regarded as a costly waste of resources by hard-pressed directors of local authorities. A debate currently exists on whether lay members of the community have a role to play in these important policy committees and, if so, what role these people should adopt.

SUMMARY

A number of promising interdisciplinary schemes to help disaffected children and youths in trouble have developed since the early 1970s. These appear to be gaining in momentum (see relevant 'Further Reading Lists' on pp. 256–7). Approaches have included school-based social work, experiments in alternative education for disaffected pupils, imaginative use of external agencies and a variety of multidisciplinary schemes, largely involving social service and educational personnel. Unfortunately, despite much lip-service, early interdisciplinary endeavours have been hampered by a host of territorial imperatives which still need to be overcome in many areas. Thus, there continue to be differences of opinion about the best courses of action to take when confronted with young people in trouble. Overriding everything, interagency liaison has to be seen to work in practice as well as in theory. Multidisciplinary approaches are the first step to resolving conflict and implementing worthwhile local policies. They are not a universal panacea.

12
CONCLUSIONS

There is currently a great deal of public and educational concern about the large numbers of pupils who absent themselves daily from schools. Despite all the structural, organizational and legislative changes which have taken place in education over the last century or so, approximately 10 per cent of secondary pupils continue to miss school daily in England and Wales; more in some regions than others. This fact alone tends to suggest that certain pupils reject the traditional aims and values of schooling and require more individual approaches which take account of their particular needs.

Truancy and absenteeism are multi-causal, multi-dimensional issues which have their roots in a wide variety of social, psychological and institutional factors. The family and home circumstances of absentees and truants are usually characterized by multiple deprivation. Not only do many absentees and truants come from unfortunate and unsupportive home backgrounds but often from unhappy homes. Some absentees and truants are inclined to have low self-concepts and to have been schooled on a diet of unrewarding academic and educational experiences. Many absentees and truants are loners, having fewer friends in school than good attenders. Absenteeism and truancy, therefore, are nurtured on failure, confrontation and disdvantage at home, in school and through anti-educational attitudes which often permeate local communities. To date, much more is known about the social and psychological than institutional aspects of truancy and absenteeism (Reid and Kendall, 1982). Far more research is needed into the educational aspects of absenteeism so that these important issues can begin to be properly understood. In particular, further school-based research is required into the link between non-attendance and the curriculum, discipline, pastoral care, teachers' attitudes and teacher–pupil relationships.

Truancy and school absenteeism are closely related to deprivation and disadvantage with all its manifestations. These include unstable home backgrounds, large families, low birth-order positions, unemployment, defective home discipline, unhealthy familial climates, low social class, histories of parental or sibling truancy, low incomes, low housekeeping standards, the mental or physical instability of parents, paternal absence from the home, anti-school and anti-authoritarian attitudes. Socio-environmental, social psychological and cultural explanations include poor housing, overcrowding, poverty, geographical location, urban–rural dimensions, community ethos and ethics, rational or irrational fears of attending school, personality factors, free school meals, peer group influences, the attraction of alternative employment, school–community conflicts and laziness. Educational and institutional factors include low intelligence, underachievement, falling behind in classwork often following an illness, school and form transfers, a fear or dislike of certain lessons, tests, examinations or teachers, boredom or inactivity at school, bullying, extortion, lack of homework, remedial or special educational provision, low teacher expectations, poor teacher–pupil and pupil–pupil relationships, teasing, defective school discipline, the application of certain school rules and punishments, organizational aspects such as those which relate to split-site schools, staff attitudes, pupil alienation, lack of a school uniform or sports kit, the curriculum, poor home–school links, negative pastoral care systems, lack of praise for the work of low ability or less able pupils and poor long-term career prospects.

Therefore, the only safe conclusion about truants and absentees is that each case is unique. Each pupil's non-attendance originates in any one or more of a combination of all these factors. Generally speaking, each case has a social, psychological and educational dimension to it in lesser or greater proportions. This makes it exceedingly difficult for teachers and social workers to implement policies which will cover every possibility and each pupil's needs, particularly as both professions tend to be so busy coping with a wide range of other educational and social matters. Unfortunately, many schools fail to come to grips with their problem of absenteeism because so few teachers are really sympathetic towards pupils like truants. After all, their absence from school is a manifestation of their low opinion of teachers and the educational goals achieved by regular schooling. The irony of their behaviour is that their non-attendance inevitably compounds their own long-term disadvantage and often exacerbates their problems, particularly as some absentees indulge in criminal activities in order to relieve their boredom when away from school. Eventually, the long-term consequences of missing school mean that society has to cater for a significant number of alienated underachievers within its midst: people who find it very hard to hold down regular employment, lead 'normal' lives and contribute positively to society (Reid, 1985a).

The media and educational reactions caused by serious disruptive behaviour at school are often out of all proportion to the actual events. In most parts of Britain, levels of disruptive and violent conduct in schools are low, although the dearth of reliable statistical evidence is a considerable handicap in making accurate judgements. Surveys suggest that, by and large, schools are well controlled, although the management of difficult pupils is not becoming any easier. Evidence from the United States shows that when discipline does break down, the long-term consequences for teachers and pupils alike are very stark and should never be underestimated. Even in Britain, however, surveys reveal that physical attacks by children on other children, repeated disruption or unruly behaviour in class, verbal abuse of teachers (including swearing, vandalism, extortion, breaking and entry of school property, arson, gang violence, attacks by pupils on teachers, racial violence and attacks on teachers by parents) do occur. For staff engaged in such confrontation, teaching can be very difficult. Their lives can be made a misery causing teachers to suffer from considerable stress. Collectively and individually, teachers must maintain order in their schools and classrooms if learning and meaningful educational activities are to take place and if teachers are to retain their dignity. Hence, all schools should have workable policies to combat disruption and absenteeism which involve the whole staff pulling together on a united front.

Like absenteeism and truancy, the aetiology of disruptive behaviour is multi-causal. Apart from the personality, temperament, ability and motivation of individual pupils, factors related to disruptive conduct include underachievement, the mores of society, peer-group relationships, familial aspects including parental attitudes and disciplinary standards, a variety of home and social background factors (many very similar to truancy and absenteeism) such as multiple adverse deprivation and disadvantage as well as the neighbourhood culture and relationships between schools and homes. Educational aspects include teachers' classroom skills, teacher–pupil relationships, situational confrontation (outbursts, over-reaction, acts of despair) all related to the mood of the moment as well as factors relating to school ethos and climate. In addition, many of the same psychological and educational issues which are linked to truancy and absenteeism are related to disruption such as intellectual ability and pupils' temperaments and personalities.

Until recently, absentees and disrupters were not considered children with special educational needs. The post-Warnock legislation means that such categories can now be included in this form of special provision. One eventual measure of the success of the 1980 Education Act will be the extent to which schools combat absenteeism and disruption through their special needs programmes. Research into school differences shows that schools do make a difference to pupil outcomes and they have it within their own means to determine the changes which they ought to make in order to improve the educational experiences of all their pupils, thereby diminishing the opportunities for misdemeanours to occur. Writers are in accord that the free, systematic use of praise and positive reinforcement are amongst the most effective ways of preventing undesirable behaviour in class from taking place, thus reducing alienation and disaffection. Although further research is necessary before too many firm conclusions are drawn on the precise relationship between disaffection and schooling, it is abundantly clear that the quality of staff in schools is a crucial part of the equation, particularly teachers' attitudes towards pupils, their classrooms and teaching competence, as well as issues relating to the curriculum. Apart from teachers, social workers and parents, researchers need to pay more attention to the views of disaffected pupils if real understanding and progress is to be made. George Kelly's (1955) maxim that if you want to understand a problem then it is best to ask the people directly concerned remains as true today as ever.

In practice, local education authorities and schools follow a variety of diverse policies for identifying and dealing with disaffected and underachieving pupils (Brighouse, 1982). One recurring problem is that schools repeatedly fail to respond to the precipitating factors which first cause non-attendance or disruptive behaviour to occur or underachievement to develop. If these behaviours are not overcome at source, they are likely to get much worse in time as pupils grow in confidence. Unfortunately, schools often do not have the time or resources they need to overcome disaffection and many pastoral care teams are institution-orientated, fostering disciplinary and administrative codes rather than pupil-orientated policies. Far more research is needed in schools on studies of pastoral care in action in order to identify good practice with disaffected pupils. Existing evidence suggests that a large number of disaffected pupils receive very little sympathetic or effective remedial treatment in school. As a consequence, many schools rely solely on the implementation of punitive measures as their only weapons against disaffected behaviour, supported by whatever help is available from the welfare agencies. Regrettably, too much pastoral care support is ill-conceived and punishment-orientated approaches often exacerbate rather than ease tension in particular situations. Far more imagination is needed by both school personnel and professionals employed in external welfare agencies before disaffected behaviour is significantly checked and overcome. Since the early 1970s a number of promising interdisciplinary initiatives have taken place to help disaffected children and youths in trouble which appear to be gaining in momentum. Too many of these early initiatives have unfortunately been hampered by professional differences including territorial imperatives. Much more thought needs to be given to establishing meaningful and workable links between professionals, especially teachers and social workers, if interagency liaison is seen to work in practice as well as in theory. There is little doubt that effective multidisciplinary approaches are one way of resolving conflict and implementing worthwhile local policies to cope with and overcome problems created and caused by disaffected pupils. They are not however, a universal panacea.

Research also shows that there is widespread variation nation-wide on the implementation, use and outcomes of formal sanctions taken by schools and courts. Whatever measures are used, they all too rarely achieve their objectives. The time may fast be approaching when more imaginative experimentation is needed to combat absence from school as well as disruptive conduct. At present, too many formal sanctions merely compound rather than ease pupils' difficulties. Few persistent absentees, for example, return to school regularly after being taken to court. Similarly, few children taken into care for disruptive behaviour repent. Rather the opposite in many cases.

Pupils' experiences in schools present considerable contrasts in context, purpose, teaching style, and quality of provision. However, some general impressions emerge. Whatever doubts may exist about the extent to which measurable learning outcomes are influenced by differences between schools in philosophy, teaching style and organization, there can be no doubting the contrasts which exist from school to school, and even from class to class within the same school, in the quality of experience enjoyed by the pupil.

Some of these variations owe much to the particular gifts and interests of different teachers. Yet many of the attributes of successful learning are capable of being achieved by planned application within schools: for example, purposeful syllabus construction; detailed schemes of work; a planned variety of activities; the active involvement of pupils and a ready and sensitive response by the teacher to their efforts; the establishment of expectations and an insistence on their attainment; and measures to detect and act upon underachievement and lack of motivation.

Fresh curricular thinking is helpful, often providing more purposeful courses for pupils and a new and challenging perspective for teachers. Successful innovation, however, depends also upon careful planning and determined application, often over several years; failing this, it can, in pupils' eyes, amount to the replacement of one type of monotonous experience by another.

Schools are first and foremost places where human beings interact. Teachers and pupils, being human, vary greatly in the gifts they bring to teaching and learning. Some teachers will always be more effective than others, but schools can do much, through encouragement, co-operative planning and the evaluation of provision to ensure that the contribution of each individual improves. A pupil, similarly, has to be respected for the progress he or she is making in relation to his or her own talents and capacities; he or she needs to feel a sense of personal value and dignity arising from his or her dealings with the school if he or she is to derive maximum benefit from the experience there. For pupils of modest academic ability and uncertain motivation, such considerations are critical and pervade most aspects of teaching and learning (Welsh Office, 1984). Within schools, far too many teachers continue to apply double standards towards their pupils; one set of criteria for able, high-fliers, another for less able pupils or those of moderate ability.

Looking to the future, the time is fast approaching when the teaching profession will have to take a much more objective and closer look at itself. This will undoubtedly be to the advantage of disaffected youngsters because the professional problems of teaching are inextricably linked to pupil alienation. Despite the fraught nature of issues like teacher effectiveness, self-evaluation and school accountability, the profession has now reached the point where it is no longer satisfactory to accept unprofessional attitudes and sub-standard teaching. For instance, teachers will soon have to decide what to do about their ineffective fellow workers. This may mean that teachers will not be given a contract for life once they have passed their probationary year. The profession has moved beyond the point where it was satisfactory for teachers to repeat their first-year experiences thirty or more times. Consequently, the profession is going to have to face up to a more vigorous examination of its initial and in-service training needs which will mean wholesale changes and developments being devised along coherent and meaningful guidelines. These will have to take account of present-day and future demands of the job. Teachers will have to be educated to the point where they understand the objectives of schooling and school management as well as specialized aspects of education. In particular, most teachers need more and better training courses on pastoral care, effective classroom and school management, coping with and over-coming disaffected and disruptive youngsters in schools through appropriate teaching and curriculum strategies, and on ways to undertake constructive self- and school evaluation programmes.

Through such initial or in-service courses, teachers should learn to detect potential or actual problems which affect secondary aged pupils as well as how to implement suitable programmes for disadvantaged and difficult pupils within schools.

Since the mid-1960s, it is probably true to say the teaching profession has lost far too much respect in the eyes of the general public, parents and pupils alike. If teachers wish to redress this balance and be regarded as well qualified, able and caring professionals, then they will have to accept more accountability by showing that their schools are well managed, their teaching effective, their curriculum appropriate and structured, and their educational outcomes suitable, satisfactory and meaningful.

The daily routine of life inside many comprehensive schools means that far too many pupils do not identify or associate themselves with their institutions, teachers or the educational philosophy or objectives of present-day educational practices. This situation is a contributory factor to existing levels of disaffection within schools. The prime requisite for combatting disaffection is the overwhelming need to make *every* pupil feel that he or she matters; the quality of their work is important, their attendance, appearance and spoken word also matter. It is when pupils feel unwanted, rejected, uncared for and disillusioned that they start to manifest their disaffection by staying away, disrupting lessons or underachieving. In this latter respect, secondary schools could learn a great deal from many of their primary counterparts.

Teachers show pupils that they care for their educational progress and social welfare through the quality of their teaching, interaction and personal relationships both inside and outside the classroom. They also show their concern through the standards they set, by arriving at lessons on time, by thorough lesson preparation, by regular and detailed correction of assignments, by participating in extra-curricular activities, by taking a personal interest in all pupils and much more besides. Until such times as these standards are adhered to by *every* professional, the educational causes of pupil disaffection will never be tackled properly.

Unless substantial changes take place within schools and society, the prognosis for pupils who manifest disaffection continues to be bleak. In a truly educated and caring society, disaffection needs both understanding and tolerance. But above all it needs eradicating if the best use is to be made of our most natural resource – people. The alternative is to allow the inequalities within society to continue and increase as employment opportunities for unskilled labour diminish in a rapidly expanding technological age. If educational and social measures are unable to solve this gigantic problem, then society is increasingly likely to feel the backlash from a substantial proportion of disaffected adults; people who have very little to look forward to and enjoy in life. Over a period of time, this disenchantment may lead to much more serious consequences than merely expanding the pool of unskilled, unemployed labour and those reliant on social security. It could contribute to a more violent society, something for which our children will never forgive us.

REFERENCES USED
IN THE TEXT

Abbott, E. and Breckinridge, S. R. (1970) *Truancy and Non-Attendance in the Chicago Schools* 2nd edn, New York, Arno Press.

Acton, T. A. (1980) Educational criteria of success, *Educational Research*, 22, 163/9.

Adelman, C. and Alexander, R. J. (1982) *The Self-Evaluating Institution*, London, Methuen.

Advisory Centre for Education (1981) Suspension: ACE Suspensions Survey, *Where*, 166, 20/6.

Anderson, R. R. (1980) *From 'List D' to Day School*, Dundee, Dundee College of Education.

Assistant Masters' Association (1978) *Proceedings of the Assistant Masters' Association Council*, 4–6 January, 1978, pp. 74/7 Appendix E, AMA Council, The Society.

Association of Assistant Mistresses (1975) *The Maintenance of Order in the School Community*, AAM, The Society.

Auld, M. (1976) *Report of the Committee of Inquiry into William Tyndale School*, London, ILEA.

Ayllon, T. A. and Roberts, M. D. (1974) Eliminating discipline problems by strengthening academic performance, *Journal of Applied Behaviour Analysis*, 7, 71/6.

Baldwin, J. and Wells, H. (1979, 1980, 1981) *Active Tutorial Work – The First–Fifth Year*, Oxford, Basil Blackwell.

Ball, C. (1983) School reports for the juvenile courts: a review of practice and procedure, *British Journal of Social Work*, 13, 2, 197/205.

Ball, C. and Ball, M. (1980) Community Works 1: Aspects of three innovatory projects, in M. Dungate, (ed.) *School's Out*, London, Community Projects Foundation.

Ball, S. (1981) *Beachside Comprehensive*, Cambridge, Cambridge University Press.

Bandura, A. and Walters, R.H. (1963) *Social Learning and Personality Development*, London, Holt, Rinehart & Winston.

Banks, O. (1979) *The Sociology of Education*, London, Batsford.

Baum, T. (1978) Surveys of absenteeism: a question of timing, *Educational Research*, 20, 3, 226/30.

Bayh, B. (1977) Challenge for the third century: Education in a safe environment, *Final Report on the Nature and Prevention of School Violence and Vandalism*, Washington, DC, US Government Printing Office.

Berg, I. (1980) Absence from school and the law, in Hersov, L. and Berg, I. (eds) *Out of School*, Chichester, John Wiley.

Berg, I., Hullin, R., McGuire, R. and Tyrer, S. (1977) Truancy and the courts: research note, *Journal of Child Psychology and Psychiatry*, 18, 359/65.

Berg, I., Consterdine, M., Hullin, R., McGuire, R. and Tyrer, S. (1978) The effect of two randomly allocated court procedures on truancy, *British Journal of Criminology*, 18, 3, 232/44. See also Berg, I., Butler, A., Hullin, R., Smith, R. and Tyrer, S. *Psychological Medicine*, 8, 447/53.

Bernstein, B. and Brandis, L. (1974) *Selection and Control*, London, Routledge & Kegan Paul.

Best, R., Jarvis, C. and Ribbins, P. (1980) *Perspectives on Pastoral Care*, London, Heinemann Educational Books.

Beynon, J. and Delamont, S. (1984) The sound and the fury: pupil-perceptions of school violence, in Frude, N. and Gault, H. (eds) *Disruptive Behaviour in Schools*, Chichester, John Wiley.

Bietzk, M. (1982) *Pilot Scheme for School Leavers*, Northampton, Northants Social Services/Southwood Upper School.

Billington, B.J. (1978) Patterns of attendance and truancy: a study of attendance and truancy amongst first-year comprehensive school pupils, *Educational Review*, 30, 3, 221/5.

Bird, C., Chessum, R., Furlong, J. and Johnson, D. (eds) (1980) *Disaffected Pupils*, Brunel University, Educational Studies Unit.

Blackham, G.J. (1967) *The Deviant Child in the Classroom*, Belmont, California, Wadsworth.

Bowlby, J. (1953) *Child Care and the Growth of Love*, Harmondsworth, Penguin.

Bowles, S. and Gintis, H. (1976) *Schooling in Capitalist America*, New York, Basic Books.

Boyson, R. (1974) The need for realism, in Turner, B. (ed.) *Truancy*. London, Ward Lock Educational.

Brighouse, T. (1981) An LEA perspective on underachievement, *Secondary Education Journal*, 12, 3, 21/23.

Brophy, J.E. and Good, T.L. (1974) *Teacher–Student Relationships: Causes and Consequences*, New York, Holt, Rinehart & Winston.

Brunel Institute of Organisation and Social Studies (1976) *The Hanworth Road Centre*, Educational Studies Unit Brunel, Brunel Institute. See also: Educational Welfare in the Borough of Hillingdon; The Education Welfare Service, Borough of Hounslow; The School Psychological Service, Education Dept., London Borough of Hounslow, all published by the Educational Studies Unit, Brunel, Brunel University.

Brunel Institute of Organisation and Social Services (1977) *The Family and Child Guidance Clinic*, Educational Studies Unit, Brunel University, Institute of Organisation and Social Studies.

Buist, M. (1980) Truants talking, *Scottish Educational Review*, 12, 1, 40/51.

Bullock Report (1975) *A Language for Life*, London, HMSO.

Button, L. (1981, 1982) *Group Tutoring for the Form Teacher: Lower and Upper Secondary School*, London, Hodder & Stoughton.

Carroll, H.C.M. (ed.) (1977) *Absenteeism in South Wales: Studies of Pupils, Their Homes and Their Secondary Schools*, Swansea, University College of Swansea, Faculty of Education.

Casburn, M. (1979) Girls will be girls: sexism and juvenile justice in a London borough, *Explorations in Feminism*, 6, Women's Research and Resources Centre Publications.

Caven, N. and Harbison, J.J.M. (1980) Persistent school non-attendance, in Harbinson, J. and Harbison, J. (eds) *A Society Under Stress: Children and Young People in Northern Ireland*, London, Open Books.

Chazan, M. (1970) *The Psychological Assessment of Mental and Physical Handicaps*, London, Methuen.

Chomsky, N. (1968) *Language and Mind*, New York, Harcourt.

Clarke, D.D., Parry-Jones, W., Gay, B.M. and Smith, C.M.B. (1981) Disruptive incidents in secondary school classrooms: a sequence analysis approach, *Oxford Review of Education*, 7, 111/17.

Clegg, A. and Megson, B. (1973) *Children in Distress*, London, Penguin Education.

Cockroft Report (1982) *Mathematics Counts*, London, HMSO.

Cohen, L. (1976) *Educational Research in Classrooms and Schools*, London, Harper & Row.

Comber, L.C. and Whitfield, R.C. (1979) *Action on Indiscipline: A Practical Guide for Teachers*, NAS/UWT in association with the Dept. of Educational Enquiry, University of Aston.

Corrigan, P. (1979) *Schooling the Smash Street Kids*, London, Macmillan Press Ltd.

Court Committee (1976) *Fit for the Future*, London, DHSS.

Covill, N., Martin, F., Taylor, J. and Tyson, M. (1984) Implications from extreme histories, in Frude, N. and Gault, H. (eds) *Disruptive Behaviour in Schools*, Chichester, John Wiley.

Cox, T. (1977) The nature and management of stress in schools, in *The Management of Stress in Schools* (Education Department, Conference Report), Mold, Clwyd County Council.

CRC (1980) *Child Guidance Service: Report 1977–1979*, Central Regional Council, Education Department.

Davie, R. (1972) Absence from school, *Education Guardian*, 12 September.

Davie, R. (1977) The interface between education and social services, in Kahan, B. (ed.) *Working Together for Children and Their Families*, DHSS/Welsh Office, HMSO.

Davie, R. (1980) Promoting school adjustment, in Pringle, M. K. (ed.) *A Fairer Future for Children*, London, Macmillan.

Davie, R., Butler, N. and Goldstein, H. (1972) *From Birth to Seven*, London, Longman in association with the National Children's Bureau.

Davie, R. et al (1983) Seven answers to Professor Wall and Professor Tizard, *London Educational Review*, 2, 2, 38/60.

Davies, B. (1976) Relations between social worker and teacher, *Social Worker Today*, 8, 8, 9/11.

Davies, B. (1977) Agency collaboration or worker control? Alternative models for more integrated services to young people, *Youth in Society*, 22, 3/6.

Davies, C. (1980) Disruptive pupils in secondary schools, *Links*, 5, 3, 10/18.

Davies, G. (1982) Newlands Centre, Baseline, *Journal of the Birmingham Association of Social Education Centres*, 2, 19/20.

Davies, L. F. (1976) Education welfare: the patchwork service, *Community Care*, 98, 16/17. See also: *Ideas*, 32, 72/6.

Davis, L. F. (1977) *Children Excluded From School: The Results of a Survey*, British Association of Social Workers and Association of Directors of Social Services.

Delamont, S. (1976) *Interaction in the Classroom*, London, Methuen.

Delamont, S. (1980) *Sex Roles and The School*, London, Methuen.

DES (1975a) *Survey of Absence from Secondary and Middle Schools in England and Wales on Thursday 17 January, 1974*, London, Dept. of Education and Science.

DES (1975b) *Survey of Violence, Indiscipline and Vandalism in Schools*, London, Dept. of Education and Science.

DES (1977) *Ten Good Schools: A Secondary School Enquiry*, carried out by HMI, London, Dept. of Education and Science.

DES (1978) Special educational needs: *Report of the Committee of*

Enquiry into the Education of Handicapped Children and Young People (The Warnock Report), Dept. of Education and Science/Welsh Office/Scottish Office, London, HMSO.

DES (1979) *Aspects of Secondary Education in England: A Survey of HM Inspectors of Schools*, London, HMSO.

DES (1981) *The School Curriculum*, London, HMSO.

DES (1982) *The New Teacher in School*, London, Dept. of Education and Science.

Dierenfield, R. (1982) All you need to know about disruption, *Times Educational Supplement*, 29 January, 1982, 72.

Docking, J. W. (1980) *Control and Discipline in Schools: Perspectives and Approaches*, London, Harper & Row.

Douglas, J. W. B. (1964) *The Home and the School*, London, MacGibbon & Kee.

Douglas, J. W. B. and Ross, J. M. (1965) The effects of absence on primary school performance, *British Journal of Educational Psychology*, 35, 28/40.

Drinkwater, C. (1981) School by beginners, *New Society*, 57, 982, 428.

Dunham, J. (1977) The effects of disruptive behaviour on teachers, *Educational Review*, 29, 3, 181/7. See also: *Educational Research*, 23, 3, 205/13.

Edmonds, R. et al (1978) *Search for Effective Schools*, Cambridge, Massachusetts, Harvard University, Centre for Urban Schools.

Erikson, E. (1963) *Childhood and Society*, New York, Norton.

Farrington, D. (1978) The family backgrounds of aggressive youths, in Hersov, L. A. and Berger, M. (eds) *Aggression and Anti-Social Behaviour in Childhood and Adolescence*, Oxford, Pergamon.

Fawcett, R. (1979) The educational psychologist and child guidance, *Journal of the Association of Educational Psychologists*, 5, 1, 8/11.

Feldhusen, J. F., Thurston, J. R. and Benning, J. T. (1973) A longitudinal study of delinquency and other aspects of children's behaviour, *International Journal of Criminology and Penology*, 1, 341/51.

Feldhusen, J. F., Roeser, T. D. and Thurston, J. R. (1977) Prediction of social adjustment over a period of 6 or 9 years, *Journal of Special Education*, 11, 29/36.

Fitzherbert, K. (1977) *Child Care Services and the Teacher*, London, Temple Smith.

Fogelman, K. (ed.) (1976) *Britain's Sixteen-Year-Olds*, London, National Children's Bureau.

Fogelman, K. and Richardson, K. (1974) School attendance: some results from the National Child Development Study, in Turner, B. (ed.) *Truancy*, London, Ward Lock Educational.

Fogelman, K., Tibbenham, A. and Essen, J. (1978) Patterns of attainment, *Educational Studies*, 4, 2, 121/30.

Fogelman, K., Tibbenham, A. and Lambert, L. (1980) Absence from school: findings from the National Child Development Study, in Hersov, L. and Berg, I. (eds) *Out of School*, Chichester, John Wiley.

Francis, P. (1975) *Beyond Control? A Study of Discipline in the Comprehensive School*, London, Allen & Unwin.

Frude, N. (1984) Framework for analysis, in Frude, N. and Gault, H. (eds) *Disruptive Behaviour in Schools*, Chichester, John Wiley.

Frude, N. and Gault, H. (eds) (1984) *Disruptive Behaviour in Schools*, Chichester, John Wiley. See also: Children's disruption at school: cause for concern, Chapter 1 in *ibid*.

Galloway, D. (1976a) Size of school, socio-economic hardship, suspension rates and persistent unjustified absence from school, *British Journal of Educational Psychology*, 46, 1, 40/7.

Galloway, D. (1976b) Persistent unjustified absence from school, *Trends in Education*, 4, 22/7.

Galloway, D. (1980) Problems in the assessment and management of persistent absence from school, in Hersov, L. and Berg, I. (eds) *Out of School*, Chichester, John Wiley.

Galloway, D. (1981) *Teaching and Counselling*, London, Longman. See also: Galloway, D. (1981) Institutional change or individual change? An overview, in Gillham, B. (ed.) *Problem Behaviour in the Secondary School*, London, Croom Helm.

Galloway, D. and Goodwin, J. (1979) *Educating Slow-Learning and Maladjusted Children: Integration or Segregation*, London, Longman.

Galloway, D., Ball, T. and Seyd, R. (1981a) Administrative and legal procedures available to local education authorities in cases of poor school attendance, *Durham and Newcastle Review*, 9, 46, 201/9.

Galloway, D., Ball, C. and Seyd, R. (1981b) The selection of parents and children for legal action in connection with unauthorised absence from school, *British Journal of Social Work*, 11, 4, 445/61. See also: Galloway, D., Ball, T. and Seyd, R. (1981), School attendance following legal or administrative action for unauthorised absence, *Educational Review*, 33, 1, 53/65.

Galloway, D., Ball, C. and Seyd, R. (1981c) Some implications for social workers of recent research on poor school attendance, *Social Work Today*, 12, 33, 15/17.

Galloway, D., Ball, T., Blomfield, D. and Seyd, R. (1982) *Schools and Disruptive Pupils*, London, Longman.

Galton, M., Simon, B. and Croll, P. (1980) *Inside the Primary School*, London, Routledge & Kegan Paul.

Galton, M. and Willcocks, J. (1983) *Moving From the Primary Classroom*, London, Routledge & Kegan Paul.

Gath, D., Cooper, B. and Gattoni, F. (1972) Child guidance and delinquency in a London borough, *Psychological Medicine*, 2, 185/91. See also: Gath, D., Cooper, B., Gattoni, F. and Rockett, D. (1977) *Child*

Guidance and Delinquency in a London Borough, Oxford, Oxford University Press.

Geddes, D. (1982) Series of articles on disruption in schools, *The Times*, 2–5 March, 1982.

Giller, H. and Morris, A. (1981) *Care and Discretion: Social Workers' Decisions With Delinquents*, London, Burnett Books.

Gillham, B. (1978) The failure of psychometrics, in Gillham, B. (ed.) *Reconstructuring Educational Psychology*, London, Croom Helm.

Gillham, B. (ed.) (1981) *Problem Behaviour in the Secondary School*, London, Croom Helm.

Gillham, B. (1984) School organization and the control of disruptive incidents, in Frude, N. and Gault, H. (eds) *Disruptive Behaviour in Schools*, Chichester, John Wiley.

Goldstein, H. (1980) Fifteen thousand hours: a review of the statistical procedures, *Journal of Child Psychology and Psychiatry*, 21, 364/6.

Graham, P. and Rutter, M. (1968) The reliability and validity of the psychiatric study of the child: II interview with the parent, *British Journal of Psychiatry*, 114, 581/92. See also: *British Medical Journal*, 3, 695/700.

Gray, G., Smith, A. and Rutter, M. (1980) School attendance and the first year of employment, in Hersov, L. and Berg, I. (eds) *Out of School*, Chichester, John Wiley.

Gray, J., McPherson, A. and Raffe, D. (1983) *Reconstructions of Secondary Education*, London, Routledge & Kegan Paul.

Green, F. L. (1980) Becoming a truant: the social administrative process applied to pupils absent from school, *Unpublished M.Sc. Thesis*, Cranfield Institute of Technology.

Gregory, R. P. et al (1981) *An Evaluation of the Effectiveness of Home Visits by an Education Welfare Officer in Treating School Attendance Problems*, Birmingham, City of Birmingham Education Dept.

Gross, N., Giacquinta, J. B. and Bernstein, M. (1971) *Implementing Organizational Innovations: A Sociological Analysis of Planned Educational Change*, New York, Harper & Row.

Grunsell, R. (1978) *Beyond Control? Schools and Suspension*, London, Writers and Readers.

Grunsell, R. (1980) *Absent from School: The Story of a Truancy Centre*, London, Writers and Readers.

Haigh, G. (ed.) (1979) *On Our Side, Order, Authority and Interaction in School*, London, Temple Smith.

Halsey, A. H., Heath, A. F. and Ridge, J. M. (1980) *Origins and Destinations*, Oxford, Oxford University Press.

Hamblin, D. H. (1978) *The Teacher and Pastoral Care*, Oxford, Basil Blackwell.

Hamblin, D. H. (1986) The failure of pastoral care, in Reid, K. (ed.) special edition of *School Organization*, 6, 1, forthcoming, on Improving Secondary School Management in an Era of Change.

Hansard (1975) cited in Tattum, D. (1982) *Disruptive Pupils in Schools and Units*, Chichester, John Wiley.

Hargreaves, D.H. (1967) *Social Relations in a Secondary School*, London, Routledge & Kegan Paul.

Hargreaves, D.H. (1980) Classrooms, schools and juvenile delinquency, *Educational Analysis*, 2, 2, 75/87.

Hargreaves, D.H. (1982) *The Challenge for the Comprehensive School*, London, Routledge & Kegan Paul.

Hargreaves, D.H. (1984) *Improving Secondary Schools*, Report of the Committee on the Curriculum and Organisation of Secondary Schools, London, ILEA.

Hargreaves, D.H., Hester, S.K. and Mellor, F.J. (1975) *Deviance in Classrooms*, London, Routledge & Kegan Paul.

Harrop, A. (1984) *Behaviour Modification in the Classroom*, London, Hodder & Stoughton Unibooks.

Hartshorn, D.J. (1983) Children and video – films at home, *Educational Studies*, 9, 3, 145/50.

Hastings, D.J. (1981) One schools's experience, in Gillham, B. (ed.) *Problem Behaviour in the Secondary School*, London, Croom Helm.

Her Majesty's Inspectorate (1977a) *Ten Good Schools: A Secondary School Enquiry*, London, HMSO.

Her Majesty's Inspectorate (1977b) *Curriculum 11–16: The Red Book*, London, Dept. of Education and Science.

Her Majesty's Inspectorate (1978) *Truancy and Behaviour Problems in Some Urban Schools*, London, Dept. of Education and Science.

Her Majesty's Inspectorate (1979) *Aspects of Secondary Education in England*, London, HMSO.

Her Majesty's Inspectorate (1980) *A View of the Curriculum*, London, Dept. of Education and Science.

Her Majesty's Inspectorate (1981) *Curriculum 11–16: A Review of Progress*, London, Dept. of Education and Science.

HMSO (1980, 1981b) *Mathematical Development: Primary Survey Reports Nos 1 and 2*: Assessment of Performance Unit, London, HMSO.

HMSO (1981a) West Indian children in our schools: *Interim Report of the Committee of Inquiry into the education of children from ethnic minority groups*, London, HMSO.

Hooper, R. (1978) Pupil perceptions of counselling: a response to Murgatroyd, *British Journal of Guidance and Counselling*, 6, 2, 198/203.

Hopkins, D. (1985) *Doing Teacher Based Research*, Milton Keynes, Open University Press.

Hopkins, D. and Reid, K. (eds) (1985) *Rethinking Teacher Education*, London, Croom Helm.

Hopkins, D. and Wideen, M. (eds) *Alternative Perspectives on School Improvement*, Lewes, Falmer Press.

Humphries, S. (1981) *Hooligans or Rebels? An Oral History of Working Class Childhood and Youth, 1889–1939*, Oxford, Basil Blackwell.

ILEA (1976) *Attendance at School*, Inner London Education Authority Schools Sub-Committee, Document, ILEA 528, ILEA.

ILEA (1977) *Keeping the School Under Review*, London, ILEA, First Version.

ILEA (1980) *Non-Attendance at School: Some Research Findings*, Inner London Education Authority Research and Statistics Branch, Document RS 760/80, ILEA. See also: Document 753/80, Attendance Survey, 1980.

ILEA (1981a) *Attendance Survey, 1981*. Inner London Education Authority Research and Statistics Branch, Document RS 791/81 ILEA.

ILEA (1981b) *Principles of Curriculum Planning: ILEA Statement on the Curriculum for Pupils Aged 5–16*, London, ILEA.

ILEA (1982) *Keeping the School Under Review*, London, ILEA, Second Version.

ILEA (1983) *Effective Learning Skills*, Learning Resources Branch, London, ILEA.

Insell, P. and Jacobson, L. (1975) *What Do You Expect?*, California, Cummings Publishing Company.

Jencks, C. et al (1972) *Inequality: A Reassessment of the Effect of Family and Schooling in America*, New York, Basic Books.

Jennings, R. (1980) The suspension of pupils from school: an aspect of juvenile justice? *Howard Journal*, 19, 3, 156/65.

Johnson, D., Ransom, E., Packwood, T., Bowden, K. and Kogan, M. (1980) *Secondary Schools and the Welfare Network*, London, Allen & Unwin.

Jones, A. (1980) The school's view of persistent non-attendance, in Hersov, L. and Berg, I. (eds) *Out of School*, Chichester, John Wiley.

Jones, A. (1981) Pastoral care and guidance, *Secondary Education Journal*, 12, 3, 18/20.

Jones, A. R. and Forrest, R. (1977) *A Continuing Approach: Fairfax House and Group 4 at Sidney Stringer School*, Coventry, Sidney Stringer School and Community College.

Jones, D. (1976) Bunking off, *Teaching London Kids*, 5, 3/8.

Kahan, B. (ed.) (1977) *Working Together for Children and Their Families*, DHSS/Welsh Office, HMSO.

Kamin, L. J. (1974) *The Science and Politics of I.Q.*, Harmondsworth, Penguin.

Kelly, G. (1955) *The Psychology of Personal Constructs*, 2 vols., New York, Norton.

Knutton, S. and Mycroft, A. (1986) Stress and the deputy head, in Reid, K. (ed.) special edition of *School Organization*, 6, 1, forthcoming, on Improving Secondary School Management in an Era of Change.

Kounin, J. S., Friesen, W. V. and Norton, E. (1966) Managing emotionally disturbed children in regular classrooms, *Journal of Educational Psychology*, 57, 1/13. See also: Kounin, J. S. (1970) *Discipline and Group Management in Classrooms*, New York, Holt, Rinehart & Winston.

Kyriacou, C. and Sutcliffe, J. (1978) Teacher stress: prevalence, sources and symptoms, *British Journal of Educational Psychology*, 48, 159/67.

Labow, W. (1975) Academic ignorance and black intelligence, in Insell, P. and Jacobson, L. (eds) *What Do You Expect?*, California, Cummings Publishing Company.

Lacey, C. (1970) *Hightown Grammar*, Manchester, Manchester University Press.

Lacey, C. (1977) *The Socialization of Teachers*, London, Methuen.

Laslett, R. (1977) Disruptive and violent pupils; the facts and the fallacies, *Educational Review*, 29, 3, 152/62.

Laufer, M. (1974) Criteria for treatment in adolescence, *Journal of Association of Workers for Maladjusted Children*, 2, 2.

Lawrence, J. (1980) *Exploring Techniques for Coping with Disruptive Behaviour in Schools*, University of London, Goldsmiths' College Educational Studies Monograph.

Lawrence, J., Steed, D. and Young, P. with Hilton, G. (1981) *Dialogue on Disruptive Behaviour: A Study of a Secondary School*, London, PJP Press.

Lawrence, J., Steed, D. and Young, P. (1977) *Disruptive Behaviour in a Secondary School*, An Educational Studies Monograph, London, Goldsmiths' College.

Lawrence, J., Steed, D. and Young, P. (1984) *Disruptive Children – Disruptive Schools?*, London, Croom Helm.

Lewis, D. G. and Murgatroyd, S. (1976) The professionalisation of counselling in education and its legal implications, *British Journal of Guidance and Counselling*, 4, 1, 2/15.

Liverpool (1974) *The Suspended Child*, Liverpool Education Committee, Teachers' Advisory Committee, Liverpool Education Committee.

Longworth-Dames, S. M. (1977) The relationship of personality and behaviour to school exclusion, *Educational Review*, 29, 3, 163/77.

Lortie, D. C. (1975) *Schoolteacher: A Sociological Study*, Chicago, University of Chicago Press.

Lowenstein, L. F. (1972) *Violence in Schools and its Treatment*, Hemel Hempstead, National Association of Schoolmasters.

Lowenstein, L. F. (1975) *Violent and Disruptive Behaviour in Schools*, Hemel Hempstead, National Association of Schoolmasters.

MacMillan, K. (1977) *Education Welfare: Strategy and Structure*, London, Longman.

MacMillan, D. L. and Morrison, G. M. (1979) Education programming, in Quay, H. C. and Werry, J. C. (eds) *Psychopathological Disorders of Childhood*, 2nd edn, New York, Wiley.

McNamara, D. (1975) Distribution and incidence of problem children in an English county, quoted in Laslett, R. (1977) Disruptive and violent pupils: the facts and the fallacies, *Educational Review*, 29, 3, 152/62.

Madaus, G. F. (1980) *School Effectiveness*, New York, McGraw-Hill.

Marsh, P., Rosser, E. and Harré, R. (1978) *The Rules of Disorder*, London, Routledge & Kegan Paul.

Marshall, M. (1981) *Burleigh College's Tutor-Mother Scheme for Students with Learning Difficulties*, Leicester, Burleigh Community College.

Marshall, T. F. and Rose, G. (1975) An experimental evaluation of school social work, *British Journal of Guidance and Counselling*, 3, 1, 2/14. See also: Rose, G. and Marshall, T. F. (1974) *Counselling and School Social Work*, Chichester, John Wiley.

Martin, F. M., Fox, S. J., and Murray, K. (1981) *Children Out of Court*, Edinburgh, Scottish Academic Press.

May, D. (1975) Truancy, school absenteeism and delinquency, *Scottish Educational Studies*, 7, 2, 97/106.

Mays, J. D. (ed) (1972) *Juvenile Delinquency, the Family and the Local Group*, London, Longman.

Mead, S. and Mead, D. (1975) Treatment opportunities in child guidance clinics, *Social Work Today*, 5, 24, 734/40.

Miller, W. B. (1958) Lower class life as a generating milieu of gang delinquency, *Journal of Social Issues*, XIV, 3, 5/19.

Millham, S. (1977) Violence in residential child care establishments, *Concern*, No. 25, Journal of the National Children's Bureau.

Millham, S. (1981) Children in trouble. *Paper Presented at All-Party Parliamentary Group for Children*, meeting of 6 May 1981, All-Party Parliamentary Group for Children.

Mills, W. P. C. (1976) The seriously disruptive behaviour of pupils in secondary schools of one local education authority, *Unpublished M.Ed. Thesis, Birmingham University*.

Milner, J. (1982) Out of bounds, *Social Work Today*, 13, 32, 16/17.

Ministry of Education (1945) *The Handicapped Pupils and School Health Service Regulations* (S.R. and O. No. 1076), London, HMSO.

Mitchell, S. and Shepherd, M. (1966) A comparative study of children's behaviour at home and at school, *British Journal of Educational Psychology*, 37, 1, 32/40.

Mitchell, S. and Shepherd, M. (1967) The child who dislikes going to school, *British Journal of Educational Psychology*, 37, 1, 32/40.

Mitchell, S. and Shepherd, M. (1980) *Persistent School Abenteeism in Northern Ireland*, Department of Education, Northern Ireland.

Moore, G. and Jardine, E. (1983) *Persistent School Absenteeism in*

Northern Ireland, Department of Education, Northern Ireland.

Mortimore, J. and Blackstone, T. (1982) *Disadvantage and Education*, London, Heinemann Educational.

Mortimore, P. (1982) Underachievement: a framework for debate, *Secondary Education Journal*, 12, 3, 3/6.

Mortimore, P., Davies, J., Varlaam, A., West, A., Devine, P. and Mazza, J. (1983) *Behaviour Problems in Schools: An Evaluation of Support Centres*, London, Croom Helm.

Mortimore, P. and Mortimore, J. (1981) Making the most of the nightschool shift!, *The Guardian*, 7 April 1981.

Mortimore, P. and team (1985) The ILEA Junior School Study: An Introduction, in Reynolds, D. (ed.) *Studying School Effectiveness*, Lewes, Falmer Press.

Murgatroyd, S. J. (ed.) (1977) Pupil perceptions of counselling: a case study, *British Journal of Guidance and Counselling*, 5, 1, 73/8.

Murgatroyd, S. J. (1980a) *Helping the Troubled Child*, London, Harper & Row.

Murgatroyd, S. J. (1980b) cited by Reynolds, D., Jones, D., St. Leger, S. and Murgatroyd, S. J., in School factors and truancy, in Hersov, L. and Berg, I. *Out of School*, Chichester, John Wiley.

Murphy, J. (1981) Class inequality in education: two justifications, one evaluation but no hard evidence, *British Journal of Sociology*, 32, 2, 182/201.

Nash, R. (1976) *Teacher Expectations and Pupil Learning*, London, Routledge & Kegan Paul.

National Association of Chief Education Welfare Officers (1975) These we serve. *The Report of a Working Party Set up to Enquire into the Cause of Absence From School*, Bedford, National Association of Chief Education Welfare Officers.

NAS/UWT (1978) *Discipline in Schools*, Hemel Hempstead, National Association of Schoolmasters and Union of Women Teachers.

NAS/UWT (1981) *Discipline or Disorder in Schools – A Disturbing Choice*, Hemel Hempstead, National Association of Schoolmasters and Union of Women Teachers.

National Education Association (1979) Teacher opinion polls, 1978/79, *The Weekly Educational Review*, 9 August 1979.

National Institute of Education (1977) *Violent Schools – Safe Schools*, Washington, DC, US Department of Health, Education and Welfare.

NUT (1976) *Discipline in Schools*, London, National Union of Teachers.

Newsom, J. and Newsom, E. (1984) Parents' perspectives on children's behaviour at school, in Frude, N. and Gault, H. (eds) *Disruptive Behaviour in Schools*, Chichester, John Wiley.

Newsom, J. and Newsom, E. (1985) *Childhood into Adolescence*, London, Allen & Unwin.

Olweus, D. (1978) *Aggression in the Schools: Bullies and Whipping Boys*,

Washington, DC, Hemisphere.

Olweus, D. (1984) Aggressors and their victims: bullying at school, in Frude, N. and Gault, H. (eds) *Disruptive Behaviour in Schools*, Chichester, John Wiley.

Ouston, J. (1981) Differences between schools: the implications for school practice, in Gillham, B. (ed.) *Problem Behaviour in the Secondary School*, London, Croom Helm.

Palfrey, C. F. (1979) The Argyle Street Project, *Community Home Schools Gazette*, 73, 202/12.

Parry, K. (1976) Disruptive children in school: the view of a class teacher and head of house, in Jones-Davies, C. and Cave, R. (eds) *The Disruptive Pupils in the Secondary School*, London, Ward Lock Educational.

Parry-Jones, W. and Gay, B. (1984) Disruptive incidents: causes and control in the secondary-school classroom, in Frude, N. and Gault, H. (eds) *Disruptive Behaviour in Schools*, Chichester, John Wiley.

Patrick, H., Bernbaum, G. and Reid, K. (1982) *The Structure and Process of Initial Teacher Education Within Universities in England and Wales*, Report, Leicester School of Education, University of Leicester.

Pedley, F. (1975) Beyond the truant, *New Society*, 31, 650, 723/4.

Phillips, D. (1978) *The Children We Fail*, London, the author. Available from 260 Wendover, Thurlow Street, London SE17 2UW.

Phillips, D. and Callely, E. (1981) Pupils' views of comprehensive schools or 'what do they think of it so far?' *Links*, 7, 1, 32/6.

Phillips, D., Davie, R. and Callely, E. (1985) Pathways to institutional development in secondary schools, in Reynolds, D. (ed.) *Studying School Effectiveness*, Lewes, Falmer Press.

Pik, R. (1981) Confrontation situations and teacher-support systems, in Gillham, B. (ed) *Problem Behaviour in the Secondary School*, London, Croom Helm.

Pollard, A. (1980) Teacher interests and changing situations of survival threat in primary school classrooms, in Woods, P. (ed.) *Pupil Strategies: Explorations in the Sociology of the School*, London, Croom Helm.

Power, M. J., Alderson, M. R., Phillipson, C. M., Schoenberg, E. and Morris, J. N. (1967) Delinquent schools? *New Society* 10, 264,542/3.

Power, M. J., Benn, R. T. and Morris, J. N. (1972) Neighbourhood, school and juveniles before the courts, *British Journal of Criminology*, 12, 111/32.

Pringle, M. L. K., Butler, N. and Davie, R. (1966) *11,000 Seven-Year-Olds*, London, Longman.

Ralphs, L. (1974) *The Role and Training of Education Welfare Officers*, Ralphs, L. chairman. Report, Local Government Training Board, HMSO.

Ravenette, A. T. (1972) Psychologists, teachers and children: how many ways to understand, *Journal of the Association of Educational Psychologists*, 3, 2, 41/7.

Raymond, J. (1982) How form tutors perceive their role, *Links*, 7, 3, 25/30.

Regan, D. (1977) *Local Government and Education*, London, Allen & Unwin.

Registrar General (1966) *Classification of Occupations*, London, HMSO.

Reid, K. (1981) Alienation and persistent school absenteeism, *Research in Education*, 26, 31/40.

Reid, K. (1982a) The self-concept and persistent school absenteeism, *British Journal of Educational Psychology*, 52, 2, 179/187.

Reid, K. (1982b) Case studies and persistent school absenteeism, *The Counsellor*, 3, 5, 25/30.

Reid, K. (1982c) Absent, Sir, *Social Work Today*, 13, 42, 12/13.

Reid, K. (1982d) School organization and persistent school absenteeism: an introduction to a complex problem, *School Organization*, 2, 1, 45/52.

Reid, K. (1982e) Persistent school absenteeism, *Westminster Studies in Education*, 5, 27/35.

Reid, K. (1983a) Institutional factors and persistent school absenteeism. *Journal of Educational Management and Administration*, 11, 17/27.

Reid, K. (1983b) Retrospection and persistent school absenteeism, *Educational Research*, 25, 2, 110/15.

Reid, K. (1983c) Differences between the perception of persistent absentees towards parents and teachers, *Educational Studies*, 9, 3, 211/19.

Reid, K. (1983d) The Management of decline: a discussion paper, *School Organization*, 3, 4, 361/70.

Reid, K. (1984a) Some social, psychological and educational aspects related to persistent school absenteeism, *Research in Education* 31, 63/82.

Reid, K. (1984b) The behaviour of persistent school absentees, *British Journal of Educational Psychology*, 54, 320/330.

Reid, K. (1984c) Disruptive behaviour and persistent school absenteeism, in Frude, N. and Gault, H. (eds) *Disruptive Behaviour in Schools*, Chichester, John Wiley.

Reid, K. (1984d) More than a matter of opinion, *Times Educational Supplement*, 5 October 1984, p. 4.

Reid, K. (1985a) *Truancy and School Absenteeism*, London, Hodder & Stoughton.

Reid, K. (1985b) *The West Glamorgan Teacher Fellowship Scheme: Leadership in the Primary School*, Swansea, West Glamorgan Institute of Higher Education, Faculty of Education.

Reid, K. (1985c) Teachers are not to blame, *South Wales Evening Post*, special article, April 1985

Reid, K. and Avalos, B. (1980) Differences between the views of teachers and students to aspects of sixth form organization at three contrasting comprehensive schools in South Wales, *Educational Studies*, 6, 3,

225/239. See also: Avalos, B. and Reid, K. (1981) Differences between graduate and non-graduate teachers to teaching sixth forms at three comprehensive schools in South Wales, *Durham and Newcastle Research Review*, IX, 46, 186/194.

Reid, K., Bernbaum, G. and Patrick, H. (1981a) Future research issues in teacher education, *Educational Review*, 33, 2, 143/150. Special edition on teacher education for the 1990s.

Reid, K., Bernbaum, G. and Patrick, H. (1981b) On course: students and the PGCE, *Unpublished Paper Presented at UCET Annual Conference, Oxford*, November 1981. See also: Bernbaum, G., Patrick, H. and Reid, K. (1985) The structure and process of initial teacher education within universities in England and Wales, in Hopkins, D. and Reid, K. (eds) *Rethinking Teacher Education*, London, Croom Helm, *and* Patrick, H., Bernbaum, G. and Reid, K. (1982) The structure and process of initial teacher education within universities in England and Wales, *Unpublished Report of DES Sponsored Project*, School of Education, University of Leicester.

Reid, K. and Kendall, L. (1982) A review of some recent research into persistent school absenteeism, *British Journal of Educational Studies*, XXX, 3, 295/314.

Reid, P. and Reid, K. (1982) Porn in a wider game, *Times Educational Supplement*, 3503, 4.

Reynolds, D. (1975) When teachers and pupils refuse a truce: the secondary school and the creation of delinquency, in Mungham, G. and Pearson, G. (eds) *Working Class Youth Culture*, London, Routledge & Kegan Paul.

Reynolds, D. (ed.) (1982) Towards more effective schooling. Special issue of the journal *School Organization*, 2, 3. See also: A state of ignorance, *Education for Development*, 7, 2, 4/35.

Reynolds, D. (1982b) The Welsh experience, *Secondary Education Journal*, 12, 3, 24/26.

Reynolds, D. (1984) The school for vandals: a sociological portrait of a disaffection-prone school, in Frude, N. and Gault, H. (eds) *Disruptive Behaviour in Schools*, Chichester, John Wiley.

Reynolds, D. (ed.) (1985) *Studying School Effectiveness*, Lewes, Falmer Press.

Reynolds, D. and Murgatroyd, S. (1977) The sociology of schooling and the absent pupil: the school as a factor in the generation of truancy, in Carroll, H.C.M. (ed.) *Absenteeism in South Wales*, University College of Swansea, Faculty of Education.

Reynolds, D. and Murgatroyd, S. (1981) Schooled for failure, *Times Educational Supplement*, 4 December 1981.

Reynolds, D. and Reid, K. (1985) The second stage – towards a reconceptualisation of theory and methodology in school effectiveness studies, in Reynolds, D. (ed.) *Studying School Effectiveness*, Lewes, Falmer Press.

Reynolds, D. and Sullivan, M. (1981) Bringing schools back in, in Barton, L.A. (ed.) *Schools, Pupils and Deviance*, London, Nafferton Books.

Reynolds, D., Jones, D. and St. Leger, S. (1976) Schools do make a difference, *New Society*, 37, 721, 223/5.

Reynolds, D., Jones, D., St. Leger, S. and Murgatroyd, S. (1980) School factors and truancy, in Hersov, L. and Berg, I. *Out of School*, Chichester, John Wiley.

Rist, R. (1974) Student social class and teacher expectations, in Insell, P. and Jacobson, L. (eds) (1975) *What Do You Expect?*, California, Cummings Publishing Company.

Robinson, T. J. (1974) Safe haven for truants, *Community Care*, 9, 10/12.

Rosenshine, B. (1978) *Instructional Principles in Direct Instruction*, Illinois, University of Illinois.

Rosenthal, R. (1975) Forward to what do you expect?, in Insell, P. and Jacobson, L. (eds) *What Do You Expect?*, California, Cummings Publishing Company.

Rosenthal, R. and Jacobson, L. (1968) *Pygmalion in the Classroom*, New York, Holt, Rinehart & Winston.

Rosser, E. and Harré, R. (1976) The meaning of disorder, in Hammersley, M. and Woods, P. (eds) *The Process of Schooling*, London, Routledge & Kegan Paul.

Roxburgh, J. M. (1972) *The School Board in Glasgow, 1873/1913*, Edinburgh, Edinburgh University Press.

Rubinstein, D. (1968) *School Attendance in London, 1870–1904*, Hull, Hull University Press.

Rutter, M. (1967) A children's behaviour questionnaire for completion by teachers: preliminary findings, *Journal of Child Psychology and Psychiatry*, 8, 1–11.

Rutter, M. (1975) *Helping Troubled Children*, Harmondsworth, Penguin.

Rutter, M. (1979) *Changing Youth in a Changing Society*, London, Nuffield Provincial Hospitals Trust.

Rutter, M. (1983) School effects on pupil progress, *Child Development*, 54, 1, 1–29.

Rutter, M. and Graham, P (1968) The reliability and validity of the psychiatric assessment of the child, *British Journal of Psychiatry*, 114, 563/79.

Rutter, M. and Quinton, D. (1977) Psychiatric disorder – ecological factors and concepts of causation, in McGuik, H. (ed) *Ecological Factors in Human Development*, Amsterdam, North Holland.

Rutter, M., Tizard, J. and Whitmore, K. (eds) (1970) *Education, Health and Behaviour*, London, Longman.

Rutter, M., Yule, W., Berger, M., Yule, B., Morton, J. and Bagley, C.

(1974) Children of West Indian immigrants: 1. Rates of behavioural disturbance and of psychiatric disorder, *Journal of Child Psychology and Psychiatry*, 15, 241/62.

Rutter, M., Cox, A., Tupling, C., Berger, M. and Yule, W. (1975a) Attainment and adjustment in two geographical areas: I. The prevalence of psychiatric disorders, *British Journal of Psychiatry*, 126, 493/509.

Rutter, M., Yule, B., Quinton, D., Rowlands, O., Yule, W. and Berger, M. (1975b) Attainment and adjustment in two geographical areas: III. Some factors accounting for area differences, *British Journal of Psychiatry*, 126, 520/33.

Rutter, M., Yule, B., Morton, J. and Bagley, C. (1975c) Children of West Indian immigrants: III. Home circumstances and family patterns, *Journal of Child Psychology and Psychiatry*, 16, 105/23.

Rutter, M., Graham, P., Chadwick, O. F. D. and Yule, W. (1976) Adolescent turmoil: fact or fiction, *Journal of Child Psychology and Psychiatry*, 17, 35/56.

Rutter, M., Maughan, B., Mortimore, P. and Ouston, J. (1979) *Fifteen Thousand Hours*, London, Open Books.

Sandon, F. (1961) Attendance through the school year, *Educational Research*, 3, 153/6.

Saunders, M. (1979) *Class Control and Behaviour Problems*, Maidenhead, McGraw-Hill.

Schein, E.H. (1980) *Organizational Psychology* (3rd edn), Englewood Cliffs, NJ, Prentice-Hall.

Schools Council (1973) *Cross'd with Adversity: The Education of Socially Disadvantaged Children in Secondary Schools*, London, Evans/Methuen Educational.

Schools Council (1981) *The Practical Curriculum*, London, Schools Council.

Scottish Education Department (1977) *Truancy and Indiscipline in Scotland*, The Pack Report, Edinburgh, Scottish Education Department.

Seabrook, J. (1974) Talking to Truants, in Turner, B. (ed.) *Truancy*, London Ward Lock Educational.

Sharp, A. (1981) The significance of classroom dissent, *Scottish Educational Review*, 13, 2, 141/51.

Shepherd, M., Oppenheim, B. and Mitchell, S. (1971) *Childhood Behaviour and Mental Health*, London, University of London Press Ltd.

Shostak, J. (1982) Black side of school, *Times Educational Supplement*, 25 June 1982, 23.

Sidaway, N.D. (1976) *No Small Change*, Carlisle, Cumbria County Council.

Skinner, A., Platts, H. and Hill, B. (1983) *Disaffection From School: Issues and Interagency Responses*, Leicester, National Youth Bureau.

Stott, D. H. (1960) Delinquency, maladjustment and unfavourable ecology, *British Journal of Psychology*, vol. 51, Part 2.

Stott, D. H. (1963) *The Social Adjustment of Children*, London, London University Press.

Stott, D. H. (1971) *The Social Adjustment of Children: Manual To The Bristol Social Adjustment Guides*, 2nd edn, London, London University Press.

Strathclyde (1977) *Report on School Attendance*, Strathclyde Regional Council Department of Education, Strathclyde Regional Council.

Stubbs, M. and Delamont, S. (1976) *Explorations in Classroom Observation*, Chichester, John Wiley.

Sullivan, R. and Riches, S. (1976) On your marks: interviews with truants in East London, *Youth Social Work Bulletin*, 3, 5, 8/10.

Tattum, D. (1982) *Disruptive Pupils in Schools and Units*, Chichester, John Wiley.

Taylor, F. (1980) Suspension, ACE Information Sheet, *Where*, 154, 23/5.

Taylor, L., Lacey, R. and Bracken, D. (1979) *In Whose Best Interests? The Unjust Treatment of Children in Courts and Institutions*, London, The Cobden Trust/MIND.

Taylor, M. (1981) *Caught Between: A Review of Research into the Education of Pupils of West Indian Origin*, Slough, NFER/Nelson.

Taylor, M., Miller, J. and Oliveira, M. (1979) The off-site unit, *Comprehensive Education*, 39, 13/17.

Tennent, T. G. (1971) School non-attendance and delinquency, *Educational Research*, 13, 3, 185/90.

The Teachers' Action Collective (1976) 'Pastoral Care': the system of control, *Teachers' Action*, 5, 22/27.

Thomas, D. (1978) *The Social Psychology of Childhood Disability*, London, Methuen.

Thomas, D. (1982) *The Experience of Handicap*, London, Methuen.

Thomas, D. (1985) Initial training needs of special education teachers, in Hopkins, D. and Reid, K. (eds) *Rethinking Teacher Education*, London, Croom Helm.

Thomas, J. (1982) Care proceedings for school non-attendance and their outcomes, *Information Sheet*, Leicester, National Youth Bureau.

Tibbenham, A., Essen, J. and Fogelman, K. (1978) Ability grouping and school characteristics, *British Journal of Educational Studies*, 26, 1, 8/23.

Tizard, J. (1973) Maladjusted children and the child guidance service, *London Educational Review*, 2, 2, 22/39.

Topping, K. J. (1976) Bibliography: special units and classes for children with behaviour problems, *Research Paper No. 7*, Halifax, Calderdale.

Topping, K. J. (1977) An evaluation of the long-term effects of remedial teaching, *Remedial Education*, 12, 2, 84/86. See also: Topping, K. J. Evaluation of psychological services and mental health consultation: *A Bibliography*, Halifax, Calderdale Psychological Services.

Topping, K. J. (1978) Consumer confusion and professional conflict in educational psychology, *Bulletin British Psychological Society*, 31, 265/7.

Topping, K.J. (1983) *Educational Systems for Disruptive Adolescents*, London, Croom Helm.

Tutt, N. (1977) Use and development of observation and assessment centres for children, *Report of a Joint ADSS/SWS Seminar*, London, DHSS. See also: Tutt, N. (1981) Treatment under attack, in Gillham, B. (ed.) *Problem Behaviour in the Secondary School*, London, Croom Helm; Tutt, N. (ed.) (1978) *Alternative Strategies for Coping with Crime*, Oxford, Blackwell; and Tutt, N. (ed.) (1977) *Violence*, London, HMSO.

Tyerman, M.J. (1958) A research into truancy. *British Journal of Educational Psychology*, 28, 217/25. See also: *Unpublished Ph.D. Thesis. Truancy*, University of London.

Tyerman, M.J. (1968) *Truancy*, London, University of London Press.

UCCA (1982) *Statistical Supplements to the 17th and 18th Reports*, London, Universities' Central Council on Admissions (UCCA).

Undeb Cenadlaethol Athrawon Cymru (1975) A *Report* by a sub-committee of members of UCAC on Truancy and Disruptive Behaviour in Schools, Cardiff, UCAC.

Upton, G. and Gobell, A. (eds) (1980) *Behaviour Problems in the Comprehensive School*, University College, Cardiff, Faculty of Education.

Varlaam, A. (1974) Educational attainment and behaviour at school, *Greater London Intelligence Quarterly*, 29, 29/37.

Warnock, M. Dame (1985) *The Richard Dimbleby Lecture*, London, BBC Publications.

Webb, S. (1980) Teething trouble: questions about the early days of units for disruptive pupils, *Unpublished Paper* available from Division 9, Education Welfare Service, ILEA. See also: Getting it Together, 2nd unpublished paper, *ibid.*

Wedell, K. and Lambourne, R. (1980) Psychological services for children in England and Wales. *Occasional Paper*, 4, 1 and 2. Division of Educational and Child Psychology, Leicester, British Psychological Society.

Welsh Office (1984) Response to underachievement: a discussion of practice in secondary schools, Cardiff, Welsh Office, October 1984, HMI Report.

West, D.J. (1982) *Delinquency*, London, Heinemann.

West, D.J. and Farrington, D.P. (1973) *Who Becomes Delinquent?*, London, Heinemann.

West, D.J. and Farrington, D.P. (1977) *The Delinquent Way of Life*, London, Heinemann Educational Books.

West Glamorgan (1980) *Research into Non-Attendance at School. Final Report*, Stage III, West Glamorgan County Council Education Committee, West Glamorgan County Council.

White, D.J. and Peddie, M. (1978) Patterns of absenteeism in primary and secondary schools, *Scottish Educational Review*, 10, 2, 37/44.

White, R. and Brockington, D. (1978) *In and Out of School: The ROSLA Community Education Project*, London, Routledge & Kegan Paul.

Wigley, V. (1980) Personal communication: cited in Mortimore, P. et al (1983) *Behaviour Problems in Schools*, London, Croom Helm.

Wilby, P. (1985) What's so wrong with Sir Keith's blueprint for the 21st century? *Sunday Times*, 31 March 1985, p. 17.

Williams, P. (1974) *Behaviour Problems in School: A Source Book of Readings*, London, Hodder & Stoughton.

Willis, P.E. (1977) *Learning to Labour: How Working Class Kids Get Working Class Jobs*, Kent, Saxon House.

Withrington, D. (1975) Anxieties over withdrawal from school: historical comment, *Research Intelligence*, 1, 20/2.

Wolstenholme, F. and Kolvin, I. (1980) Social workers in schools: the teachers' response, *British Journal of Guidance and Counselling*, 8, 1, 44/5.

Wood, J. (1981) The behavioural approach to non-attendance cases. Division 7, Education Welfare Service, *ILEA*, see also, in Dunn, J. (ed.) Partnership in education and social sciences: some school problems, *Joint Occasional Publication No. 2*, University of Lancaster, 1981.

Woods, P. (1984) A sociological analysis of disruptive incidents, in Frude, N. and Gault, H. *Disruptive Behaviour in Schools*, Chichester, John Wiley.

Wragg, E.C. (ed.) *Classroom Teaching Skills*, London, Croom Helm.

Wragg, E.C. and Kerry, T.L. (1979) *Classroom Interaction Research*, Nottingham, University of Nottingham School of Education.

Wright, H.J. and Payne, T.A.N. (1979) *An Evaluation of a School Psychological Service: The Portsmouth Pattern*, Hampshire Education Dept.

York. R., Heron, J. and Wolff, S. (1972) Exclusion from school, *Journal of Child Psychology and Psychiatry*, 13, 259/66.

Young, P., Lawrence, J. and Steed, D. (1979) Local education authority responses to disruptive behaviour: a research note, *Policy and Politics*, 7, 4, 387/93.

Young, P., Steed, D. and Lawrence, J. (1980) Local education authorities and autonomous off-site units for disruptive pupils in secondary schools, *Cambridge Journal of Education*, 10, 2, 55/70.

Younghusband, E., Davie, R., Birchall, D. and Pringle, M.L.K. (1970) *Living With Handicap*, London, National Children's Bureau.

Yule, W., Berger, M. and Wigley, V. (1984) Behaviour-modification and classroom management, in Frude, N. and Gault, H. (eds) *Disruptive Behaviour in Schools*, Chichester, John Wiley.

FURTHER READING LISTS

This reading list is subdivided into sections by chapter as appropriate. Owing to constraints imposed by space, time and style, the section inevitably includes a number of books, articles and reports which are excluded from the references cited in the text. Nevertheless, all these primary sources, besides many others, were read and digested before *Disaffection From School* was written. Interested parties are thoroughly recommended to read these materials because they add a great deal of detailed information to many of the points covered in the text. This is particularly true for chapters 7, 8, 9, 10 and 11.

CHAPTER 1

Blackburn, K. (1975) *The Tutor*, London, Heinemann.
Blackburn, K. (1983) *Head of House, Head of Year*, London, Heinemann.
Cannings, B. (1983) *The School Leaver's Book*, London, Longman.
Cheston, M. (1979) *It's Your Life*, Oxford, Wheaton & Co., Pergamon.
Coles, M. and White, M. (1982) *How to Study and Pass Exams*, London, Collins Educational.
Hamblin, D. H. (1986) *The Pastoral Curriculum*, Oxford, Basil Blackwell.

Hargreaves, D.H. (1984) *Improving London Schools*, Report of the committee on the curriculum and organisation of secondary schools, London, ILEA.

Hunt, M. and John, R. (1985) *Pause and Think*, London, Universities Tutorial Press.

McKeown, S. (ed) (1983) *Effective Learning Skills: A Teacher's Guide*, London, ILEA.

Marland, M. (1975) *The Craft of the Classroom*, London, Heinemann.

Reid, K. (1985) *Truancy and School Absenteeism*, London, Hodder & Stoughton.

Thompson, J. (1978) *It's a Matter of People*, London, Hutchinson.

CHAPTER 2

Craik, J.B. (1985) Attitudes to school of poor attenders, *Unpublished M.Phil thesis*, Milton Keynes, The Open University.

Hersov, L. and Berg, I. (eds) (1980) *Out of School*, Chichester, John Wiley.

Reid, K. (1985) *Truancy and School Absenteeism*, London, Hodder & Stoughton.

See also various publications on persistent school absenteeism by Galloway, D., Reid, K. and Reynolds, D. included in the References Used in the Text and elsewhere.

CHAPTER 3

Children's Defense Fund (1975) *School Suspensions: Are They Helping Children?*, Cambridge, Mass.

Frude, N. and Gault, H. (eds) (1984) *Disruptive Behaviour in Schools*, Chichester, John Wiley

Galloway, D., Ball, T., Blomfield, D. and Seyd, R. (1982) *Schools and Disruptive Pupils*, Harlow, Longman.

Gallup, G.H. (1977) Ninth annual Gallup poll of the public's attitudes toward the public schools, *Phi Delta Kappan*, 59, 1, 33/48.

Gawthorne-Hardy, J. (1977) *The Public School Phenomenon*, London, Hodder & Stoughton.

Grace, G.R. (1978) *Teachers, Ideology and Control*, London, Routledge & Kegan Paul.

Rubel, R.J. (1977) *The Unruly School*, Lexington, Mass., Lexington Books.

Tattum, D. (1982) *Disruptive Pupils in Schools and Units*, Chichester, John Wiley.

CHAPTER 4

Barton, L. and Meighan, R. (eds) *Schools, Pupils and Deviance,* Driffield, Nafferton Books.

Bird, C., Chessum, R., Furlong, J. and Johnson, D. (eds) *Disaffected Pupils,* Educational Studies Unit, Brunel University.

Coulby, D. and Harper, T. (1985) *Preventing Classroom Disruption,* London, Croom Helm.

Delamont, S. (1976) *Interaction in the Classroom,* London, Methuen.

Dobbins, D. A. (1984) *The Prevalence and Characteristics of Children with Specific Learning Difficulties,* 2 vols. Report of a sponsored DES project, Swansea: University College of Swansea, Department of Education.

Dobbins, D. A. (1985) *A Longitudinal Study of the Reading Attainment and Related Variables of Unexpected Underachievers, Low Achievers and Normal Readers from 9–14 years,* Swansea, West Glamorgan Institute of Higher Education, Faculty of Education.

Furlong, V. (1976) Interaction sets in the classroom: towards a study of pupil knowledge, in Stubbs, M. and Delamont, S. (eds) *Explorations in Classroom Observation,* Chichester, John Wiley.

Lawrence, J., Steed, D. and Young, P. with Hilton, G. (1981) *Dialogue on Disruptive Behaviour: A Study of a Secondary School,* London, PJP Press.

Lawrence, J. and Steed, D. (1985) *Disruptive Children: Disruptive Schools,* London, Croom Helm.

Meyenn, R. J. (1980) Schoolgirls' peer groups, in Woods, P. (ed.) *Pupil Strategies: Explorations in the Sociology of the School,* London, Croom Helm.

Pollard, A. (1980) Teacher interests and changing situations of survival threat in primary school classrooms, in Woods, P. (ed.) *Pupil Strategies: Explorations in the Sociology of the School,* London, Croom Helm.

Reynolds, D. (1976) The delinquent school, in Hammersley, M. and Woods, P. (eds) *The Process of Schooling,* London, Routledge & Kegan Paul.

Tajfel, H. (1981) *Human Groups and Social Categories,* Cambridge, Cambridge University Press.

Warnock, H. M. (Chairman) *Special Educational Needs: Report of the Committee of Enquiry into the Education of Handicapped Children and Young People,* DES/Welsh Office/Scottish Office, HMSO.

Willis, P. (1977) *Learning to Labour,* Farnborough, Saxon House.

CHAPTER 5

Leach, D. (1977) Teacher perceptions and 'problem' pupils, *Educational Review,* 29, 3, 188/203.

Leach, D.J. and Raybould, E.C. (1977) *Learning and Behaviour Difficulties in Schools*, London, Open Books.

North Carolina State Department of Public Instruction (1977) *Emotionally Handicapped Pupils: Developing Appropriate Educational Programs*, Raleigh, USA, NCSDPI.

Quay, H.C. and Werry, J.S. (eds) (1979) *Psychopathological Disorders of Childhood*, 2nd edn, New York, John Wiley.

Reinert, H.R. (1980) *Children in Conflict*, 2nd edn, St Louis, C.V. Mosby.

Rutter, M. and Hersov, L. (eds) (1977) *Child Psychiatry: Modern Approaches*, Oxford, Basil Blackwell.

Rutter, M., Tizard, J. and Whitmore, K. (eds) (1970) *Education, Health and Behaviour*, London, Longman.

Sindelar, P.T. and Deno, S.L. (1978) The effectiveness of resource programming, *Journal of Special Education*, 12, 17/28.

Topping, K. (1983) *Educational Systems for Disruptive Adolescents*, London, Croom Helm.

CHAPTER 6

Hargreaves, D.H. (1967) *Social Relations in a Secondary School*, London, Routledge & Kegan Paul.

Hargreaves, D.H. (1972) *Interpersonal Relations and Education*, London, Routledge & Kegan Paul.

Hargreaves, D.H., Hester, S.K. and Mellor, F.J. (1975) *Deviance in Classrooms*, London, Routledge & Kegan Paul.

Lacey, C. (1970) *Hightown Grammar*, Manchester, Manchester University Press.

Reynolds, D., Jones, D., St. Leger, S. and Murgatroyd, S. (1980) School factors and truancy, in Hersov, L. and Berg, I. (eds) *Out of School*, Chichester, John Wiley.

Reynolds, D. (ed.) (1985) *Studying School Effectiveness*, Chichester, Falmer Press.

CHAPTER 7

Bird, C., Chessum, R., Furlong, J. and Johnson, D. (eds) *Disaffected Pupils*, Educational Studies Unit, Brunel University.

Blackie, P. (1980) Not quite proper, in Reedy, S. and Woodhead, M. (eds) *Family, Work and Education*, London, Hodder & Stoughton.

Burgess, R.G. (1983) *Experiencing Comprehensive Education*, London, Methuen.

Delamont, S. (1976) *Interaction in the Classroom*, London, Methuen.

Fogelman, K. (1978) School attendance, attainment and behaviour, *British Journal of Educational Psychology*, 48, 2, 148/58.

Frude, N. and Gault, H. (eds) (1984) *Disruptive Behaviour in Schools*,

Chichester, John Wiley.

Furlong, J. (1976) Interaction sets in the classroom: toward a study of pupil knowledge, in Stubbs, M. and Delamont, S. (eds) *Explorations in Classroom Observation*, Chichester, John Wiley.

Furlong, J. (1977) Anacy goes to school: a case study of pupils' knowledge of their teachers, in Woods, P. and Hammersley, M. (eds) *School Experience*, London, Croom Helm.

Galloway, D., Ball, T., Blomfield, D. and Seyd, R. (1982) *Schools and Disruptive Pupils*, London, Longman.

Galton, M. and Moon, B. (eds) (1983) *Changing Schools: Changing Curriculum*, London, Harper & Row.

Gannaway, H. (1976) Making sense of school, in Stubbs, M., and Delamont, S. (eds) *Explorations in Classroom Observation*, Chichester, John Wiley.

Grunsell, R. (1980) *Beyond Control: Schools and Suspension*, London, Writers and Readers.

Hargreaves, D. H. (1982) *The Challenge for the Comprehensive School*, London, Routledge & Kegan Paul.

Hargreaves, D. H. (1984) *Improving Secondary Schools*, Report of the committee on the curriculum and organisation of secondary schools, London, ILEA.

Hargreaves, D. H., Hester, S. K. and Mellor, F. J. (1975) *Deviance in Classrooms*, London, Routledge & Kegan Paul.

Judge, H. (1984) *A Generation of Schooling*, Oxford, Oxford University Press.

Lawrence, J., Steed, D. and Young, P. with Hilton, G. (1981) *Dialogue on Disruptive Behaviour: A Study of a Secondary School*, London, PJP Press.

Lawrence, J. et al (1981) *Dialogue on Disruptive Behaviour: A Study of a Secondary School*. London, PJP Press.

Marsh, P., Rosser, E. and Harré, R. (1978) *The Rules of Disorder*, London, Routledge & Kegan Paul.

Muncie, J. (1984) *The Trouble With Kids Today*, London, Hutchinson.

Musgrove, F. and Taylor, P. H. (1969) *Society and the Teacher's Role*, London, Routledge & Kegan Paul.

Nash, R. (1976) Pupils' expectations of their teachers, in Stubbs, M. and Delamont, S. (eds) *Explorations in Classroom Observation*, Chichester, John Wiley.

Reid, K. (1985) *Truancy and School Absenteeism*, London, Hodder & Stoughton.

Reynolds, D. (ed.) (1985) *Studying School Effectiveness*, Chichester, Falmer Press.

Rosser, E. and Harré, R. (1976) The meaning of disorder, in Hammersley, M. and Woods, P. (eds) *The Process of Schooling*, London, Routledge & Kegan Paul.

Rutter, M., Maughan, B., Mortimore, P. and Ouston, J. (1979) *Fifteen Thousand Hours*, London, Open Books.

Shaw, B. (1983) *Comprehensive Schooling: The Impossible Dream?*, Oxford, Basil Blackwell.

Varlaam, A. (1974) Educational attainment and behaviour at school, *Greater London Intelligence Quarterly*, 29, 29/37.

Woods, P. (1979) *The Divided School*, London, Routledge & Kegan Paul.

Woods, P. (1981) *Schools and Deviance*, Milton Keynes, Open University Press.

York, R., Heron, J. and Wolff, S. (1972) Exclusion from school. *Journal of Child Psychology and Psychiatry*, 13, 259/266.

CHAPTER 8

Association of Northern Ireland Education and Library Boards (1976) *Vandalism and Indiscipline in Schools: Report of the Working Party*, ANIELB.

Ball, C. and Ball, M. (1980) School's out, in Dungate, M. (ed.) *Community Works I: Aspects of Three Innovatory Projects*, London, Community Projects Foundation.

Best, R., Jarvis, C. and Ribbins, P. (eds) (1980) *Perspectives on Pastoral Care*, London, Heinemann.

Bird, C, Chessum, R., Furlong, J. and Johnson, D. (eds) (1980) *Disaffected Pupils*, Educational Studies Unit, Brunel University.

Blackburn, K. (1975) *The Tutor*, London, Heinemann.

Blackburn, K. (1983) *Head of House, Head of Year*, London, Heinemann.

Brunel Institute of Organisation and Social Studies (1976) *The Hanworth Road Centre*, Educational Studies Unit, Brunel Institute.

Cleveland Education Authority (1978) *Disruptive and Violent Behaviour in Schools*, Cleveland Education Authority.

Cumbria Education Dept. (1976) *No Small Change: The Report of the Working Party on Problem Children in Schools*, Cumbria Education Dept.

Davis, L. F. (1977) *Children Excluded From School: The Results of a Survey*, London, British Association of Social Workers and Association of Directors of Social Services.

Devon County Council Education Dept. (1975) *Disruptive and Violent Behaviour in Schools*, Devon County Council.

Disruptive Pupils Study Group (1979) *Report of the Disruptive Pupils Study Group*, Northants Education Dept.

Dorset Social Services Dept. (1976) *Disruptive Pupils and Their Problems: Report of the Working Party*, Dorset County Council.

Galloway, D., Ball, T., Blomfield, D. and Seyd, R. (1982) *Schools and Disruptive Pupils*, London, Longman.

Gath, D., Cooper, B., Gattoni, F. and Rockett, D. (1977) *Child Guidance and Delinquency in a London Borough*, Oxford, Oxford University Press.

Gillham, B. (ed.) (1981) *Problem Behaviour in the Secondary School: A Systems Approach*, London, Croom Helm.

Gillham, B. (1984) School organization and the control of disruptive incidents, in Frude, N. and Gault, H. (eds) *Disruptive Behaviour in Schools*, Chichester, John Wiley.

Grunsell, R. (1980) *Absent from School: The Story of a Truancy Centre*, London, Writers and Readers.

Hamblin, D.H. (1978) *The Teacher and Pastoral Care*, Basil Blackwell, Oxford.

Hamblin, D.H. (ed.) (1981) *Problems and Practice of Pastoral Care*, Oxford, Basil Blackwell.

Hamblin, D.H. (1986) *The Pastoral Curriculum*, Oxford, Basil Blackwell.

Hampshire Education Authority (1979) *Help for Difficult Pupils: Report of a Working Party of the Hampshire Education Authority*, Hampshire Education Authority.

Hoghughi, M. (1978) *Troubled and Troublesome*, London, Burnett Books.

Inner London Education Authority (1978) *Disruptive Pupils: Report of the Schools Sub-Committee to the Education Committee*, London, ILEA.

Isle of Wight Education Committee (1979) *Report of the Working Party Set Up To Consider The Needs Of Disturbed and Disturbing Pupils on The Isle of Wight*, Isle of Wight Education Committee.

Johnson, D., Ransom, E., Packwood, T., Bowden, K. and Kogan M. (1980) *Secondary Schools and the Welfare Network*, London, Unwin Educational.

Jones, A. (1984) *Counselling Adolescents: School and After*, 2nd edn, London, Kogan Page.

Lawrence, J., Steed, D. and Young, P. (1977) *Disruptive Behaviour in a Secondary School*, Educational studies monograph No. 1, University of London, Goldsmiths' College.

Lawrence, J. et al (1981) *Dialogue on Disruptive Behaviour*, London, PJP Press.

Liverpool Education Committee (1974) *The Suspended Child*, Teachers' Advisory Committee, Liverpool Education Committee.

Liverpool Education Committee (1979) *Interim Report of the Standing Committee for Disruptive Pupils*, Schools and legal working parties, Liverpool, Liverpool Education Committee.

Nelson-Jones, R. (1982) *The Role and Practice of Counselling Psychology*, London, Holt, Rinehart & Winston.

Nelson-Jones, R. (1983) *Practical Counselling Skills*, London, Holt, Rinehart & Winston.

North Yorkshire Teachers' Association Consultative Panel (1977) *Report on Disruptive Pupils*, NYTACP.

Robinson, M. (1978) *Schools and Social Work*, London, Routledge & Kegan Paul.

Robinson, Y.J. (1974) Safe Haven for Truants, *Community Care*, 9, 10/12.

Simmond, C. and Wade, W. (1984) *I Like to Say What I Think*, London, Kogan Page.

Staffordshire Education Committee (1977) *Disruptive Pupils in Schools*, Staffordshire Education Committee.

Strathclyde Regional Council of Education (1977) *Report on School Attendance*, Strathclyde Regional Council.

Suffolk Secondary Education Sub-Committee (1976) *Report of a Working Party of the Education Service*: Disruptive Pupils in Secondary Schools, Suffolk County Council.

Tattum, D. (1982) *Disruptive Pupils in Schools and Units*, Chichester, John Wiley.

Topping, K. (1983) *Educational Systems for Disruptive Adolescents*, London, Croom Helm.

West Glamorgan County Council Education Committee (1980) Research into Non-Attendance at School, *Final Report – Stage III*, West Glamorgan County Council.

CHAPTER 9

Blackburn, K. (1975) *The Tutor*, London, Heinemann.

Blackburn, K. (1983) *Head of House, Head of Year*, London, Heinemann.

Cannings, B. (1983) *The School Leaver's Book*, London, Longman.

Cheston, M. (1979) *It's Your Life*, Oxford, Wheaton & Co., Pergamon.

Coles, M. and White, M. (1982) *How to Study and Pass Exams*, London, Collins Educational.

Delamont, S. (1976) *Interaction in the Classroom*, London, Methuen.

Evans, M. (1981) *Disruptive Pupils*, Schools Council Programme 4: Individual pupils, London, Schools Council.

Hamblin, D.H. (1974) *The Teacher and Counselling*, Oxford, Basil Blackwell.

Hamblin, D.H. (1978) *The Teacher and Pastoral Care*, Oxford, Basil Blackwell.

Hamblin, D.H. (1983) *Guidance 16–19*, Oxford, Basil Blackwell.

Hamblin, D.H. (1986) *The Pastoral Curriculum*, Oxford, Basil Blackwell.

Hargreaves, D.H., Hestor, S. and Mellor, F. (1975) *Deviance in Classrooms*, London, Routledge & Kegan Paul.

Hargreaves, D.H. (1984) *Improving Secondary Schools*, Report of the committee on the curriculum and organization of secondary schools, London, ILEA.

Hoghughi, M. (1978) *Troubled and Troublesome*, London, Burnett Books.

Holden, A. (1969) *Teachers as Counsellors*, London, Burnett Books.

Holden, A. (1972) *Counselling in Secondary Schools*, London, Constable.

Hopkins, D. and Wideen, M. (eds) (1984) *Alternative Perspectives on School Improvement*, Lewes, Falmer Press.

Hunt, M. and John, R. (1985) *Pause and Think*, London, UT Press.

Johnson, D., Ransom, E., Packwood, T., Bowden, K. and Kogan, M. (1980) *Secondary Schools and the Welfare Network*, London, Unwin Eductional.

Jones, A. (1984) *Counselling Adolescents: School and After*, London, Kogan Page.

Laslett, R. (1977) Disruptive and violent pupils: the facts and the fallacies, *Educational Review*, 29, 3, 152/62.

Lytton, H. and Lytton, M. (1974) *Craft Guidance and Counselling in British Schools*, 2nd edn, London, Edward Arnold.

McKeon, S. (ed.) (1983) *Effective Learning Skills: A Teacher's Guide*, London, ILEA.

Marland, M. (1975) *The Craft of the Classroom*, London, Heinemann.

Nelson-Jones, R. (1982) *The Roles and Practice of Counselling Psychology*, London, Holt, Rinehart & Winston.

Nelson-Jones, R. (1983) *Practical Counselling Skills*, London, Holt, Rinehart & Winston.

Wilson, M. and Evans, M. (1980) *Education of Disturbed Pupils*, Schools Council Working Paper, No. 65, London, Methuen Educational.

CHAPTER 10

Davie, R. (1977) The interface between education and the social services, in Kahan, B. (ed.) *Working Together for Children and Their Families*, DHSS/Welsh Office, HMSO.

Galloway, D., Ball, T. and Seyd, R. (1981) Administrative and legal procedures available to local education authorities in cases of poor schools attendance, *Durham and Newcastle Research Review*, IX, 46, 201/9.

Giller, H. and Morris, A. (1981) *Care and Discretion: Social Workers' Decisions With Delinquents*, London, Burnett Books.

Gillham, B. (ed.) (1981) *Problem Behaviour in the Secondary School*, London, Croom Helm.

Johnson, D., Ransom, E., Packwood, T., Bowden, K. and Kogan, M. (1980) *Secondary Schools and the Welfare Network*, London, Allen & Unwin.

Mortimore, P., Davies, J., Varlaam, A., West, A. with Devine, P. and Mazza, J. (1983) *Behaviour Problems in Schools*, London, Croom Helm.

Pack, D.C. Chairman (1977) *Truancy and Indiscipline in Schools in Scotland*, Scottish Education Dept., HMSO.

Reid, K. (1985) *Truancy and School Absenteeism*, London, Hodder & Stoughton.

Staffordshire Education Committee (1977) *Disruptive Pupils in Schools*, Staffordshire Education Committee.

Strathclyde Regional Council Department of Education (1977) *Report on School Attendance*, Strathclyde Regional Council.

Tattum, D. (1982) *Disruptive Pupils in Schools and Units*, Chichester, John Wiley.

Topping, K. (1983) *Educational Systems for Disruptive Adolescents*, London, Croom Helm.

West Glamorgan County Council Education Committee (1980) *Research into Non-Attendance at School: Final Report – Stage III*, West Glamorgan County Council.

CHAPTER 11

Austin, S. (1975) *To be Called Stupid*, Schools Curriculum Project, Northern Ireland Polytechnic.

Ball, C. and Ball, M. (1980) School's out, in Dungate, M. (ed.) *Community Works 1: Aspects of Three Innovatory Projects*, London, Community Projects Foundation.

Bond, C. M. (1981) *Partnership in Practice: A Study of the Pastoral Care System and its Interaction with a School Social Worker in a Haringay Comprehensive School*, Polytechnic of North London, Survey Research Visit.

Derrick, D. (ed.) *Social Work Support Team: Grange County Comprehensive School*, London, Centre for Information and Advice on Educational Disadvantage.

Derrick, D. and Watkins, R. (1977) *Co-operative Care: Practice and Information Profiles*, London, Centre for Information and Advice on Educational Disadvantage.

Dinnage, R. (1978) Social work in a school setting, *Social Work Today*, 10, 2, 12/14.

Dunn, J. (ed.) (1982) *Education and Social Services: Models of Partnership*, joint occasional publication No. 3, University of Lancaster.

Dunn, J. et al (1981) *Education and Social Services: A Partnership*, joint occasional publication No. 1, University of Lancaster.

Firth, R. (1977) *Hillhead Junior High School Services Truancy Project*, London, Centre for Information and Advice on Educational Disadvantage.

Francis, N. (1977) Working in no man's land, *Times Educational Supplement*, 11 March, 20/1.

Galloway, D. M. and Goodwin, C. (1979) *Educating Slow-Learning and Maladjusted Children: Interpretation or Segregation*, London, Longman.

Galway, J. (1979) What pupils think of special units, *Comprehensive Education*, 39, 18/20.

Gillham, B. (ed.) *Reconstructing Educational Psychology*, London, Croom Helm.

Groves, I. (1980) Devising a treatment model based on 'girls only' method, *Social Work Today*, 11, 48, 12/13.

Harding, R. (1975) Towards a more effective use of social workers in schools (Parts 1 and 2), *Association for Counselling and Social Care Bulletin*, 2, 9/13 and 3, 3/8.

Harvey, L., Kolvin, I., McLaren, M., Nicol, A.R. and Wolstenholme, F. (1977) Introducing a social worker into schools, *British Journal of Guidance and Counselling*, 5, 1, 26/40.

Johnson, S. (1977) *School-based Social Workers in Haringay*, London, Centre for Information and Advice on Educational Disadvantage.

Llewelyn-Davies, J. et al (1977) Birmingham home–school liaison officers, Educational Action Projects, Vol. 1, London, Dept. of the Environment.

Loxley, D. (1976) Community psychology: an alternative perspective, *Unpublished Paper*, Sheffield, Sheffield Education Dept., Psychological Service.

Loxley, D. (1979) Community Psychology and Education, *Unpublished Paper*, given at Psychology and Education Conference, Keele Educational Research Association.

Marshall, T.F. and Rose, G. (1975) An experimental evaluation of school social work, *British Journal of Guidance and Counselling*, 3, 1, 2/14.

Morris, P. (1978) Teacher with a foot in both camps, *Community Care*, 238, 20/1.

Mulholland, M. et al (1980) *Turf Lodge Teenage Project Intermediate Treatment Group Report*, London, Save the Children Fund.

Padmore, K. (1981) *Social Education in a Secondary School*, Nottingham Young Volunteers.

Pitts, J. (1974) Preventative work in the school. *Youth Social Work Bulletin*, 1, 2, 3/8.

Pritchard, J. (1981) Untapped source, *Times Educational Supplement*, 16 October 1981, p. 20.

Rock, D. and Taylor, N. (1980) Out of site: alternative provision, *Teaching London Kids*, 15, 17/19.

Rose, G. and Marshall, T.F. (1974) *Counselling and School Social Work*, Chichester, John Wiley.

Sampson, O.C. (1975) Dream that is dying, *Bulletin of the British Psychological Society*, 28, 380.

Staines, L. et al (1981) *Moat Project*, Leicester, Leicestershire Social Services Project.

Topping, K.J. and Quelch, T. (1976) *Special Units and Classes for Children with Behaviour Problems: an Informal Survey of LEA Practice*, Psychological Service Research Paper No. 6, Calderdale Education Dept., Metropolitan Borough of Calderdale.

Ward, D. and Pearce, J. (1979) Breaking down the professional barrier, *Social Work Today*, 10, 36, 19/21.

Wolstenholme, F. and Kolvin, I. (1980) Social workers in schools: the teachers' response, *British Journal of Guidance and Counselling*, 8, 1, 44/56.

CHAPTER 12

Hargreaves, D.H. (1984) *Improving Secondary Schools*, Report of the committee on the curriculum and organisation of secondary schools, London, ILEA.

Reid, K. (1985) *Truancy and School Absenteeism*, London, Hodder & Stoughton.

SUBJECT INDEX

absenteeism and the law 178–83
absenteeism *per se* 1–15, 16–28,
  218–20; *see also under specific
  subheadings*
absentees' sex differences 26
aetiology of disruptive behaviour 46–69
alternative education 205–7

bullying 123

case studies 1, 21–2, 32–4, 43–5,
  50–2, 65, 67–9, 83–6, 128–9, 135,
  160–75, 184–5, 189, 190–201
categories of absenteeism 22, 81–3
Child Guidance Service xiv, 208, 211
classroom management 119–23
comparisons between non-attenders and
  disrupters 189–90, 221
conclusions 218–26
curriculum 11–15, 53, 55–60, 111–12,
  151–7, 219, 223

deviance 75–7
diagnosing disruptive behaviour 78–80

disruption in schools 1–15, 29–45,
  46–69, 70–87, 220–2; *see also under
  specific subheadings*
disruptive behaviour and absenteeism
  80–6

educational change 157–9
educational research 88–93
Educational Welfare Service xiv, 160–6,
  207–10, 213–14
examinations 53
external referrals 207–12
extortion 43

familial factors and disruption 60–2
form tutors 143–7
formal sanctions 177–202
formal sanctions and disruptive
  behaviour 183–9
further reading lists 247–58
future outlook 86–7
future outlook and disruption 86–7,
  221–6

general public, attitude of towards disruption 67–9

higher education 52
history of absenteeism 24
home, school and disruption 62–5
home and school 62–4

identification 133–6
in loco parentis concept 7
initial teacher education 4, 31, 54, 158, 224
inter-agency change 215–17

LEA policies 131–3

maladjustment and disruptive behaviour 70–3
managing disruptive pupils in classrooms 121–3
Manpower Services Commission 9, 158
measurement 91–3
multidisciplinary perspectives 6–8, 203–26

parental perspectives 107–11
parental-condoned absence 23
parents 9
pastoral care and counselling 147–8
pastoral care systems 9–15, 141–3
pastoral-academic dichotomy 125–9
peer-group relationships and disruption 65–7
prevention of disruptive behaviour 148–50
problem of absenteeism 16–17
psychiatric disorders 77–8
psychology 6, 8
pupils' perceptions 104–7, 147–8
racism 54–5
rape 43
rates of absenteeism 24–7
rationale xi–xiv, 1–15
references 227–46
robbery 43
roots of absenteeism 17–21

school change 15, 157–9
school effectiveness 53
school factors 88–124, 218–26
school improvement 12–14, 100–1, 150–7
school initiatives 141–76, 223–6
school organization 93–100
school phobia 23
school policies 129–31
School Psychological Service xiv, 208, 210–11
school rules 112–14
school-based social work 204–5
sexism 53–4
soccer violence 3–6
social services 203–17
sociology 7, 8
special educational needs and disruptive behaviour 73–5
staff development 100–1

teacher expectations 114–16
teacher stress 43
teacher-baiting 5–6
teacher-pupil relationships 116–19, 224–6
teachers and social workers 212–17
teachers' views 32–4
territorial imperatives 212–17
TVEI 158
types of absenteeism 23–4

underachievement 47–60, 89, 136–8, 219
underachievement and disruption 138–40, 222–6
United States 25, 31, 42–3, 45, 89, 102

vandalism 2, 8, 43, 88, 220

weapon violence in schools 43
what is disruptive behaviour? 34–6
William Tyndale Enquiry 90

young offenders xiii, *see also case studies in chapter 10*

NAME INDEX

(references in the further reading lists are excluded)

Abbott, E. and Breckinridge, S. R. 25
Acton, T. A. 91
Adelman, C. and Alexander, R. J. 107
Advisory Centre for Education 184,
    185, 186, 187
Anderson, R. R. 112, 116
Assistant Masters' Association 186
Association of Assistant Mistresses 186
Auld, M. 90
Ayllon, T. A. and Roberts, M. D. 94

Baldwin, J. and Wells, H. 145, 146
Ball, C. 182
Ball, C. and Ball, M. 134
Bandura, A. and Walters, R. H. 71
Banks, O. 114
Baum, T. 24
Bayh, B. 43
Berg, I. 25, 178
Berg, I. et al 180, 181
Bernstein, B. and Brandis, L. 114
Best, R. et al 143

Beynon, J. and Delamont, S. 123, 124
Bietzk, M. 206
Billington, B. J. 8, 107
Bird, C. et al 61, 62, 91, 112, 116, 134,
    142, 143
Blackham, G. J. 75
Bowlby, J. 71
Bowles, S. and Gintis, H. 89
Boyson, R. 27, 137
Brighouse, T. 9, 222
Brophy, J. E. and Good, T. L. 53
Brunel Institute of Organisation and
    Social Studies 134, 211
Buist, M. 112
Bullock Report 153
Button, L. 145

Carroll, H. C. M. 23, 25, 26
Casburn, M. 181
Caven, N. and Harbison, J. J. M. 23, 25
Chazan, M. 71
Chomsky, N. 47

Clarke, D. D. et al 122
Clegg, A. and Megson, B. 95, 130
Cockroft Report 153
Cohen, L. 78
Comber, L. C. and Whitfield, R. C. 8, 38
Corrigan, P. 113
Court Committee 61
Covill, N. et al 143
Cox, T. 123
CRC 211

Davie, R. 83, 109, 122, 133, 203
Davie, R. et al 26, 52, 61, 83, 211
Davies, B. 208, 212, 215, 216
Davies, C. 131
Davies, G. 206
Davis, L. F. 72, 186
Delamont, S. 114, 117, 118
DES 24, 25, 31, 88, 94, 118, 153
Dierenfield, R. 32
Docking, J. W. 46, 119
Douglas, J. W. B. 71
Douglas, J. W. B. and Ross, J. M. 26
Drinkwater, C. 205
Dunham, J. 75, 117

Edmonds, R. et al 53
Erikson, E. 71

Farrington, D. 8
Fawcett, R. 211
Feldhusen, J. F. et al 62, 63
Fitzherbert, K. 131, 208
Fogelman, K. 26, 76, 111
Fogelman, K. et al 26, 52
Fogelman, K. and Richardson, K. 26
Francis, P. 122
Frude, N. 6, 113, 119
Frude, N. and Gault, H. 32

Galloway, D. 7, 23, 24, 27, 89, 142, 143, 188, 190
Galloway, D. and Goodwin, J. 71, 73, 136
Galloway, D. et al 8, 23, 32, 35, 73, 77, 91, 95, 119, 146, 179, 180, 181, 182, 184, 186, 187, 188
Galton, M. et al 80
Galton, M. and Willcocks, J. 153
Gath, D. et al 91
Geddes, D. 89
Giller, H. and Morris, A. 183
Gillham, B. 96, 100, 101, 214

Goldstein, H. 91
Graham, P. and Rutter, M. 77
Gray, G. et al 27
Gray, J. et al 102
Green, F. L. 179, 180
Gregory, R. P. et al 209
Gross, N. et al 93
Grunsell, R. 61, 62, 91, 134, 186, 187, 188, 205, 206

Haigh, G. 122
Halsey, A. H. et al 52
Hamblin, D. H. 11, 145
Hansard 39
Hargreaves, D. H. 12, 18, 66, 90, 91, 95, 109, 113, 140, 151
Hargreaves, D. H. et al 18, 66, 79, 109, 112, 117, 118, 119, 122
Harrop, A. 122, 137
Hartshorn, D. J. 68
Hastings, D. J. 96
Her Majesty's Inspectorate 40, 153
HMSO 54, 55
Hooper, R. 148
Hopkins, D. 92
Hopkins, D. and Reid, K. 145
Hopkins, D. and Wideen, M. 151
Humphries, S. 24

ILEA 24, 153, 155, 156
Insell, P. and Jacobson, L. 115

Jencks, C. et al 89, 102
Jennings, R. 183, 186
Johnson, D. et al 142, 143, 147, 213
Jones, A. 117, 133, 143
Jones, A. R. and Forrest, R. 134
Jones, D. 61

Kahan, B. 203, 212
Kamin, L. J. 114
Kelly, G. 22, 122, 222
Knutton, S. and Mycroft, A. 117
Kounin, J. S. et al 122
Kyriacou, C. and Sutcliffe, J. 117

Labow, W. 115
Lacey, C. 62, 66, 90
Laslett, R. 38, 71
Laufer, M. 71
Lawrence, J. 71, 122
Lawrence, J. et al 35, 95, 98
Lewis, D. G. and Murgatroyd, S. 142
Liverpool 136

Longworth-Dames 188
Lortie, D. C. 120
Lowenstein, L. F. 31, 35, 37

MacMillan, K. 208, 213
MacMillan, D. L. and Morrison, G. M.
94
McNamara, D. 41, 88
Madaus, G. F. 102
Marsh, P. et al 8, 113, 117, 121
Marshall, M. 205
Marshall, T. F. and Rose, G. 204
Martin, F. M. et al 180, 181, 182
May, D. 7, 8, 135
Mays, J. D. 62, 65
Mead, S. and Mead, D. 211
Miller, W. B. 65
Millham, S. 71, 183
Mills, W. P. C. 41
Milner, J. 135
Ministry of Education 71
Mitchell, S. and Shepherd, M. 26, 66,
71
Moore, G. and Jardine, E. 27
Mortimore, J. and Blackstone, T. 52
Mortimore, P. 48, 52, 53, 98, 100, 139
Mortimore, P. et al 61, 79, 102, 119
Mortimore, P. and Mortimore, J. 53
Murgatroyd, S. J. 127, 142, 148
Murphy, J. 52

Nash, R. 114
NACEWO 24, 25
NAS/UWT 36, 83, 186
National Education Association 43
National Institute of Education 43
NUT 31, 32, 186
Newsom, J. and Newsom, E. 107

Olweus, D. 123
Ouston, J. 101

Pack Committee 4, 69, 95
Palfrey, C. F. 134
Parry, K. 35
Parry-Jones, W. and Gay, B. 123
Patrick, H. et al 62, 75
Pedley, F. 209
Phillips, D. 62
Phillips, D. and Callely, E. 105
Phillips, D. et al 124
Pik, R. 101, 121
Pollard, A. 113
Power, M. J. et al 90, 91

Pringle, M. L. K. et al 71

Ralphs, L. 208
Ravenette, A. T. 211
Raymond, J. 145
Regan, D. 73
Registrar General 109
Reid, K. xii, 7, 9, 18, 19, 21, 22, 27, 64,
66, 79, 80, 81, 82, 83, 92, 100, 106,
112, 133, 135, 152, 153, 156, 157,
178, 187, 190, 201, 212, 220
Reid, K. and Avalos, B. xii
Reid, K. and Kendall, L. 219
Reid, K. et al 4, 47, 54, 62, 75
Reid, P. and Reid, K. 68
Reynolds, D. 66, 88, 89, 102, 116, 127,
138
Reynolds, D. and Murgatroyd, S. 24,
130, 138
Reynolds, D. and Reid, K. 90, 102, 103
Reynolds, D. and Sullivan, M. 91
Reynolds, D. et al 27, 90, 91, 93, 100
Rist, R. 115
Robinson, T. J. 134
Rosenshine, B. 53
Rosenthal, R. 114
Rosenthal, R. and Jacobson, L. 114
Rosser, E. and Harré, R. 120, 121
Roxburgh, J. M. 24
Rubinstein, D. 24
Rutter, M. 52, 60, 63, 64, 71, 76, 91,
102
Rutter, M. and Graham, P. 77
Rutter, M. and Quinton, D. 78
Rutter, M. et al 25, 27, 41, 53, 61, 71,
76, 78, 80, 89, 91, 93, 94, 100, 118,
155

Sandon, F. 24
Saunders, M. 122
Schein, E. H. 93
Schools Council 130, 153
Scottish Education Dept. 23, 25, 32, 36,
67, 83, 95
Seabrook, J. 62
Sharp, A. 116, 118
Shepherd, M. et al 75
Shostak, J. 118
Sidaway, N. D. 41
Skinner, A. et al 141, 214, 217
Stott, D. H. 71, 72, 76
Strathclyde 133
Stubbs, M. and Delamont, S. 7, 19
Sullivan, R. and Riches, S. 134

Tattum, D. 32, 35, 38, 64, 69, 91, 113, 119
Taylor, F. 184, 187
Taylor, L. et al 179
Taylor, M. 55
Taylor, M. et al 134
Teachers' Action Collective, The 143
Tennent, T. G. 26
Thomas, D. 74, 75
Thomas, J. 181, 182
Tibbenham, A. et al 102
Tizard, J. 71, 211
Topping, K. J. 35, 72, 210, 214
Tutt, N. 71
Tyerman, M. J. 7, 18, 22, 23, 26, 80, 89

UCAC 83
UCCA 54
Upton, G. and Gobell, A. 211

Varlaam, A. 61

Warnock 74

Webb, S. 208
Weddell, K. and Lambourne, R. 210
Welsh Office 55, 137, 224
West, D. J. 26
West, D. J. and Farrington, D. P. 26, 63
West Glamorgan 133, 179
White, D. J. and Peddie, M. 24, 26
White, R. and Brockington, D. 206
Wigley, V. 79
Wilby, P. 159
Williams, P. 24
Willis, P. E. 66, 113
Withrington, D. 24
Wolstenholme, F. and Kolvin, I. 213
Wood, J. 208, 209
Woods, P. 120
Wragg, E. C. 122
Wragg, E. C. and Kerry, T. L. 122
Wright, H. J. and Payne, T. A. N. 210

York, R. et al 95, 186, 187
Young, P. et al 131
Younghusband, E. et al 71, 73
Yule, W. et al 122